THE STUDENT ATHLETE'S GUIDE
TO GETTING RECRUITED

"Stewar ⸻ make a
very difficult decision much easier. This book is designed to help anyone
who is interested in competing in college athletics. Brown's insight will
help you become more successful both as a student and as an athlete."
— SCHELLAS HYNDMAN, MEN'S SOCCER COACH,
SOUTHERN METHODIST UNIVERSITY

"Stewart Brown has captured the complex process of college recruiting
in a very readable how-to guide. *The Student Athlete's Guide to Getting
Recruited* provides a map for the student-athlete and her family to help
navigate the difficult waters of college recruiting. This is a must read for
any high school athlete interested in competing on the college level."
— GARY CLARK, DIRECTOR OF ATHLETICS, FURMAN UNIVERSITY

"Stewart Brown has used his knowledge as a college and high school
coach to give outstanding advice to high school athletes wanting to play
college sports. Any high school athlete aspiring to play college sports will
benefit from reading this book."
— RANDY ALLEN, ATHLETIC DIRECTOR AND HEAD FOOTBALL COACH,
HIGHLAND PARK HIGH SCHOOL

"The transition from high school to college athletics can be an exciting
time but can be also a time full of confusion. This book is the first that
can successfully guide a student from high school to excelling in athletics
in college."
— BROADUS WHITESIDE, JR., DIRECTOR OF COMPLIANCE,
SOUTHERN METHODIST UNIVERSITY DEPARTMENT OF ATHLETICS

"Intercollegiate athletics adds richness to our institutions of higher education and to the experiences of those student-athletes fortunate enough
to participate. There are significant challenges, however, in moving from
a successful high school student-athlete to a successful college student-
athlete, and Stewart Brown's book do
letes and their parents through this co
cal information and solid illustrations
athlete immensely."
— ROBERT A. HYNES, PH.D., ASSISTA⸻
SUPPORT SERVICES, FIT⸻

"Stewart Brown captures all the information needed for the college bound student-athlete and their parents in *The Student Athlete's Guide to Getting Recruited*. This is an invaluable resource filled with great tips. It is a must read for any young person considering playing sports in college at any level."

—MICHAEL SCERBO, WOMEN'S LACROSSE COACH, DUQUESNE UNIVERSITY

"Stewart Brown has done an excellent job in portraying the recruiting process. Most importantly he provides valuable information for students, parents and coaches. This book is an outstanding aid in helping students understand the recruiting process."

—CHARLES BREITHAUPT, DIRECTOR OF ATHLETICS, TEXAS UNIVERSITY
INTERSCHOLASTIC LEAGUE (UIL)

"Future college athletes will learn many tips on how to succeed. As a former Academic All-American, I believe this information to be relevant to all high school and college athletes who want to succeed in the classroom and within the competitive arena of college sports. I will be helping my athletes utilize these tips for their own success."

—KIM COLON, WAKELAND HIGH SCHOOL HEAD SOCCER COACH AND
ACADEMIC ALL-AMERICAN AT SOUTHERN METHODIST UNIVERSITY

"This book is an insider's look that provides the much needed roadmap to navigating your way through the often confusing recruitment process. This is a MUST read for any parent with an aspiring student-athlete."

—TERRI MCCRACKEN, PARENT OF HIGH SCHOOL
STUDENT-ATHLETE, CARROLLTON, TX

"Entering the process of preparing to be a successful student-athlete without a plan is like sending your team to a championship game without a coach. Stewart Brown's book should become part of the family library and the knowledge base that will help them successfully navigate the recruitment process."

—BOB COLLINS, EDITOR, STUDENT ATHLETE SCHOLARSHIPS FOUNDATION

"I found *The Student Athlete's Guide to Getting Recruited* to be very complete in its content. The organization makes it easy to get the information you need quickly, and above all, I feel it embodies the 'current' state of college athletic recruiting in a way that benefits the student-athlete and the concerned parent."

—JOHN COSSABOON, WOMEN'S SOCCER ASSISTANT COACH,
GONZAGA UNIVERSITY

The Student Athlete's Guide to

GETTING RECRUITED

*How to Win Scholarships, Attract Colleges
and Excel as an Athlete*

STEWART BROWN

The Student Athlete's Guide to Getting Recruited: How to Win Scholarships, Attract Colleges and Excel as an Athlete

By Stewart Brown

Published by SuperCollege, LLC
3286 Oak Court
Belmont, CA 94002
www.supercollege.com

Credits: Cover: TLC Graphics, www.TLCGraphics.com. Design: Monica Thomas Layout: The Roberts Group, www.editorialservice.com

Trademarks: All brand names, product names and services used in this book are trademarks, registered trademarks or tradenames of their respective holders. SuperCollege is not associated with any college, university, product or vendor.

Disclaimers: The author and publisher have used their best efforts in preparing this book. It is sold with the understanding that the author and publisher are not rendering legal or other professional advice. The author and publisher cannot be held responsible for any loss incurred as a result of specific decisions made by the reader. The author and publisher make no representations or warranties with respect to the accuracy or completeness of the contents of the book and specifically disclaim any implied warranties or merchantability or fitness for a particular purpose. The accuracy and completeness of the information provided herein and the opinions stated herein are not guaranteed or warranted to produce any particular results. The author and publisher specifically disclaim any responsibility for any liability, loss or risk, personal or otherwise, which is incurred as a consequence, directly or indirectly, from the use and application of any of the contents of this book.

ISBN13: 9781932662290

Manufactured in the United States of America
10 9 8 7 6 5 4 3 2 1

Library of Congress Cataloging-in-Publication Data

Brown, Stewart.

     The student athlete's guide to getting recruited : how to win scholarships, attract colleges and excel as an athlete / Stewart Brown.

        p. cm.

     ISBN 978-1-932662-29-0 (alk. paper)

     1. College athletes--Recruiting--United States. 2. College sports--Scholarships, fellowships, etc.--United States I. Title.

GV350.5.B76 2008

796.071173--dc22

2008012282

DEDICATION

To Mum and Dad in Scotland, to Julie who lived and breathed every word and punctuation mark throughout this project, and finally to all the people who have given input to this project—college coaches, experts, parents and young athletes.

CONTENTS

INTRODUCTION

The school gossip announces, "Did you hear that Julie—you know, the runner in my chemistry class—got a full scholarship to compete at Athletic University?"

"Yes, I did! Jimmy who lives down the street also got a full scholarship to play baseball. And so did the annoying kid you used to play soccer with," replies Gossip's mom. "*Everyone* gets a full scholarship to college—well, if you are an athlete that is."

Myth Number One: Every athlete gets a full scholarship to participate in collegiate athletics. This is not usually the case. Some athletes do receive full rides (NCAA I football, basketball, women's tennis, and volleyball do offer full scholarships), but the majority of athletes fund their college from academic scholarships in addition to the lucky few who receive athletic scholarships.

Myth Number Two: Only the top athletes get actively recruited by college coaches. This, again, is not true. Top athletes get recruited to top programs; but every college program is looking for a balance of student-athletes, and many high school athletes that were not heavily recruited do succeed. There is a college for every student and a program for every athlete; and if you—as an athlete—want to pursue college athletics, you can recruit yourself to programs at different levels.

Myth Number Three: Your parents—well, the genetics they share with you—are responsible for your athletic performance. This is partially true, but it is also a cop-out! You can better develop as an athlete by following well documented and scientifically proven methodology and making correct choices in all aspects of your life.

Myth Number Four: Once a college coach says you can be part of their program, your work is done. Again, not true. There are many things that a prospective student-athlete needs to achieve once he or she has found and

1

been offered the opportunity to compete in collegiate athletics. Minimally, the student-athlete still needs to be accepted academically to the institution, complete the NCAA eligibility requirements and re-focus his or her academic and athletic goals.

Myths Number Five and Six: You have a scholarship for all four years but the college coach can take it back from you if you do not perform well. Neither of these is true. An athletic scholarship is year-to-year; however, a college coach has to renew your scholarship and will likely do so unless you break team rules, become academically ineligible or decide to quit on your own.

The majority of high school student-athletes are bombarded with myths and hand-me-down ideas from various sources regarding how best to become a competent and successful collegiate student-athlete. Due to these various interpretations, the high school student can get confused and frustrated about college and athletic recruitment which may lead to disappointment—and this is why every high school athlete and parent should read this book.

The eye-opening journey that is *The Student Athlete's Guide to Getting Recruited* takes you through true and real-life examples as they are shared. Get ready to find out the good—and the bad—from stories demonstrating what options are available and what pitfalls to avoid during the recruiting process. You'll also gain insights into the preparation for college athletics, the visitations, and what to expect once you, the student-athlete, complete the transition from high school to college athletics.

Here's what you'll learn in this book:

CHAPTER ONE: Navigating through the Rules
Follow three high school students during the recruiting process: Jacob (sophomore soccer player), Julie (junior tennis player) and Michael (senior lacrosse player). Each athlete takes you through what to expect during the corresponding recruitment phase and explains the NCAA rules that control and protect both the prospective student-athlete and the recruiting college coach. A recruiting timeline is included.

CHAPTER TWO: I'm Eligible, Why Take the SAT Again? Scholarships and Financial Aid
Follow Steve (baseball), Dave (swimming) and Kelly (volleyball) as they prepare to make choices concerning their college careers. Addressing NCAA eligi-

bility, financial aid and admission standards, each story creates a foundation on which to build college decisions.

CHAPTER THREE: What College Coaches Really Want
Candid insight into what a college coach really looks for during the recruitment process is outlined by individual sport. Interviews with top college coaches from NCAA I, II, and III schools provide great insight into their sports and recruiting practices—including the academic, athletic and psychological aspects of college athletics.

CHAPTER FOUR: Bigger, Faster, Stronger...Smarter: Develop Yourself for College Athletics
Follow Julie (tennis) and Bryan (track) as they work toward fitness in a bid to compete at the highest levels. These athletes learn about their training and their own physical make-up. In addition, two strength and conditioning experts give advice that will be helpful in preparing a high school athlete for the rigors of college athletics.

CHAPTER FIVE: Your Body as an Athletic Temple
Gary (swimming) makes good life choices in a bid to achieve his own sporting goals. Experts from the fields of sport nutrition and athletic training give their valuable insight into how athletes can better prepare themselves away from the playing field. Information focuses on living a healthy lifestyle, including how drugs, alcohol, negative sleep patterns and dehydration can negatively affect athletic performance.

CHAPTER SIX: Tuck in Your Shirt and Pull up Your Socks: Attract College Coaches
Follow Coach McNeil (college soccer coach), Liz (field hockey) and Jonathan (cross-country) during the early recruitment phases. You will learn what coaches see during recruitment events and how it influences them. Additionally, Liz and Jonathan will take you through their communication issues and how to assure a smooth recruiting experience.

CHAPTER SEVEN: Not a 48-Hour Vacation: College Visits
Simon and Philip (golf) take unofficial visits, with one a success and the other not. In addition, Sonia (gymnastics), Jasmine (basketball) and Tony (football) experience different types of official visits that highlight good and bad behaviors that may influence their prospects.

CHAPTER EIGHT: What is Next? Transition Smoothly to College

The summer prior to college enrollment is a very important time for preparation if the student-athlete is to experience success at a high level. Jose (soccer), Marlo (volleyball) and Arthur (basketball) highlight pitfalls prior to enrolling that influence a longer duration of their collegiate career. Jenna (softball) travels a path, when already in school, that anyone would want to avoid at all costs.

EXPERT INSIGHT: Developmental Challenges for First-Year Student-athletes

Dr. Robert Hynes: Director of Counseling Services and Assistant Dean for Student Support Services, Fitchburg State College (Fitchburg, MA)

CHAPTER NINE: When Do I Get a Day Off? Develop a Schedule That Allows You to Succeed

Time management is a very important aspect of being a college student and student-athlete. Athletic Trainer Rita and student-athlete Gavin (baseball) highlight the help given to students from the NCAA regarding time limitations and schedule their very hectic lives as student-athletes. Additionally, daily college training schedules are presented.

CHAPTER TEN: The Rules Are There to Protect You

College life for Nick (football), Erica (lacrosse), Lynn (rowing) and Jeff (track) does not go as planned, or as promised, which causes great distress in their lives. However, there are options—if they know about them—that can correct their situations by proper management and using the NCAA rules to their advantage.

APPENDIX

Web Site Resources
College Coach and Expert Biography and contact information

NAVIGATING THROUGH THE RULES

High school student-athletes rarely commit to a college or university without visiting other institutions to compare athletic, academic, social and other considerations. This is wise. Seniors who make snap choices about where they plan to spend the next four or five years often regret not having made a more thorough evaluation of their options while in high school. The following stories about Jake, Julie and Michael provide examples of situations that many high school athletes have experienced during the recruiting process as they passed through their secondary school years and began college. You will see their thought processes and actions while they navigated their way through the labyrinth of NCAA rules, interacted with college coaches and committed to what they hoped would be the institution of their dreams.

SOPHOMORE YEAR: JAKE'S STORY

In the youth soccer world, it is very common for parents to be involved in marketing their sons and daughters to colleges. They typically walk around the field handing out brochures to the college coaches watching the games. During that time, the parents take notes on who has been at which game and who had asked questions about which player. This can be useful information for their children, but it can lead to frustration too.

HIGH SCHOOL VS. CLUB SPORTS

For some sports and athletes, there is the debate on whether an athlete should focus on high school athletics, focus on club athletics or attempt to find a balance between both. Each college coach will have his or her own philosophy of the good and bad of either scenario and as a prospective student-athlete, you should ask several coaches for opinions.

Benefits of High School Sports over Club Sports:

- Athletes get the opportunity to play with and against older and younger athletes (similar to college).

- Athletes are in an environment of hierarchy—they learn the roles expected of being a freshman, senior and the two years in-between.

- Representing a high school (sometimes a community) can create a feeling of pride, passion and belonging that may not occur within club sports.

- Competitive club players may not get to develop strong leadership roles in club sports, but they may get that opportunity at the high school level, especially in the latter years.

- Athletes experience another coaching style and philosophy that will allow them to grow in their knowledge of the sport—every coach has something to teach.

Benefits of Club Sports over High School Sports:

- Athletes experience playing with and against athletes of the same age and similar talent level.

- Without a hierarchy of ages an athlete may feel more comfortable accepting and developing a leadership role within the team.

- Club teams tend to travel farther and are exposed to different teams, styles of play, and philosophy—more than most high schools.

- Club teams tend to have like-minded athletes around them which can create an environment of synergy as the athletes set and attain their goals.

- There are fewer restrictions on practice and game schedules, which can create more learning opportunities for the athlete.

For sports that do not offer club teams, many experts see the benefit of having down-time from their training and competition time. This may keep the student-athlete fresher both physically and mentally. High school athletes that participate in both club and high school sports all year may be overcome by the burden of practicing and competing year round. The frustration may lead to burn-out (overtraining) and each athlete must be careful to schedule some down-time. It is important that a high-school-aged athlete have time to *just be a kid*.

It is not critical for recruitment that a high school athlete play club sports or participate in regional and/or developmental junior Olympic programs. However, college coaches want to see their prospects competing at the highest level available to them (either high school or club) and training in the most competitive environment possible to develop them further as athletes (some may have geographical issues related to playing club sports and coaches will understand this). Each college coach is looking to recruit athletes that have been challenged, pushed, developed and grown within an environment that will lead to the same development and success expected in college.

If a high school athlete's team is not very good and has poor commitment, it may be difficult to attract the attention of college coaches. In this circumstance, it is vitally important student-athletes communicate regularly with college coaches and create a recruitment video that highlights his or her strengths. A prospect in this predicament may be asked to walk on for the first year to allow a better evaluation (NCAA II programs may ask you to try out during a campus visit for evaluation) before scholarship monies are offered.

It is always in the best interest of athletes to be in a successful environment whenever possible—whether high school, club or both.

Jake, a high school sophomore, knew that he had been the standout at a winter soccer tournament. In one key game, he had scored two goals and assisted on another. His extra effort in competitive situations, persistence in penetrating tough defenses and focus on winning contributed significantly to two upset victories. This enabled his team to advance out of the group stages. Through his parents' sideline scouting, he knew that coaches from two of his top three college choices had watched his performance.

Jake could not wait to check his email and sort through all the letters and recruiting materials from the college coaches he had impressed during the tournament! After all, he had sent letters inviting many of them to watch him play and he had enclosed his team schedule. Later, he had sent emails to each of the coaches thanking them for coming to the tournament. In short, Jake had done all the advance work and follow-up his team coaches had suggested. Now it was time to reap the benefits.

Much to Jake's disappointment, college coaches did not respond to his emails or letters. He wondered why invitations to visit campuses and scholarship offers were not filling up his mailbox and jamming his cell phone. Jake did not understand the rules.

- NCAA recruiting rules restrict any written correspondence between coaches and high school athletes before their junior year.

- When an athlete begins ninth grade, he or she becomes a recruitable student-athlete, what the NCAA calls a "Prospective Student-Athlete", "Prospect", or "PSA." He or she remains a PSA until preseason practice begins prior to the first semester in college or when classes start, whichever occurs first. At this time, the young man or woman become a "student-athlete."

Therefore, no matter how much Jake impressed college coaches, they could not initiate correspondence to let him know how impressed they were with his performance at the tournament. NCAA rules restrict coaches from sending Jake email, text messages or letters containing any athletic program information. Coaches can only send non-athletic program information such as these:

- A college summer camp brochure that has open enrollment.

- A recruiting questionnaire for the student to return to the coaches and/or the school's athletic department.

- Educational information on the university but no information regarding the athletic program.

MIND THE RULES: Men's basketball prospects can receive athletically related material on June 15 following their sophomore year.

> **MIND THE RULES:** College coaches have to wait until September 1 of a PSA's junior year to send any written correspondence regarding their athletic programs. They can send either a recruiting brochure or media guide, but not both. At this point, coaches can communicate via email, text messages, letters, instant message (IM) or fax.

The rules do not make restrictions on college coaches conversing with high school or club coaches. After Jake's winter tournament, the college coaches told Jake's club coach about their interest, and his club coach delivered the message. Once Jake understood why the college coaches were not able to respond to his letters, he sent them the following email:

TO: CoachRenaldo@email.university.edu

FROM: JakeLastname@email.com

SUBJECT: Jake Lastname Class of 2010

Dear Coach Renaldo,

Thank you for taking time to watch me play during the winter tournament. I understand you were at the game when I scored two goals and assisted one of my teammates on the third. I hope you liked my overall attitude toward the game! I believe that I would be a great addition to Soccer University.

I know that there are many restrictions on our contact until September 1, but please feel free to contact my coach. If there is anything you would like me to do, he will be happy to relay that information. Coach Haynes can be reached via email at mysoccercoach@mysoccercoach.com or by phone at 555-777-8888.

I look forward to hearing from you and receiving more information from your Admissions Department. I have kept up to date with everything going on at SU via your Web site and I am continually impressed.

Yours in soccer,

Jake

Sure enough, on September 1 of his junior year, the letters, emails and recruiting materials that Jake had been expecting since the tournament his sophomore year began pouring in from college coaches.

Depending on the talent level of the prospect, the eye for talent of the recruiting coaches (and what they want for their programs) and the need for specific types of athletes/players, most high school athletes do not receive random letters of interest from their dream colleges. For all but the best-of-the-best, the recruiting process begins with the prospects initiating an interest in specific programs and encouraging the coach to recruit them.

Every high school student-athlete interested in participating in college athletics needs to initiate contact with the coaching staff—no matter how talented the students are in the athletic arena. Very rarely do prospects receive an initial contact and then a scholarship offer from the college of their dreams. It is the prospect's responsibility to alert the college coaches of his or her interest in specific programs and educational institutions.

JUNIOR YEAR: JULIE'S STORY

At any time prospects, or their parents, can initiate calls to college coaches. If the coaches are unavailable, however, and the caller leaves a message, he or she should be prepared to play one-way phone tag.

Julie, a high school junior and a highly rated tennis player, was the number one seed on her high school state championship winning team. Very active and successful on the national youth circuit, Julie attracted coaches from both small liberal arts schools and large state schools. Julie had an amazing ability to play doubles with anyone. She drew attention to herself with aggressive net play and dynamic personality on the court. Every coach saw her as the perfect team player, especially for a non-team sport.

As anticipated, on September 1, Julie was flooded with recruiting correspondence from most major women's tennis programs throughout the nation. A few programs piqued her interest that she had not previously considered. Overwhelmed with all this new and somewhat unsolicited attention, Julie needed a plan. Julie found that the recruiting process can be made easier with the right plan and a commitment to follow through with the plan.

First, Julie needed to be honest with herself and her family regarding each institution's ability to realistically fit her needs. Considering different factors, including the academic, athletic and social environments of each campus, she created a list of potential schools. Julie needed to be honest

with the coaches energetically pursuing her. Being courteous and express-
ing her needs for her collegiate experience was a large part of her plan.
When a school did not fit these needs, Julie explained this to the coaches,
which helped manage her feelings of being overwhelmed. Being able to
take ownership of her recruiting efforts by using a workable list removed
much of her tension and anxiety.

Second, Julie needed to understand that college coaches accept rejec-
tion from recruits all the time. Each college coach does not expect to
receive a signed National Letter of Intent from every prospect. Therefore,
they over-recruit every year. Coaches constantly update their recruiting
lists, adding to and subtracting from, with every commitment or rejec-
tion. When a prospect commits to the institution, the coach progresses to
the next PSA. When a recruit says "no," the coach fills that opening with
another prospect. In that way, coaches work down from their "top" recruit
of that class, to "walk-on" athletes that they would like to have as part of
their program.

By returning an email and/or letter to the recruiting coach, Julie
showed a great deal of respect for the process. She replied to every text
message, letter and email in a positive way, knowing that she could renew
recruiting opportunities later if her circumstances changed.

TO: CoachEvert@email.statecollege.edu

FROM: JulieLastname@email.com

SUBJECT: Julie Lastname Class of 2009

Dear Coach Evert,

Thank you very much for your continued interest in me as a student-
athlete for Tennis State College. At this time, however, I am pursuing
other academic opportunities that are a better fit for my educational
needs. If things change, I will contact you. I wish you good luck with
your upcoming season and recruiting efforts.

Thanks again,

Julie

Many coaches wrote back. They appreciated her honesty and thanked
Julie for her information, while bestowing best wishes on her for the future.
Others replied to her saying that if anything changed, a door would always

be open for her—even if it were a couple of years down the road. Julie was initially afraid to hurt the college coaches' feelings but after reading their appreciation of her honesty, her anxiety decreased. Honesty allowed everyone to direct his or her recruiting efforts in a positive manner.

Not *every* coach understands and is courteous, however. There are always coaches who do not reply. Even worse, some will tell recruits that they are making a huge mistake. Julie did the right thing. She remembered that college coaches are prepared to sign only a percentage of their recruiting list and they always have a back-up plan, so she felt she could be honest with the coaches. She narrowed down her choices and told the coaches she was interested—or not interested—depending on the program and/or school.

By early November, Julie had worked through all the information she received and replied to all correspondence. She narrowed her choices down to five schools. The next stage of Julie's plan was to call and discuss unofficial visits with the head coaches of these five tennis programs.

Julie had mixed luck reaching the five coaches. One coach never replied to several voice mails she left. At another school, Julie left messages with an administrative assistant, but still no response came from the coach. Julie's excitement about two programs began to fade. Did they lose interest in her all of a sudden? Why were they not calling her back?

> **MIND THE RULES:** PSAs cannot receive phone calls from NCAA Division I college coaches until July 1 between their junior and senior years. The exceptions to the July 1 telephone call rules include the following:
>
> - A football prospect can receive one phone call in May of his junior year from any institution.
>
> - A men's basketball player can receive one phone call per month from June 15 prior to his junior year until June 30 prior to his senior year. Starting July 1 of his senior year, he can receive a weekly call.
>
> - A women's basketball player can receive one phone call in April and one phone call in May of her junior year.

Many college coaches acknowledge that there is a problem with prospective student-athletes' lack of knowledge regarding the rules. In an attempt to alleviate this frustration, a coach may place on his/her voicemail a message ending like this:

> *"If you are a junior or younger, or a parent of a junior or younger, due to NCAA rules, I cannot call you back. Please keep trying. I look forward to hearing from you soon."*

RULES INFO

NCAA Division II programs: A coach can initiate a phone call on June 15 prior to the senior year.

NCAA Division III programs: A coach can initiate a phone call immediately after the completion of a PSA's junior year.

After Julie understood that college coaches cannot initiate the calls but can communicate in writing (including text messages), Julie continued to call in hopes of eventually catching the coach. She left the following voicemail:

> *"Coach Connors, this is Julie Lastname again. I know you cannot call me back because I am a junior, so I will keep trying. Please feel free to text me at 555-555-5555 when you are available and I will call you. I look forward to talking with you soon."*

Julie further expressed her interest in the program with the following email:

TO: CoachConnors@email.university.edu

FROM: JulieLastname@email.com

SUBJECT: Excited about TU

Dear Coach Connors,

Thank you for your continued correspondence with me via email and regular mail. As you can tell by the messages I have left on your office voicemail, I am very excited about the prospect of learning more about Tennis University, how I may fit into your plans and how TU fits my educational and athletic needs. I would really like the opportunity to talk with you soon.

When would be a good time for me to call you? If we have trouble reaching each other, my cell phone number is 555-555-5555 and you can text me when you are available for me to call you. You can always call my high school coach, Coach Jones, on 555-555-6666 and she will be happy to let me know when I should call you.

I look forward to talking to you soon,

Julie Lastname

If Coach Connors sends a text message while Julie is not available, she should follow up with an explanation:

Coach Connors, I was in a study group and missed your text message. Is this a good time to call you? Julie Lastname

Obviously, the more options Julie provides, the greater chance she has of connecting with Coach Connors. The worst thing Julie could have done was to have given up and to have stopped trying. But by working within the constraints of the rules, Julie made the recruitment process a success. With a couple of voicemails, a few text messages back and forth, and help from her high school tennis coach, Julie and Coach Connors finally talked.

During the initial phone call, Julie encouraged the coach to do most of the talking. She wanted to leave her questions until a future call or when sitting face to face during an unofficial visit. Open-ended and simple questions during the first call allowed Coach Connors the opportunity to sell her program. She gave Julie her insight about the institution from an academic, athletic and social perspective. Listening intently, Julie could tell what Coach Connors liked about each area. For this first phone call, Julie kept her questions simple:

- Please tell me about your tennis program.

- Please tell me more about the academic areas of your university.

- Please tell me about the city Tennis University is in.

Knowing that the initial call is also an opportunity to sell herself, Julie was prepared to answer the following questions from the coach:

- Have you taken your SAT/ACT and if yes, what scores did you get?

- What is your current cumulative GPA and your most recent GPA?

- Have you registered with the NCAA Eligibility Center?

- What academic area(s) are you interested in?

- Why are you interested in Tennis University?

- When and where are your next tournaments/competitions?

Julie knew that honesty was important as well as detailed answers. She knew that answering *"somewhere in the 1300 range"* when the coach asked for her SAT scores would not be sufficient. Any college coach needs specific scores to determine the following:

- Whether the academic profile of the PSA fits that of the institution.

- Whether the PSA will require admission assistance.

- Whether the PSA will qualify for academic scholarship opportunities.

Julie planned to take the SAT/ACT again on the next available date and her organizational skills impressed Coach Connors. Julie showed that she understood the importance of the recruiting and admission process as well as being in control of her academic future.

Julie also knew to be honest about her test scores and grades. She knew not to promise a 4.0 GPA and a 1600 on her SAT* when a more realistic score for her would be an 1100 on her SAT and a 3.3 GPA. Coach Connors was appreciative of Julie's veracity and openness. The coach also liked that Julie did not apologize for her grades or create excuses. The fact that Julie promised to improve academically also showed Coach Connors that she understood the institution's academic profile.

The most important question Julie had to answer was why she was interested in Tennis University. After researching the academic and athletic aspects of the university, she knew how to answer that question. Julie also explained any concerns she had about TU, allowing Coach Connors the opportunity to address these reservations. Coach Connors appreciated Julie's thoughtful preparation.

The conversation between Coach Connors and Julie went very well. Both received the information they needed and agreed to continue to the next step in the recruiting process. Coach Connors encouraged Julie to

---

*Colleges and the NCAA Eligibility are currently only taking into consideration the Critical Reading and Math sections of the SAT.

talk with her parents and arrange an unofficial visit to Tennis University. Throughout their telephone conversation, Julie took detailed notes that she could use for questions during their face-to-face meeting.

> **MIND THE RULES:** An unofficial visit is a meeting on campus where the prospective student-athlete visits the educational institution at the student's expense.
>
> ● The institution cannot provide any transportation to/from campus.
>
> ● The institution cannot pay for any meals and or lodging.
>
> ● A prospective student-athlete can stay on campus but must pay the regular institutional rate for lodging.
>
> ● During the visit, the prospective student-athlete and his or her parents, guardians and/or spouse may receive free admission to an on-campus athletic event.
>
> ● A coach can provide transportation to an off-campus sporting event or athletic facility only if it is within 30 miles of the campus.

It is important for junior prospective student-athletes to go on unofficial visits. During this time, the prospective student-athletes and their parents have unlimited contact with the coaching staff. It is a great opportunity for the student to sell him/herself to the institution and to have the coaches and student-athletes market the institution to prospects. Talking with the coaching staff and interacting with current student-athletes, Julie received insight into the institution, the tennis program and the coaches. All of this was invaluable when it was time for her to choose where she wanted to attend school.

Julie wanted to visit four institutions: two schools were local and the other two were out of state. Julie's family began to plan how they could provide the time and money to visit each of these schools. The two local institutions were of course most accessible. During a day off from school, Julie walked around the two local campuses to get a feel for the overall environment before meeting with the coaches. Julie knew by walking around campus that she could see herself living at these institutions and she felt comfortable within the academic and social environment. Therefore, she arranged a meeting with the coaches and asked for the opportunity to spend time with current student-athletes.

Visiting the remaining two out-of-state schools required resourceful thinking as the funds were not readily available for Julie and her family. Julie's parents knew that one of her choices was very similar to another school within their state. They were not convinced that Julie would like the large school environment in a small rural town, but a trip to the closer school would give Julie the chance to see if she liked the environment there. If Julie felt at home in the similar school, her parents could arrange to fly her to visit the out-of-state school. However, if Julie did not like the school, then there would be no need for the out-of-state trip and they would not have wasted their money.

The second out-of-state school on Julie's list was a very small school in a large city. Again, Julie's parents found a similar school within driving distance and arranged an unofficial visit to that institution. If Julie liked that school environment, they would spend the money to send her to the actual out-of-state school. The unofficial visits were successful in that they gave Julie exposure to schools similar to her choices and helped Julie confirm that Tennis University was the best overall fit for her.

When Julie became a senior, Coach Connors attended a local satellite tournament to watch Julie play. After the event, Coach Connors discussed Julie's future at Tennis University with her parents. Understanding NCAA rules, Julie joined the conversation only after her high school coach dismissed her at the end of the tournament.

> **MIND THE RULES:** A High School/Club coach must dismiss the PSA at the conclusion of an event before the PSA can talk to the college coach.

Julie expressed her delight that Coach Connors made the trip to see her compete and her excitement at the thought of attending TU strengthened. She understood that NCAA rules restrict coaches to when, where and how often they can talk with the parents of a prospect, or a PSA, and when they can watch a prospect compete in an event. During this visit, Coach Connors used one **CONTACT** and one **EVALUATION**.

MIND THE RULES: The NCAA allows coaches seven **total** contacts and evaluations per prospective student-athlete with a maximum of four contacts throughout the complete recruitment process.

- Seven total = four contacts + three evaluations; or three contacts + four evaluations; but NOT six contacts + one evaluation

CONTACTS

The NCAA considers any off-campus face-to-face encounter a **contact** and this is only allowed during a PSA's senior year.

Accidental contact is a greeting between the coach and the PSA or the parents, but the conversation does not progress further than a "hello" and no recruiting conversation occurs. This does not count toward the coach's four-contact limitation.

Illegal contact is a conversation that occurs between a coach and a PSA, or between the coach and the parents, when it is not allowed by NCAA rules. Examples of illegal contacts include any of the following:

- Recruiting conversation between a senior PSA or parent *during* an event, including a multi-day tournament. All contact must wait until *after* the event has concluded.

- Recruiting conversation with a PSA who is younger than a senior.

- Recruiting conversation during a **quiet period** or **dead period**.

CONTACT PERIOD: This is the time when NCAA allows personal off-campus contact between a coach and a PSA.

QUIET PERIOD: Coaches cannot recruit off campus but they can communicate via phone calls or in writing.

DEAD PERIOD: NCAA does not permit any contact at all between a coach and a PSA.

Coach Connors spent a couple of days during the weekend tennis tournament watching Julie's attention-grabbing performances. Evaluating her athletic ability, Coach Connors wanted to confirm Julie could perform at the level expected by Tennis University. Even though Coach Connors watched Julie play several times during the weekend, NCAA considers this one EVALUATION because the tournament occurred on consecutive days.

EVALUATIONS

- Coaches can evaluate a PSA of any age during the appropriate times.

- A coach can evaluate a PSA a maximum of seven times prior to signing a National Letter of Intent.

- The NCAA describes an **evaluation** as any off-campus activity designed to assess the academic or athletic ability of the prospective student-athlete.

The NCAA can change the rules that apply to contact between prospects and coaches, including the availability of text messaging. For the purpose of this book, we have included text messaging as part of the communication between coaches and prospects, projecting that text messaging will remain part of recruiting process.

Please check www.StudentAthletesGuide.com for updated information regarding all rules governing correspondence.

SENIOR YEAR: MICHAEL'S STORY

Michael, a lacrosse player who had just completed his junior year, visited a large state university close to home. He discovered he did not like the idea of being in a large auditorium with 300 other students; he desired the smaller school setting where he could have a more personal relationship with his professors. With this decision, Michael narrowed his choices from seven schools to three.

As a lacrosse player, Michael knew his big day for receiving phone calls from college coaches would be July 1. Prior to this date, he sent an email explaining his availability to each of three coaches:

TO: CoachCooper@email.College.edu

FROM: MichaelLastname@email.com

SUBJECT: July 1 Phone Call

Dear Coach Cooper,

As July 1 approaches, I am looking forward to being able to talk with you on a more regular basis. As you know, I am volunteering at the Red Cross this summer and I will be working on July 1. However, I will have my cell phone with me (number 222-222-2222) and I will be available during my break between 10:00 and 10:30 a.m. Our lunch break is from 12:30 until 1:30. I normally eat with the other volunteers, but I will answer my phone if you call during that period.

If these two times do not work for you, I will be finished at 4:30 p.m. and will be free all evening.

I look forward to your phone call and to setting up a home visit with you in the very near future.

Thank you,

Michael Lastname

The email Michael wrote respected the coach's time and expressed his interest and excitement about Lacrosse Liberal Arts University.

MIND THE RULES: NCAA rules restrict the college coach to one initiated telephone call per week during a PSA's senior year. However, prospects or their parents can initiate a phone call to a college coach at any time.

When a coach leaves a voicemail or message with anyone who answers the phone call, it is his or her one phone call for that week. Remembering that recruiting goes two ways, Michael always had the courtesy to return calls to coaches, even those who were involved in programs that no longer held his attention. Michael had already established alternate communication methods during his junior year including email, text messaging, letters, faxes and instant messaging. He knew these forms of communications were useful when he missed a phone call from the coaches.

After narrowing down his choices, Michael expected three phone calls on July 1, one from each of the programs on his short list. However, additional calls came from coaches of programs he had declined previously. Obviously, these coaches wanted to put Michael back on their recruiting list. They believed they could convince Michael that their schools and programs fit his needs. This is a common tactic for some persistent coaches.

Michael was surprised to receive these calls and during a conversation with Coach Cooper, he asked for advice on how to handle it. During the next unsolicited telephone call, Michael was able to express his decision in a polite but direct manner:

"Coach, I appreciate your call but I have done a lot of research over the past 18 months and I have narrowed down my choices to three schools. I am very confident that one of these three institutions is

where I will enroll next year. If anything changes, I will research your school and program again and if it fits my needs, I will give you a call. Thank you for your interest and good luck!"

During a further conversation with Coach Cooper, Michael and his family arranged a home visit for the following week. Coach Cooper planned to offer Michael a scholarship and discuss his academic options at LLAU.

MIND THE RULES: On the day of the home visit, the telephone rules change.

- On any date where a coach is due to visit a senior prospective student-athlete for an evaluation and/or contact, the coach can call the prospective student-athlete unlimited times.

There are a few other times when the one weekly phone call rule changes:

- The day of National Letter of Intent signing, coaches can call unlimited times.

- Five days prior to an official visit, coaches can call unlimited times.

- After the signing of a National Letter of Intent, coaches can call unlimited times.

Reported as a contact, home visits are becoming less popular due to prospective student-athletes verbally committing to institutions prior to their senior year. Michael was different. He wanted a home visit, and he was looking forward to his official visit so that he could gather information that would help him make this major life decision.

The home visit can be an important step in the recruitment process. In Michael's case, it was a chance for Coach Cooper to learn more about Michael and his family, and it was a perfect opportunity for Michael and his family to learn more about LLAU, Coach Cooper and his programs. In any home visit, both parties need to ask—and answer—pointed and fact-seeking questions. Honesty is important. Both parties need to assess if it is truly a good fit.

Michael drew on the support of his family in preparation for his home visit. Coach Cooper arrived promptly Saturday morning after breakfast and everyone gathered at the dining room table for the discussion. Coach Cooper walked through a short PowerPoint presentation on the benefits of attending and playing lacrosse at LLAU. He covered the academic success of his program as well as the strength of the university's job placement program. Highlighting areas of the admissions publication and a lacrosse media guide, Coach Cooper spoke strongly of the program in hopes to sway Michael toward LLAU.

Michael and his family sat and listened politely until he was finished. Coach Cooper closed his presentation and opened up the floor for questions. Wisely, Michael's parents allowed him to take the lead and ask his questions first. Only after Michael was finished did his parents ask their questions regarding the time line of recruiting and financial aid.

As the relationship and reciprocal interest strengthened, it was time for Michael to plan his official visits—not just to Lacrosse Liberal Arts University, but to the other two institutions that held his interest as well.

OFFICIAL VISITS

- An official visit is one for which the educational institution shoulders the expense, i.e. the institution will pay all expenses or a portion of the expenses attendant to the visit.

- Each prospective student-athlete is allowed a *maximum* of five official visits.

- Each PSA can only make one official visit to each institution—(when a prospective student-athlete is a two-sport athlete, he or she can still only take five visits and only one per institution).

- An official visit can occur any time after the first day of the prospective student-athlete's academic senior year.

Being proactive, Coach Cooper had previously encouraged his prospects to take the SAT or ACT in their junior year as a prerequisite for their official visits. Had Michael not taken a standardized test on an official test date or at an appropriate test site, he would not have been allowed an official visit. Michael had taken Coach Cooper's advice, and as instructed, he mailed the coaching staff a copy of his transcripts and test scores at the end of his junior year. This assured the coaches of his eligibility so that they could schedule his official visit.

Michael knew the official visit was a crucial last step in the assessment process. What happened during these 48 hours could "make or break" his decision to wear the yellow and blue of the LLAU Bulldogs. This was the final test to see if Lacrosse Liberal Arts University was the correct academic, athletic and social environment for his collegiate tenure, so he soaked in the atmosphere. For two days, Michael experienced life as a student-athlete. He attended classes, watched training, and attended sporting events that occurred on campus. Michael not only began to understand the dynamics of the school better—the quality time he spent with his future teammates left a lasting impression.

MIND THE RULES: According to NCAA rules regarding official visits, institutions can provide PSAs with the following:

- A 48-hour maximum visitation time limit
- Commercial air transportation in coach class to and from his home town airport
- Transportation to and from campus and the local airport
- A student-host who is given $30 per day for entertainment
- A maximum of three meals per day during his visit
- Transportation by the student-host for entertainment purposes, only within a 30 mile radius of campus
- A place to stay for the two nights of his visit (hotel or dorm room)
- Tickets to home athletic events for the prospect and his parents (or spouse)

After each visit, Michael sent thank-you notes to all the coaches for their hospitality:

Dear Coach Cooper,

Thank you for providing me with an official visit this past week-end. I enjoyed my two days on campus, especially the time I spent with the players. Fred did a wonderful job as my host as he showed me around campus and introduced me to everyone. I now have a much better appreciation for life as a student-athlete and I believe that Lacrosse Liberal Arts University is a valid choice for my college education. I look forward to hearing from you soon and discussing what our next step will be.

Sincerely,

Michael Lastname

Writing the notes helped Michael understand more about his likes and dislikes as he found words that expressed his feelings regarding each of the schools. For example, he knew Small Lacrosse College was not for him. The university's excessive party atmosphere turned him off completely; he was looking for a stronger academic environment. Michael decided to let the coach know, via email, he was no longer interested in attending that school.

TO: CoachBush@email.lacrosse.edu

FROM: MichaelLastname@email.com

SUBJECT: Class of 2008

Dear Coach Bush,

After careful consideration, I need to inform you of my decision to attend another institution. I was very impressed by you and your program's winning traditions but academically it is not what I am looking for. I wish you and your program the best of luck in the future. I also appreciate all the time and effort you have put toward my recruitment.

It has been a great pleasure getting to know you and learning about your program.

Thank you and good luck!

Michael

Michael narrowed down his choices to two schools: Lacrosse Liberal Arts University and Private Lacrosse College. Both institutions had very similar dynamics and each could offer Michael what he was searching for in further education. However, Michael was not ready to make a final decision.

MONEY AS A DECISION FACTOR

For many future collegiate athletes, the amount of scholarship money offered— or more to the point, the amount of out-of-pocket expenses they and their parents have to prepare to handle—becomes a major decision in choosing the college they will attend. Fortunately for Michael, he did not need to worry about those factors.

In Chapter Seven, this book acknowledges that it is okay to ask a college coach about the potential for athletic aid when you either know that you want to attend that institution or you have an offer from another institution. College coaches understand that the cost of attending college is an important factor for most parents and prospects, and they will be ready to talk about scholarship options (academic, athletic, etc.) with you. However, college coaches would prefer you choose their program and institution because of other factors such as the academics, their program and the opportunities their institution will provide you when you graduate.

Attempting to play one coach against another financially will undoubtedly harm your reputation and scholarship opportunities. Telling one coach that you received scholarship X from institution Y, especially if it is not true, will alert the coaching staff (maybe incorrectly) that you are only interested in money. But, it is okay to tell a coach that you…

● Have received a scholarship offer from one or more institutions (be prepared to tell them which ones if they ask).

● Would like to attend their institution, but as it stands, your family cannot financially afford *all* the out-of-pocket expenses.

● Are willing to share with the coach the financial gap between what your parents can afford to pay and what they are expected to pay.

● Are exploring other avenues for scholarships and financial aid—academic, governmental financial aid and private scholarships.

Remember, honesty in all your communication with college coaches is important at every level—especially financial aid.

Although some college athletes receive a full scholarship, you should not enter a conversation with any coach believing that you will receive a full scholarship or that you deserve one. Coaches make financial choices based on certain criteria:

- The amount of money they have available for that given year.
- Your talent relative to the talent of the student-athletes within the program.
- Your talent relative to the talent of student-athletes of the institutions they compete against.
- The need for your position during that given recruitment class.
- Their prediction on your development over the coming years and how that fits into the program's future.

Michael had the interest of two coaches from the final two schools on his short list. At this point, both coaches were feeling pressure and wanted an answer. They needed to know if Michael was going to join their program. His decision would not only affect their immediate recruiting needs, but it could change recruiting efforts two and three years down the road.

Coach Hunter from Private Lacrosse College chose the pressure tactic in his final dealings with Michael. He demanded Michael make a decision by Friday afternoon at 4:00 p.m. The aggressiveness and lack of understanding from Coach Hunter raised alarm bells. Michael knew he had to make a decision but he did not appreciate the pressure. At the end of the day, it was his life and his choice, and he was the one in control. Michael felt that it was his decision and no one should put pressure on him to make it by a certain time. Only one person was in charge of his recruiting process: **MICHAEL!**

Coach Cooper from LLAU, however, understood Michael needed more time to consider his options. Although he strongly believed his institution was a better fit for Michael, he wanted Michael to make that choice for himself. His patience and understanding won Michael over. Coach Hunter's gamble of putting pressure on Michael had backfired, while Coach Cooper's support helped Michael feel that LLAU was where he was genuinely valued, wanted and needed. On Thursday evening, Michael excitedly committed to LLAU, the lacrosse program and Coach Cooper.

The recruiting process can be long and tricky at times and each prospective student-athlete will encounter all types of people along the way. It is a great adventure and a time for the prospects to learn more about themselves while they learn about other people in their lives as well. Michael received pressure and advice from many individuals who believed they had the right answers for him. It was important for him to gather information from people he trusted and respected. His parents, teachers and coaches helped Michael navigate through the recruiting process.

Michael did have one last athletic step to take before he enrolled at Lacrosse Liberal Arts University. He signed a **National Letter of Intent** on signing day and a financial aid letter, which contractually bound Michael to LLAU for at least one year.

Each sport has different signing days. Some sports have two; some have one. Depending on the sport and year, the dates vary. Below are estimates of signing dates per sport:

Sport	Initial Signing Date	Final Signing Date
Basketball (Early Period)	2nd Wednesday in November	3rd Wednesday in November
Basketball (Regular)	3rd Wednesday in April	3rd Wednesday in May
Football (Midyear JC Transfer)	3rd Wednesday in December	3rd Wednesday in January
Football (Regular)	1st Wednesday in February	1st Tuesday in April
Field Hockey	1st Wednesday in February	August 1st
Soccer	1st Wednesday in February	August 1st
Track and Field	1st Wednesday in February	August 1st
Cross-Country	1st Wednesday in February	August 1st
Men's Water Polo	1st Wednesday in February	August 1st
All Other Sports (Early)	2nd Wednesday in November	3rd Wednesday in November
All Other Sports (Regular)	2nd Wednesday in April	August 1st

THE NATIONAL LETTER OF INTENT

Over 500 academic institutions participate in the National Letter of Intent (NLI) program for the benefit of prospective student-athletes and their athletic programs.

By signing an NLI, the prospect agrees to attend that institution for a minimum of one academic year. In return, the institution agrees to provide athletically related financial aid (scholarship/grant-in-aid) for the same time period (the financial agreement is signed on the same day as the NLI). After signing the NLI, the prospective student-athlete is no longer a recruitable prospect to other institutions that participate in the NLI program and these other programs are required to cease recruitment of the prospect immediately.

When a prospect signs an NLI, they are signing for an institution and not a specific coach. If the coach leaves the program, the prospect is still committed to attend and participate in the program for that university or college.

Finally, even when a prospect signs a National Letter of Intent they still are required to gain admission to the institution and to be certified by the NCAA Eligibility Center before becoming a collegiate student-athlete. If a prospect does not gain admission to the institution or if he or she is deemed ineligible by the NCAA Eligibility Center, the NLI becomes void.

For more information and conditions of the National Letter of Intent Program, please check out their Web site at www.national-letter.org.

CHAPTER ONE: GLOSSARY

Prospective Student-Athlete (PSA): any high school student-athlete that is entering ninth grade

Student-Athlete: enrolled and eligible college athlete

Written Correspondence: letter, note, postcard, email, text message, instant message or fax

Coach-to-Coach Contact: unlimited conversation between college coaches and club/HS coaches

Unofficial Visit: campus visit where the PSA visits the educational institution at his or her own expense: unlimited

Official Visit: the institution pays for the visit: five max per student

Home Visit: visit by the college coach to the home of the PSA

SAT: standardized test used for NCAA Eligibility and college placement

ACT: standardized test used for NCAA Eligibility and college placement

Contact: off-campus face-to-face encounter between PSA and coach: maximum 4

Evaluation: off-campus activity designed to access the academic or athletic ability of PSA: maximum seven

Contact Period: when a coach can have in-person, off-campus recruiting contacts and evaluations.

Evaluation Period: when a coach can assess the academic and athletic abilities of a PSA

Quiet Period: no off-campus contacts or evaluations although on-campus contacts are permitted

Dead Period: no in-person contacts or evaluations on- or off-campus

National Letter of Intent: signed commitment to attend and compete at an educational institution

NCAA Eligibility Center: a department within the NCAA that decides if a high school athlete has met the minimum academic standards to participate in college athletics

YEARLY ALLOWANCES

Freshman/Sophomore Year

PSA can do any of the following:

- Call
- Send email
- Send letter
- Send resume
- Send transcript
- Send text message to coach
- Attend an unofficial visit

College coach can do any of the following:

- Send camp brochure
- Send athletic questionnaire
- Send general educational information
- Evaluate prospects

Junior Year

PSA can do any of the following:

- Call
- Send email
- Send letter
- Send resume
- Send transcript
- Send text message to coach
- Attend an unofficial visit

College coach can do any of the following:

- Send letters
- Send emails
- Send faxes
- Send instant messages
- Text message

- Send athletic publication
- Evaluate

(Some sports: football, men's and women's basketball can have limited phone contact)

Senior Year

PSA can do any of the following:

- Call
- Send email
- Send letter
- Send resume
- Send transcript
- Send text message to coach
- Attend an unofficial visit
- Receive a home visit
- Attend an official visit
- Sign NLI

In addition to sophomore and junior years, college coach can do any of the following:

- Make one weekly phone call
- Have face-to-face contact at permitted times
- Attend a home visit
- Offer official visits to PSAs

SUMMARY

- Email coaches prior to competition and invite them to watch. (ALL YEARS)

- Email coaches and thank them for attending. (ALL YEARS)

- Answer all emails and letters. (JUNIOR & SENIOR YEAR)

- Be honest and forthright with everyone, especially yourself. (ALL YEARS)

- Call coaches and express your interest in their programs. (ALL YEARS)

- Set up unofficial visits. (JUNIOR YEAR)

- Give coaches your cell phone number so they can text you. (JUNIOR & SENIOR YEARS)

- Call on a regular basis to institutions of interest. (JUNIOR & SENIOR YEARS)

- Ask open questions to coaches. (ALL YEARS)

- Let the coach talk about his/her program and institution. (ALL YEARS)

- Take the SAT/ACT early and often. (JUNIOR & SENIOR YEARS)

- Send transcripts to institutions you are recruiting and being recruited by. (JUNIOR YEAR)

- Know why you like a certain educational institution. (ALL YEARS)

- Return phone calls to coaches. (SENIOR YEAR)

- Send thank-you cards after unofficial and official visits. (JUNIOR & SENIOR YEAR)

IMPORTANT DATES

June 15 prior to Junior Year: Men's basketball coaches can call PSAs once a month

Throughout Junior Year: Make unofficial visits to schools to see what types of school environments you prefer

September 1 Junior Year: PSA can receive written athletic material from college coaches

April/May Junior Year: Women's basketball can make one call per month

May Junior Year: Football coaches can make one phone call to each PSA

End of Junior Year: Send end-of-year transcripts to coaches/Admissions Office. NCAA III institutions can contact PSA by telephone

June 15 prior to Senior Year: NCAA II institutions can contact PSA by telephone weekly

July 1 prior to Senior Year: NCAA I institutions can contact PSA by telephone weekly

1st Day of Senior Year: PSA can attend official visits to a maximum of five institutions

EXAMPLE HIGH SCHOOL RECRUITING TIMELINE

Sophomore Year	
Meet with HS Counselor to assure correct academic track for NCAA Eligibility	August
Start to compile list of academic institutions that interest you	Fall–Winter
Draft and complete recruiting resume	Fall–Winter
Write to coaching staff expressing an interest in their program	Early Spring
Decide which camps (if any) you will attend that summer	Late Spring
Junior Year	
Meet with HS Counselor to assure correct academic track for NCAA Eligibility	August
Register with NCAA Eligibility Center	Fall
Register and take SAT and/or ACT	Fall
Have standardized tests sent to NCAA and institutions	After Testing
Correspond with all college coaches	Fall
Write again to any coach that has not replied to you	Fall
Call your top choices to see their level of interest	Fall
Schedule unofficial visits to different types of institutions	During Season
Narrow down choices by types of institution	After Visits
Continue to correspond via text, email and phone	After Visits
Complete pre-financial aid paper work	Spring
Narrow down choices to five or less (programs that you are interested in official visit) Spring	
Express your level of interest to each college coach/program	Spring
Send junior year-end transcripts to NCAA Eligibility Center	Early Summer

Senior Year	
Meet with HS Counselor to assure correct academic track for NCAA Eligibility	August
Complete academic applications	August–October
Schedule official visits	August–October
Continue correspondence with college coaches	All Year
Choose institution/program	When Ready
Explain to coaches your choice	When You Know
Complete financial aid information	January–February
Complete housing forms	Spring
Sign NLI	Signing Date
Send final transcript to institution and NCAA	Graduation
Talk with strength coaches about summer workout program	April–May
Follow summer workout and be physically and mentally ready for the start of school	Summer

Note: This timeline is a guide. Some PSAs will move more quickly than others and may commit as juniors or even earlier.

CHAPTER TWO

I'M ELIGIBLE, SO WHY TAKE THE SAT AGAIN?

Every college has its own standard for academic achievement and admittance. Some academic institutions even have different standards for athletes, which can be weaker. The confusing part is that these standards can vary tremendously from those of the NCAA (each division has its own standards), from institutions within their conference, or even among schools with similar standing nationally. It is crucial that PSAs understand the standards of the NCAA and the programs they are interested in, and know whether the institutions can help with admissions if needed.

STEVE'S STORY

Steve was interested in three programs that had academic merit, as well as the possibility of four years of significant playing time. In addition, each program competed very well within their conferences, and at a regional and national level. The three schools—Baseball University, Brainy Baseball University, and Smart Baseball College—all had different academic and socio-economic profiles. Each had different admissions standards that varied from one to the other (regardless of whether the prospective student was an athlete or not), even though they competed within the same athletic conference.

Steve assumed that because the two colleges competed against each other within the same athletic conference, the institutions would have the same academic standards. This was not the case. Each school set their own standards for academic achievement and admissions acceptance.

In preparation for official visits, and under the suggestion of his coaches, Steve began the NCAA Eligibility Center process prior to the end of his junior year. He knew it was important to begin mid-spring to avoid the junior rush at the end of the spring, as well as the summer rush from graduating seniors.

The NCAA Eligibility Center is more commonly known as the NCAA Clearinghouse or The Clearinghouse.

Steve went online to register and completed all personal and high school information so that at the end of his junior year, his transcripts and test scores would be sent to the NCAA Eligibility Center to establish his standing. Even though Steve had achieved an appropriate SAT score and a high enough GPA and had completed his core classes by the end of his junior year, the Eligibility Center could still not deem him eligible to compete in NCAA athletics until he had actually graduated from high school.

NCAA ELIGIBILITY CENTER PROCEDURE

- Log on to www.ncaaclearinghouse.net

- Click on *Prospective Student-athletes*

- Click on *Domestic Student Release Form* and enter your information

  ✔ Personal Information: full name, address and country of citizenship

  ✔ High School Information: H.S. Code, entering and graduation dates—NCAA High School Code can be found by using a link on the page

  ✔ Other High School Information: H.S. Code, entering and graduation dates

✔ If a PSA has attended more than one high school this information is required for each school

✔ If a PSA attends more than one high school the NCAA Eligibility Center requires a transcript from each school

✔ Anticipated College Enrollment Period and Sport(s)

✔ Choice of correspondence media: the registering PSA can choose to receive NCAA Eligibility Center via email or regular mail

✔ Personal Identification Number (PIN): this number is used when logging onto the Web page for updates.

✔ Payment: The cost to register with the NCAA Eligibility Center is $50.

   ○ Payment can be made on the Web site using a credit card.

   ○ Payment can be made with a check by sending your confirmation paperwork with a check to the NCAA Eligibility Center.

   ○ Some PSAs may qualify for the fee waiver.

✔ Signature of Approval and Release—must be agreed on by both the Prospect and the Parent (if PSA is under 18)

✔ Submit

    Address: NCAA Eligibility Center
                 301 ACT Drive
                 Box 4043
                 Iowa City, IA 52243-4044

NCAA ELIGIBILITY CENTER FEE WAVIER

For a prospect to be eligible for a waiver of the NCAA Eligibility Center fees, the prospect must be eligible for an ACT or SAT fee waiver.

● The prospect must check with his or her high school counselor and the counselor must submit an electronic fee-waiver confirmation form to the NCAA Eligibility Center.

SAT Fee Waiver:

The SAT fee waiver is available to high school juniors and seniors in the US, Puerto Rico or US Territories who cannot afford the testing fees. Only high school counselors can award the Fee Waiver Card.

● Covers basic test fees (SAT or SAT Subject)

- May qualify student for application fee waiver to academic institutions

- Waivers can only be used for regular registration; however, for the October testing date, the Waiver Card may be used for late registration.

Eligibility:

- US citizen or foreign national testing in US

- US citizen living outside US

- Meet financial eligibility guidelines—participation in Federal Free and Reduced Lunches/National School Lunch Program

- Home-schooled students must prove eligibility to local high school counselor

Steve completed all the relevant personal information, then reached the signature page. This is extremely important. Steve's signature confirmed that all information was correct. He understood that furnishing improper information to the NCAA could result in the permanent ineligibility at NCAA member institutions. Further, his signature authorized the NCAA to use his academic and personal information in several ways:

- All listed high schools are allowed to send transcripts, proof of graduation and other relevant information regarding academics or athletic eligibility to the Eligibility Center.

- The Center can authorize the release of all academic information to NCAA member institutions (colleges and universities) that requested the information.

- The prospect cannot request information be sent to a member institution; the institution must request it. If there is no request by a member institution, the NCAA will not complete the certification process.

- NCAA is permitted to release information to outside sources, including the media, to correct any inaccuracies.

- NCAA is allowed to collect information to be used for research regarding eligibility, academic preparation, and academic performance, research that may be released and published.

After the submission of the signature page and agreement to all NCAA regulations regarding the Eligibility Center, Steve had to complete a questionnaire. The NCAA Eligibility Center requires all prospective student-athletes to complete an *Amateurism Questionnaire,* which is a series of questions validating their amateur status.

AMATEURISM QUESTIONNAIRE

- Has the PSA been marketed by anyone regarding athletic ability and/ or accepted benefits from an athletic agent?

- Has the PSA received prize money, had expenses paid, or paid to compete in any athletic event?

- Has the PSA been associated with a professional sports team or received expenses from a professional team?

- Has the PSA previously attended a two- or four-year school?

- Has the PSA attended a two- or four-year school on a full-time basis?

Steve answered all the questions and agreed that his responses were correct. Clicking on the confirmation button, Steve attested that his responses were true and that he was in fact an amateur athlete.

Steve was persistent with his counselors to send his transcripts to the NCAA. He knew at the beginning of every summer they were swamped with transcript requests, so he was diligent about turning in his requests on time.

To qualify and become eligible to compete in NCAA athletics, Steve had to complete all four of the NCAA standards for eligibility:

1. Graduate from HS

2. Complete NCAA stated core curriculum

3. Attain a minimum GPA from the 16 core classes

4. Attain a minimum SAT or ACT score

NAIA is another collegiate athletic association that works primarily with smaller schools. NAIA eligibility is different from that of the NCAA. To be eligible for NAIA competition, the student must graduate from an accredited high school or be accepted as a student of good academic standing at their currently enrolled institution (college or university). In addition, the prospect must meet two of the three criterions listed below:

- Achieve a minimum of 18 on the enhanced ACT or 860 on the SAT (Critical Reading and Math sections)

- Achieve an overall GPA during high school of 2.000 or better

- Graduate in the upper 50 percent of his or her high school graduating class

A "Non-qualifier" is a student-athlete who does not attain all the standards set forth by the NCAA.

A "partial-qualifier" is a student-athlete at the NCAA II level that meets one of the two qualifying standards. If a student-athlete is a partial-qualifier, he or she is eligible to practice with their team at their home practice facility and to receive athletic aid. When the student-athlete becomes academically eligible the following year, he or she can participate in four seasons of competition.

A qualifier is eligible to practice, compete, and receive athletically related financial aid.

The core curriculum considered by the NCAA consists of 16 classes (each a year long, or two classes combined to make a year-long credit). The eligibility guidelines for a student's Grade Point Average vary, dependent on the SAT or ACT scores. With a sliding scale such as this, a GPA of 3.55 or better can have an SAT as low as 400 (Math and Critical Reading combined) while an SAT score of 1010 can have a GPA as low as 2.00 to allow the PSA to certify as a qualifier.

The NCAA Academic Core consists of:

- 4 credits (4 years) of English

- 3 credits of math (Algebra 1 or higher)

- 2 years of natural or physical science (at least one lab-based course)

- 1 additional year of English, math or science

- 2 years of social science

- 4 years of additional classes (foreign languages, philosophy, non-doctrine religion)

It is imperative that each high school student know where they stand regarding their eligibility. High school students can complete a NCAA Eligibility Worksheet to determine their NCAA Eligibility Grade Point Average which can be different from the high school's calculation of overall GPA. The NCAA Eligibility GPA is determined from a student's group of core classes only.

To obtain an up-to-date copy of NCAA I and NCAA II eligibility worksheets, visit the NCAA at https://web1.ncaa.org/eligibilitycenter/hs/wksheet.pdf to print off a copy and complete the forms to determine your eligibility. It will be helpful to enlist the help of your high school guidance counselor to ensure you are calculating your GPA based on the appropriate core classes.

Steve's school, like every high school, is evaluated independently from other schools throughout the country. To insure a proper progress toward graduation and NCAA eligibility, Steve met with his guidance counselor yearly to assess his classes and to make sure they were all counting toward the NCAA core. Steve had learned a lesson from an older friend who thought he was taking the same classes as someone else from another school who was eligible; but because the schools rated their classes differently, Steve's friend could not become eligible.

Each of the high school core classes must meet standards set forth by the NCAA.

- The course must be recognized as an academic course and qualify toward graduation.

- The class must be considered college prep by the high school, meaning it prepares the student academically to enter a four-year college upon graduation.

- A mathematics class must be at or above an Algebra 1 level.

- Any course must be taught by a qualified instructor defined by the appropriate authority.

- A core class must be taught at or above the high school's regular academic level.

At the conclusion of Steve's junior year, his SAT score was 1180 and his core GPA was 3.45, which mirrored his over-all grade point average. Proud of this, he relayed his scores to the coaches at the institutions in which he was interested. Steve assumed he would receive a positive response from the coaches and was surprised at how each one reacted differently to his scores and future NCAA Eligibility Center report. Steve had estimated that once his high school graduation was complete, he was eligible, and that meant that he could get in to any school he wanted. He was, after all, not just an athlete, but a *heavily recruited* athlete.

Coach Jefferson from Brainy Baseball University received a copy of Steve's transcripts and test scores, which he promptly sent to the Admissions Department for evaluation. Upon receiving the transcript back from the Admissions Department, Coach Jefferson notified Steve that although his grades and scores were impressive for a large majority of academic institutions, there was no way—even with a stellar senior year and a large jump in his SAT score—that he would be admitted to BBU. Steve followed up with an email to the coach and asked for admissions help from the Athletic Department and/or baseball program.

TO: Coach_Jefferson@BrainyBaseballU.edu

FROM: BaseballSteve@email.com

SUBJECT: Admissions

Coach Jefferson, with regard to my grades and the admissions standards at BBU, is there any possibility that the Athletic Department could help with my process? You have recruited me for over a year and I have been very impressed with your program and BBU as an academic institution. If you could provide some admissions help, I would be very grateful as I know that I can succeed as a student and as an athlete within your program.

I look forward to hearing from you in the very near future.

Steve Lastname

Even if Coach Jefferson could have helped Steve, he would not put his reputation on the line, nor did he want to add a potential academic headache to his program. He wished Steve great success in his college search.

The coaches at Smart Baseball University wanted to consider admissions options for Steve and seemed more willing to help than BBU. Upon receiving Steve's transcripts, Coach Rodriguez met with the admissions counselor who supervised athletic admissions. Although Steve was competitive for other schools in the conference, he was not competitive with the caliber of prospective students and the prospective student-athletes that apply to SBU. Even though he was a recruited athlete, Steve was still competing academically against everyone else that applied to the university as well.

Coach Rodriguez notified Steve that even with admissions help from the baseball program, he would still need to take the SAT again and achieve a 100 to 200 point jump from his previous results. In addition, he would need to take a couple of advanced classes his senior year, and pass with a B or better before he could be considered for admission to SBU.

TO: BaseballSteve@email.com

FROM: CoachRodriguez@smartbaseballuniversity.edu

SUBJECT: Recruitment Opportunities

Steve,

Thank you for your consistent correspondence with me regarding your desire to attend Smart Baseball University and to be a member of our baseball program. I appreciate your sending us a copy of your high school transcript and SAT test scores and this has allowed us to review your academic profile and how it fits into SBU.

As you know, SBU is a very strong academic institution. Acceptance into our university requires all our recruits to be very competitive, which at times prohibits recruitment into our baseball program. Although your transcripts and test scores are very impressive, our Admissions Department does not feel your academic profile is strong enough for acceptance at SBU.

If there was anything I could do above the avenues that we have already explored for you, I would! I believe that you have a very bright future as a baseball player and student. Until your academic profile meets our desired admissions standards, however, we cannot offer you a position within our program.

Please keep me updated as to your academic advancement.

Coach Rodriguez

Baseball University was much more accepting of Steve's hard work in the classroom and of his SAT scores. Steve's grades were sufficient to be admitted to the university, even without additional help from the baseball program. In fact, Coach Pierce wanted to see what academic scholarships Steve would qualify for in addition to his baseball scholarship.

At some universities, athletes can receive an admissions waiver if they fall below normal admissions standards for freshman students. In some instances, universities allow a total number of waivered athletes, while others may allow a certain number in each recruiting class. If the coach, and his or her program, has shown strong academic success with previous students, there may be more waivers available for the coach to use. There are also universities that have different admission standards for athletes because they believe that being an athlete, especially at a highly competitive level, is beneficial to the institution. However, every university and program is different.

Steve should have asked the coaches early in the recruiting process what test scores, grades and classes he needed to have on his transcript. That way Steve could have prepared for those institutions he wanted to attend. In addition, Steve could have saved himself some energy in the recruiting process by not pursuing a program where he had no possibility of being accepted. He could have found a better "reach school" than Brainy Baseball University. It is important that a "reach" school is not an impossible reach.

Steve was confused about the large discrepancy in the reactions from each academic institution. Even though he was well on his way to being declared eligible by the NCAA and graduating from his high school, Steve did not understand that academically he was competing against every other person his age that was applying to the school. There are academic gray areas that colleges and universities can recruit within, but coaches never guarantee that they can secure a PSA a spot on the roster or the acceptance list.

Steve decided that he would take the challenge from Smart Baseball College and retake the SAT as soon as the fall began. Steve also enrolled in two advanced placement classes with the determination to get A's. He wanted to get accepted to SBC, compete for Coach Rodriguez and prove to everyone that he deserved to attend an academic institution like Smart Baseball College.

The final part of Steve's journey to becoming a qualifier by NCAA standards was to send his official transcript to the NCAA Eligibility Center as soon as he graduated. Once again he was persistent with his high school counselors and had them send out the transcripts in a timely manner.

Only an NCAA qualifier can receive an athletic scholarship!

DAVE'S STORY

Dave and his family were not only worried about the cost of tuition, his books, and room and board, but they were also concerned regarding the *additional* costs that a student generally accrues at college. With great guidance from Coach Spitz, his swimming coach, Dave and his family began to explore their options. They came to understand that as a student-athlete, Dave could attain scholarship monies and grants from various organizations, as long as he was qualified. As Dave neared the end of high school, he received athletic and academic scholarships that would cover approximately 50 percent of his college expenses. But there was still a lot of money to make up—50 percent was not nearly enough, given his family's financial situation—especially when he took into account the total cost of attendance, which was above and beyond the cost of tuition, room, board, books and fees.

Dave knew he had to find other scholarships; but before he began his search, he contacted the Financial Aid Department of Super Swim University and asked for an estimate of the total cost of attendance for the upcoming academic year.

Using federal guidelines and regulations, each institution's Financial Aid Office can determine the monetary value of the total cost of attendance, including the following:

- Total cost of tuition and all fees

- Room and board—the cost of room and board to live on campus, not off campus

- Books and educational supplies

- Transportation to and from the institution

- Additional expenses related to attendance

Determined to save his parents and himself the burden of student loans, Dave aggressively sought different scholarships from every possible angle he could think of. Researching on the Internet and reading a couple of books that his parents had been using for research, Dave found many scholarships that he qualified for. Luckily Dave was a red head, had a strong Scottish ancestral line, and was skilled at using duct tape—this alone qualified him for three scholarships!

There are scholarships based on every talent, achievement, academic interest and career interest that you can imagine.

Logging onto the Web, Dave filled out a personal profile on scholarship sites, including his interests, his family background, his academic achievement and interests, as well as random information for the out-of-the-box scholarships. On a regular basis, Dave received potential scholarship opportunities. It was very important for Dave and his family that he create time in his weekly schedule to sort through them, complete the applications and send them off. Every Sunday afternoon, the family sat down and worked their way through Dave's academic expenses, continually adjusting and modifying their family plan for payment of Dave's college expenses as he found more scholarships that would help him achieve his goal of attending Super Swim University.

When reviewing various scholarships, Dave had to be careful that the scholarships he was applying for did not compromise his NCAA eligibility or have a possible negative effect on the swimming program or the overall athletic or academic standing of Super Swim University. Each scholarship Dave accepted had to meet stringent regulations set forth by the NCAA. This meant that Dave had to look for scholarships that were...

- Part of scholarship programs that were established and recognized and that would continue as scholarship programs in the future.

- Awarded with absolutely no regard to his athletic ability and potential at the given university.

If an established and recognized program awards a scholarship where part of the award criteria is based on athletic participation, the award must meet specific standards set forth by the NCAA. Acceptable awards are those where...

- The award is made based on specific and measured athletic criteria based on past performance.

- The award is paid directly to the institution and is only available for the educational expenses of the student-athlete.

- The scholarship award is not restricted to specific educational institutions (or athletic departments).

- The donor, or decision maker, of the award is not considered a "representative of athletic interest."

- The value of the award does not exceed the "total cost of attendance."

- The award is provided only once.

- The scholarship is not awarded from an outside sports team or organization.

A representative of athletic interest: An individual, independent agency, corporate entity or organization that is known to promote, make financial contributions, assist in recruiting or provide benefits to enrolled student-athletes and/or an institution's athletic department

---

As a swimmer, Dave could receive any percentage of a scholarship that offered 1 percent to 100 percent of a full grant-in-aid. As Coach Spitz explained to Dave, swimming was an *equivalency* sport. In simple terms, Dave understood that Coach Spitz had a maximum of 9.9 full grant-in-aids that he could split between all his athletes. Some of the athletes could receive more than others, while some of the athletes could get no athletically related scholarship monies, and a few could receive *full scholarships.*

Early in the recruiting process, Coach Spitz had explained to Dave that each coach was different in his or her approach to determining scholarships. Just as every institution determines its own admissions process, each athletic department determines how much of the maximum awards will be issued on a sport-by-sport basis.

Even though the NCAA maximum for men's swimming is 9.9 (women's is 14) not every program will award the maximum. In addition, different programs may offer the same athlete different percentages of a scholarship—this will be determined by the need for that athlete in a given year or the amount of scholarship money available based on the previous year's recruiting and the current recruiting environment.

In his selection process, Dave took into consideration many factors. He considered the academic opportunities offered by each institution and he weighed the financial implications for his family. In the end, he narrowed down his choices to two schools. Private Swim College offered Dave a 50 percent athletic scholarship, while Coach Spitz at Super Swim University had only been able to offer him 40 percent. Although the scholarship offer from PSC was a higher percentage and a higher monetary value, it was still cheaper for Dave to attend Super Swim University, since Private Swim College was a much more expensive school. Dave's family was not concerned about the higher percentage but the total out-of-pocket cost of his education.

A **full grant-in-aid** is the monetary value of tuition, room, board, books and fees at the institution. This value may change on a yearly basis (it normally increases by approximately 5 percent every year).

During the recruitment phase, Dave encountered several coaches who laid out a complicated matrix regarding his scholarship opportunities. Some coaches offered him a small percentage his first year with incremental increases the following years. They promised that this was a guarantee, but under the guidance of his high school swim coach, Dave knew that a collegiate coach could not guarantee these additions. A scholarship agreement is awarded yearly and is only for *one* year.

Dave understood the complications of a convoluted agreement, and he was aware that a few unscrupulous coaches try to use such offers as bait to lure prospects into their programs. It is very easy for a coach to keep a scholarship award at the initial amount and not increase it as promised. Dave had agreed with his parents that when he accepted a scholarship amount, he would be happy with that, and his family would budget that amount for four years. If Dave were to get a scholarship increase in the following years, Dave and his family would consider it a bonus.

With his strong academic profile, the Admissions Department at Super Swim University awarded Dave an academic scholarship. According to NCAA rules, Dave could receive the award only if it were based solely on his academic achievements. In addition, the award of the scholarship met standards that had been previously established by the institution. With this generous addition to his athletic scholarship, Dave's total package was over 50 percent.

Like most academic scholarship awards, the one offered by SSU was contingent on Dave maintaining a high academic standard during his time at the university. Super Swim University, like many educational institutions, set minimum standards and expected awardees to maintain them.

If a scholarship recipient drops below a college or university's standards, one of three changes may occur:

- The student might be placed on probation regarding his or her academic scholarship. The institution might allow the student a semester or two to achieve the standards before rescinding the award.

- The academic institution may not re-award the scholarship automatically, but can allow the student the opportunity to receive the award again when academic standards are reached and maintained.

- The academic institution may automatically rescind the scholarship permanently.

Dave had worked diligently in completing scholarship applications for everything he believed he might possibly win. All his hard work paid off. During his first year at SSU, he qualified for the total amount of the cost of attendance at the institution.

With his tuition, room, board and fees all paid for, the Financial Aid Office sent him reimbursement checks on a regular basis to make up the difference in the cost of the institution and the total cost of his scholarships. The additional money was used by Dave to pay for his books, supplies and any additional educational expenses he had accrued, up to the total cost of attendance.

During Dave's second year, he decided to live off campus. Every month he received a stipend check from his scholarship monies to pay for his apartment, food, and general living and educational expenses.

KELLY'S STORY

As a head-count sport, volleyball coaches can only offer their prospects a full grant-in-aid (full scholarship) or nothing. Therefore, Kelly applied for various scholarships from many different sources—the government, independent scholarship sources and Volleyball State College, where she wanted to attend.

Kelly's family consisted only of herself and her dad. As a single parent, her dad worked hard to provide her with every opportunity he could. Kelly also worked after school. Over the course of two years, Kelly saved money toward her college tuition. Nevertheless, this was just a small drop in the ocean compared to the high costs of tuition and academic expenses.

During her junior year, Kelly's dad wanted to get a better understanding of what he was facing when it came to sending his daughter to college. A volleyball scholarship was always an option but due to various reasons, he was not convinced that she would pursue that avenue. Therefore, in anticipation of having to choose a college based on finances, he proactively began searching for ways to pay for college.

The first step for Kelly's dad was to apply for federal aid. Even though Kelly was still a junior, her dad went online to complete a FAFSA4caster (www.fafsa4caster.ed.gov). Anticipating that his income and tax status would not change significantly from one year to the next, Kelly's dad completed the form using all his previously filed tax information. Once this was done, he received an EFC number from the government. The acronym EFC stands for Expected Family Contribution, a sum based on family members' past tax information. In Kelly's case, the figure came from her dad's tax information (income, savings, investments, etc.) as well as her own and was the estimated amount the government believed Kelly's dad and Kelly could contribute toward her college education.

It was important for Kelly's dad to fill out the EFC form early, in order to help Kelly make her college selection. If Kelly were to choose a college in the fall of her senior year but her dad could not complete the FAFSA until the spring of her senior year, they could not plan properly. With an early estimate, it was easier for Kelly and her dad to work with the Financial Aid Office. It helped them determine the amount of aid she would qualify for and it gave them an early start on any loans or additional grants or scholarships for which she was eligible.

STAFFORD LOAN

A Stafford loan is a low interest loan from the government that is available to most students. An athlete can take out the loan over and above his or her scholarship.

PELL GRANT

Student-athletes can receive a Pell Grant over and above their scholarship monies, if they qualify.

WORK-STUDY

Kelly, just like every other student-athlete, has to work within the NCAA rules when it comes to income. Even though she would not be a scholarship athlete during her first year, she could still only receive NCAA approved aid.

During a conversation with her financial aid representative, Kelly heard about the Work Study program at Volleyball State College. Kelly found that she could work on campus within the program and earn extra money that she could put toward her educational expenses or for anything else she needed. As long as Kelly received a pay rate that was standard for the position and was only paid for the work performed, she could participate in the program. The money that she made through the Work Study program was over and above the dollar amount that the Financial Aid Office documented as the total cost of attendance.

Due to Kelly and her dad's proactive approach to understanding their financial aid situation, they were able to work with the Financial Aid Office earlier than most other students. This allowed Kelly the opportunity to apply sooner for need-based grants awarded by the institution.

Kelly could not ask Coach Fillmore or anyone else in the Athletic Department to help her apply for these grants. The coaching staff and other Athletic Department staff have to allow the Financial Aid Office and grant issuing bodies to make the decision with no bias toward any athlete and without consideration of anyone's athletic ability.

SUMMARY

- Be aware that all academic institutions do not have the same academic standards, even when they compete in the same conference.

- Understand that every institution sets its own standards for academic achievement and admissions.

- Know what academic standards each institution expects from you.

- Ask the coach early in the recruitment process if your academic profile fits the institution.

- Register early (end of junior year) with the NCAA Eligibility Center.

- Request that your high school counselor send your academic transcripts to the Eligibility Center.

- Check with your high school counselor to see if you qualify for the ACT, SAT or NCAA Eligibility Center fee waiver.

- Meet with your high school counselor to insure that you are taking the correct classes relative to the NCAA core classes and athletic eligibility.

- Read and understand the confirmation information in the Eligibility Center application.

- Make sure that you supply all the correct information to the NCAA—especially concerning your amateur status.

- Be certain that you have your test scores sent directly to the NCAA Eligibility Center from the ACT or SAT.

- Know what GPA you must attain relative to your SAT/ACT score for NCAA Eligibility.

- Ask the coaches or admissions representatives which classes you should take your senior year to be better prepared for college.

- Send your transcripts to the NCAA Eligibility Center and your future institution *immediately* upon graduation from high school.

- Take into consideration the total cost of attendance and additional expenses when planning college costs.

- Research and apply for various additional scholarships.

- Know whether your sport is a *head-count* or *equivalency* sport.

- Ask the recruiting coaches if they receive the full allotment of scholarship money.

- Know that scholarship monies are not guaranteed to increase–even if promised.

- Accept a scholarship that you are going to be happy with—consider any increase a bonus.

- Understand the minimum standards you must meet in order to maintain any academic or outside scholarships.

- Complete scholarship and federal aid applications early.

- Attain an EFC number in your junior year if possible.

NCAA I SCHOLARSHIPS BY SPORT

Head Count Sports: Only offer full grant-in-aid or nothing

Women's Sports	Men's Sports
Basketball (15)	Basketball (13)
Volleyball (12)	Football (85 I-A or 63 I-AA)
Gymnastics (12)	
Tennis (8)	

Equivalency Sports: The coach can divide the scholarships

Women's Sports	Men's Sports
Archery (5)	Baseball (11.7)
Badminton (6)	Cross Country/Track & Field (12.6)
Bowling (5)	Fencing (4.5)
Cross Country/Track & Field (18)	Golf (4.5)
Equestrian (15)	Gymnastics (6.3)
Fencing (5)	Lacrosse (12.6)
Field Hockey (12)	Rifle (3.6)
Golf (6)	Skiing (6.3)
Lacrosse (12)	Soccer (9.9)
Rowing (20)	Swimming and Diving (9.9)
Rugby (12)	Volleyball (4.5)
Skiing (7)	Water Polo (4.5)
Soccer (14)	Wrestling (9.9)
Softball (12)	
Squash (12)	
Swimming and Diving (14)	
Synchronized Swimming (5)	
Team Handball (10)	
Water Polo (8)	

NCAA II SCHOLARSHIPS BY SPORT

Women's Sports	Men's Sports
Archery (9)	Baseball (9)
Badminton (10)	Basketball (10)
Basketball (10)	Cross Country/Track (12.6)
Cross Country/Track (12.6)	Fencing (4.5)
Equestrian (15)	Football (36)
Fencing (4.5)	Golf (3.6)
Field Hockey (6.3)	Gymnastics (5.4)
Golf (5.4)	Ice Hockey (13.5)
Gymnastics (6)	Lacrosse (10.8)
Ice Hockey (18)	Rifle (3.6)
Lacrosse (9.9)	Skiing (6.3)
Rowing (20)	Soccer (9)
Rugby (12)	Swimming and Diving (8.1)
Skiing (6.3)	Tennis (4.5)
Soccer (9.9)	Volleyball (4.5)
Softball (7.2)	Water Polo (4.5)
Squash (9)	Wrestling (9)
Swimming and Diving (8.1)	
Synchronized Swimming (5)	
Team Handball (12)	
Tennis (6)	
Volleyball (8)	
Water Polo (8)	

The above information is taken from the NCAA Manual.

IN WHICH DIVISION SHOULD YOU COMPETE?

The above question is one that only you, the prospective college student-athlete, can answer. The general theory is that NCAA I schools have better athletics, better funding, and a better education than either NCAA II or NCAA III institutions, but this is not true in all cases.

Remember, there is a place for everyone! As you will see by the numbers given in the table at the end of this chapter, there are far more opportunities at the NCAA II and III levels than there are at the NCAA I level.

In fact, there are NCAA II and NCAA III athletic programs that are better than the division above them, and there are many NCAA II and NCAA III institutions that are ranked higher academically and can provide a better education for you than the athletically divided schools above them.

When choosing which college or university to attend, the first priority should be academics—no matter the athletic program. When choosing an athletic program, your philosophy and approach to athletics is key. Ask yourself what you would like to gain from the experience. As a future college student-athlete, you need to decide what you want from athletics in all avenues.

- What are your individual goals?
- Do you want to play a lot or be a role/fringe player?
- Do you want to compete for conference and/or national championships?
- Is athletics a social component of your education?
- Are you prepared to miss two/three days of class every week to travel for athletics?
- Are you prepared to give up school holidays and days off for your athletic program?

Some college athletes are happy being part of a successful team even though they do not play much. Others would rather play for a "lower" level team and play more—and have the opportunity to be a team captain and starter.

You may be faced with choosing between a good mid-major NCAA I program with a partial scholarship or an NCAA II program that has the same—or better—scholarship opportunity and competes for a national championship. Or maybe the opportunity to attain a very coveted degree from an NCAA III institution and the opportunity to play within a very highly competitive program is a better option than playing at an NCAA II school without the academic rigor or sitting on the bench for four years at an NCAA I institution.

Some PSAs just want the opportunity to say they are college athletes and enjoy the experience—no matter the level or division. Saying you are an NCAA I athlete may be impressive to your parents' friends, but ultimately you want to be happy and successful academically, athletically and socially—and you can accomplish that at any division as long as the institution, coaches and program fit your needs and mesh with your philosophy of approach to reaching your collegiate goals.

The three divisions of NCAA athletics vary in different manners:

An **NCAA I** institution must offer seven sports for both men and women (or six for men and eight for women) with a minimum of two team sports for each gender. Each gender must participate in all three sporting seasons sponsored by the NCAA. In addition, NCAA I football programs must meet minimum attendance requirements. Each NCAA I institution must meet the minimum athletic scholarships for each sponsored sport.

NCAA II institutions must offer five sports for both men and women (or four for men and six for women) with a minimum of two team sports for each gender. Each gender must participate in all three sporting seasons sponsored by the NCAA. Each sport has maximum scholarship opportunities per sport, but no minimum (which are fewer than NCAA I programs) and most student-athletes create a financial aid package with a combination of athletic scholarship, academic awards, and other awards, loans and grants. NCAA II institutions tend to play in regionalized conferences and recruit more local prospects.

NCAA III institutions must offer five sports for both men and women (or four for men and six for women) with a minimum of two team sports for each gender. Each gender must participate in all three sporting seasons sponsored by the NCAA. Student-athletes do not receive athletically related financial aid with the emphasis being placed on student participation. In other words, the student-athlete's experience is the primary focus of an institution's athletic department.

While the philosophy of NCAA III athletics does not include awarding athletically related scholarships, a coach that is recruiting you may be able to direct you to appropriate academic and private scholarships within the institution that can help you and your parents pay for educational expenses. There are also some NCAA III institutions that provide financial aid to students that cannot afford to attend their schools—such an institution will scholarship the difference between the student's EFC (from FAFSA) and the cost of attendance at the institution.

Number of Programs*

SPORT	NCAA I	NCAA II	NCAA III	Number of Athletes
Women— Championship				
Basketball	325	286	428	15,096
Bowling	24	15	5	383
Cross Country	322	265	371	13,228
Fencing	26	4	14	658
Field Hockey	77	27	154	5,468
Golf	231	130	143	3,981
Gymnastics	65	6	15	1,414
Ice Hockey	31	2	42	1,727
Lacrosse	80	38	153	5,999
Rifle	27	3	7	217
Rowing	86	15	41	6,902
Skiing	16	9	15	503
Soccer	301	220	409	21,709
Softball	267	266	399	16,609
Swimming/Diving	188	72	237	11,011
Tennis	310	218	360	8,534
Indoor Track	289	117	224	19,090
Outdoor Track	299	165	258	20,871
Volleyball	311	269	412	14,010
Water Polo	31	10	20	1,173
Total	**3,306**	**2,137**	**3,707**	**170,526**
Women— Participation				
Archery	2	0	0	21
Badminton	0	0	3	30
Equestrian	15	6	24	1,286
Rugby	1	1	2	149
Squash	8	0	18	360
Synch. Swimming	4	1	3	97
Total	**30**	**8**	**50**	**1,943**

SPORT	NCAA I	NCAA II	NCAA III	Number of Athletes
Men— Championship				
Baseball	286	241	363	28,767
Basketball	326	289	398	16,571
Cross Country	299	234	346	11,893
Fencing	20	3	12	632
Football	235	153	230	61,252
Golf	287	214	276	8,250
Gymnastics	17	0	2	321
Ice Hockey	58	7	68	3,973
Lacrosse	56	34	132	7,871
Rifle	26	2	8	207
Skiing	14	8	14	525
Soccer	199	166	387	19,135
Swimming/Diving	139	52	190	7,771
Tennis	266	173	315	7,599
Indoor Track	242	108	217	19,135
Outdoor Track	265	155	250	22,075
Volleyball	22	15	45	1,210
Water Polo	21	9	15	942
Wrestling	87	44	97	6,139
Total	**2,865**	**1,907**	**3,365**	**224,926**
Men—Participation				
Archery	1	0	0	21
Badminton	0	0	0	0
Bowling	0	1	1	33
Equestrian	0	0	8	95
Rowing	26	4	30	2,139
Rugby	0	0	2	84
Sailing	7	1	16	417
Squash	8	0	17	395
Total	**42**	**6**	**74**	**3,184**

*Based on the NCAA Participation Report 2005-2006

Many young athletes dream of being professional athletes and pursue college athletics to make it happen. Below is data estimated from the NCAA that compares participation rates of six sports and the percentage of students that achieve their goal of participating in college athletics and then professional sports.

Student Athletes

	Men's Basketball	Women's Basketball	Football
High School Student Athletes	546,335	452,929	1,071,775
High School Senior Student Athletes	156,096	129,408	306,221
NCAA Student Athletes	16,571	15,096	61,252
NCAA Freshman Roster Positions	4,735	4,313	17,501
NCAA Senior Student Athletes	3,682	3,355	13,612
NCAA Student Athletes Drafted	44	32	250
Percent High School to NCAA	3.0%	3.3%	5.7%
Percent NCAA to Professional	1.2%	1.0%	1.8%
Percent High School to Professional	0.03%	0.02%	0.08%

Source: www.ncaa.org

Student Athletes

	Baseball	Men's Ice Hockey	Men's Soccer
High School Student Athletes	470,671	36,263	358,935
High School Senior Student Athletes	134,477	10,361	102,553
NCAA Student Athletes	28,767	3,973	19,793
NCAA Freshman Roster Positions	8,219	1,135	5,655
NCAA Senior Student Athletes	6,393	883	4,398
NCAA Student Athletes Drafted	600	33	76
Percent High School to NCAA	6.1%	11.0%	5.5%
Percent NCAA to Professional	9.4%	3.7%	1.7%
Percent High School to Professional	0.45%	0.32%	0.07%

Source: www.ncaa.org

CHAPTER THREE

COLLEGE COACHES–WHAT THEY WANT

Every coach looks for different athletic and psychological/emotional attributes in their athletes. These characteristics can vary from coach to coach within a sport or athletic conference, and they can differ from one region of the country to another. The interesting thing about athletics and coaches is that an evaluation of a prospective student-athlete is mostly subjective. What one coach likes, another may dislike.

There are some sports such as golf, track, cross-country and swimming, however, where times and/or scores speak volumes about the athlete's ability. Each coach is looking for the best student-athlete for his or her program.

Beyond the accomplished high school student-athlete, coaches are always looking for future collegiate student-athletes who have not yet "peaked." Athletes mature at different rates throughout their career and consequently peak at different stages as well. Development may depend on other sports in which an athlete competes, his or her physical maturity, and the length of time the athlete has competed in that sport. Many high school "superstars" peak too early and do not have an accomplished collegiate career.

Every year college coaches are pleasantly surprised at the development of a relatively unaccomplished student-athlete who turns out to be a very successful college student-athlete. One of the most famous examples of this is David Robinson, who played just one year of high school basketball but developed tremendously both physically and technically during his time at the Naval Academy. David Robinson is now considered to have been one of the best players to ever play in the NBA.

Every sport is different, but it is helpful to know what coaches look for when they recruit, regardless of their particular sport. The following coaches are all at the top of their respected fields. They have coached teams through NCAA Championships, developed professional and Olympic athletes and have received NCAA National Coach of the Year honors.

COLLEGE COACHES SPEAK

BASEBALL

Rich Hill, University of San Diego

ACADEMICS:

"A-to-Z recruitment and development" is the philosophy of Coach Hill. Whether in the classroom or on the baseball field, he prepares his student-athletes to achieve peak performance at everything they do. Coach Hill wants everyone in his program to be a success and he believes that starts in the classroom.

ATHLETICS:

First View: Coach Hill trusts his instincts when it comes to recruiting. While watching a prospect, he thinks about who that player reminds him of—and whether they were a success. It is important to Coach Hill to keep an open mind as he watches a youth baseball game, but above all, he is looking for "talent" in both position players and pitchers.

For pitchers, Coach Hill looks for a young man that has great arm strength and who can effectively change his pitches to create the "knock-out pitch" that will win the game. In addition, a pitcher should have great command of his mound and have the potential to develop when he enters college, something Coach Hill calls the player's "project-ability."

For a positional player, the first thing Coach Hill evaluates is the athleticism of the prospect. The ease at which the athletes play is important, in addition to their arm strength, feet set up, reaction time and instinct. Bat speed, timing and loft are other characteristics that Coach Hill evaluates. However, Coach Hill acknowledges that he cannot always get the "blue chipper." On many occasions, the development potential is an important factor during the recruitment process. Considering that the University of San Diego Baseball program sends four to eight student-athletes to the professional ranks every year, it is fair to say that Coach Hill is excellent at evaluating talent.

THE PERFECT ATHLETE AND RECRUIT:

- Talented player—pitcher ranked in top 50 nationally
- First round draft potential
- Extreme commitment to college—most important for USD Baseball
- Strong family background
- Good character
- Great student
- Commitment to train
- Mental toughness

MOST IMPORTANT ATHLETIC CHARACTERISTICS:

- Power
- Speed
- Agility
- Balance—during swing
- Technique—both left- and right-handed hitting
- Strength—core specific
- Flexibility

PSYCHOLOGICAL AND EMOTIONAL:

A baseball player at the University of San Diego has one focus every day. "Your only job is to be great today," says Coach Hill as he emphasizes process-oriented goals rather than results-oriented goals. With the use of two team psychologists, the athletes spend significant time channeling their energy by breathing and visualizing the success of the team. At USD, Coach Hill and his staff train their athletes to have a mental edge.

Additionally, Coach Hill uses a network of coaches to insure that the prospect has the right character for USD—a strong and positive mental attitude and selflessness is essential. Coach Hill also understands that 17- to 20-year-old males can be emotionally volatile. He believes that there is always a good person waiting to come out. "With the correct structure, discipline and positive environment, everyone can succeed within our program," he adds.

BEST PIECE OF ADVICE:

"Watch the movie *The Peaceful Warrior*," says Coach Hill. "Living in the moment is very important. Watch it and you will understand!"

In addition, Coach Hill emphasizes the need for efficient time management for entering freshmen. The combination of academic and athletic commitments can leave first year student-athletes feeling overwhelmed, but there are resources to help them develop good time management skills. They just need to take advantage of them.

BASKETBALL

Coach David Hixon, Amherst College

ACADEMICS:

Amherst College is one of the most academically competitive institutions in the country and also boasts an NCAA Championship winning basketball team. Because of the high academic standards, educational strength is very important to Coach Hixon. He does not want a student-athlete who is miserable because of academic difficulty. Although Coach Hixon does not normally recruit student-athletes who he thinks will struggle academically at Amherst, he knows student-athletes who ask for help will get the assist that they need. Usually during the first year, student-athletes figure out the resources available to them so that they can succeed in the class-room as well as on the court.

ATHLETICS:

First View: The first thing that catches Coach Hixon's eyes during the recruiting process is the internal drive of prospects. "What is their competitive nature?" Coach Hixon asks. He believes being competitive is the most important aspect of success for any athlete. "Is he aggressive with the ability to bounce back repeatedly?" A prospect that handles failure and continues to try to improve and succeed shows he has a strong competitive spirit.

In addition to a competitive spirit, Coach Hixon looks for a basketball player that is technically strong and has the ability to make shots, especially in big situations. When looking at a technically gifted player, Coach Hixon considers if he will fit the needs of the team and if he is able to defend.

In most instances, Coach Hixon trusts his gut instinct with recruiting. He has found that his intuition can lead him to a player that will develop into a successful collegiate student-athlete. When a basketball player demonstrates raw athletic talent and can score points, then he has a future. However, Coach Hixon believes guards are harder to develop at the college level although working daily with a competitively driven center will enable them to develop their technical ability faster.

THE PERFECT ATHLETE AND RECRUIT:

- Smart

- Aggressive/competitive

- Confident

- Athletic

MOST IMPORTANT ATHLETIC CHARACTERISTICS:

- Quickness

- Physical strength

- Timing

- Coordination

- Jumping ability

- Agility—not as important for the "big banger" (center)

PSYCHOLOGICAL AND EMOTIONAL:

Competitive drive and confidence are two factors that will allow an athlete to survive. "During the first year as college student-athletes, they need to be prepared for their confidence and ego to become bruised," says Coach Hixon.

He explains that first year student-athletes are normally used to having been among the better high school athletes (and students), but as college freshman, they are among better, stronger and more disciplined athletes. In addition, they are required to do freshmen chores, such as picking up equipment, etc. Freshman athletes also have to be prepared to sit on the bench. Coach Hixon feels the successful student-athlete does not get discouraged and does not wait until it is too late to seek advice from his teammates and/or coaches.

When asked about winning the National Championship in 2007, Coach Hixon responded that the team's chemistry was what won the tournament. Having been to the Final Four a few times previously, the seniors had the experience to make shots at the right time. More importantly for the team, the seniors were able to allow younger players to draw from their strength and experience. Strong team chemistry and a strong belief in their ability drove the program to achieve at the highest level.

BEST PIECE OF ADVICE:

"Do not get discouraged," states Coach Hixon. "There will be disappointments along the way, but the ability to fight through these disappointments is what will build a successful character that everyone will be able to turn to in the future. Everyone experiences disappointment, but how a person responds to setbacks tells a lot."

In addition, Coach Hixon would like to see freshmen understand defense better before they enter college. Having a solid knowledge of various defensive options—and the desire to defend—can help freshmen separate themselves from others.

CROSS COUNTRY/TRACK

Matthew Morris, Western Illinois University

ACADEMICS:

Believing that strong students are more compliant student-athletes, the first thing Coach Morris notices is a recruit's academic profile. Because Western Illinois is a tier-one academic institution, a successful academic profile is necessary during the recruitment process. High SAT/ACT scores and GPAs can usually help student-athletes receive scholarship assistance.

Coach Morris has brought runners into his programs that were borderline students, and they have succeeded by learning more efficient ways to study. He believes that once students learn what works for them academically, they will succeed. "Student-athletes [can] be successful with a structured study-hall program and a good work ethic with energy directed to their studies."

ATHLETICS:

First View: "Are the student-athletes good at what they do?" That's a question that Coach Morris always asks during the recruitment process. Running times and race placement is just the start. What the prospects did in the past is not as important as what they will do in the future. Coach Morris feels every athlete matures differently, and projection of potential is important during the recruitment process.

Coach Morris believes entering female freshmen student-athletes generally have matured fully, while males still have much more growth potential. The physical maturity of an athlete can limit his or her future. In cross-country, it is unusual for males to score well their freshman year, while female runners can do very well as freshmen since they may have reached physical maturity already.

High school students that come from "low mileage" (40 miles per week) programs have the opportunity to develop, says Coach Morris. With more mileage and a well-designed training program, a runner can grow and improve. Coach Morris acknowledges that his program is a "fairly low mileage" college program, but it is a great deal harder than most student-athletes experience at high school. At WIU, female runners put in 70-80 miles a week and male runners 80-85 miles weekly. Development potential can only occur if the athletes' bodies can handle that type of training and the student-athletes stay free of injury.

THE PERFECT ATHLETE AND RECRUIT:

- Good student

- High sport intelligence—understands racing strategies and has the ability to make adjustments

- Good personality—has the ability to lead and make everyone strive to be better

- Talented

- Raw physical—fast responder, high VO_{2max}, high Lactate Threshold

- Mental ability—strong internal drive, stays focused at all times (best indicator)

- Strong work ethic

MOST IMPORTANT ATHLETIC CHARACTERISTICS:

- Technique—running efficiency and running economy

- High VO_{2max}

- High Lactate Threshold

- Strength—physical and mental

PSYCHOLOGICAL AND EMOTIONAL:

During the recruitment process, Coach Morris believes it is important for the coaches and current student-athletes to spend as much time with prospects as allowed by the NCAA. Whether a prospect "fits in" with the program and with the school is vitally important. "For a student-athlete to succeed, he or she must fit the philosophy of the program and the school," Coach Morris explains.

In addition to being physically strong, the importance of mental strength and focus is vital to becoming a successful runner. Coach Morris feels everyone has bad days, but great runners can compete on those days because of their internal drive to fight through the barriers and succeed.

Coach Morris is always looking for the runners that emotionally commit themselves to winning a race. "Great runners are never afraid to fail— and bounce back strongly if they do." He believes talent can be a limiting factor for many runners but it is the athletes that set long-term goals and remain single-minded in achieving those goals that succeed beyond everyone else. In addition, the ability to use their internal drive, especially in big occasions, will separate the top runners from the rest. Coach Morris asks the running "demons," "What *makes* you run?"

BEST PIECE OF ADVICE:

"Be ready to work really hard," states Coach Morris. Most runners making the transition from high school to college will experience an increase in academic and training workload and they need to be ready. In addition, athletes must be prepared for delayed gratification—it may take up to two years for them to achieve the success that they experienced in high school. Entering college athletics, a student-athlete is competing against older and stronger athletes. Freshmen need to be ready to work hard in order to move up.

GOLF

Mike McGraw, Oklahoma State University

ACADEMICS:

The ultimate goal for every golfer that enters Oklahoma State University is to graduate. Although academics is one of the last components that Coach McGraw learns about a prospect, it is vitally important that they have the potential to succeed academically when they enroll as freshman at OSU. Every coach is looking for a successful team in the classroom. "No one wants an academic headache," states Coach McGraw.

ATHLETICS:

First View: A golf coach notices a prospect's score; but more than that, Coach McGraw looks for the *finishing* scores. "When the pressure is on, does the prospect stay resilient?" Coach McGraw pays attention to how a golfer stays composed. He also notices how he treats his playing partner, parents and tournament volunteers.

Due to the influence of professional golfers like Tiger Woods, golf is becoming more athletic in nature. Coach McGraw considers an athletic golfer a "bonus" for his program.

Coach McGraw evaluates prospects on their ability to deal with adversity. "A golfer who can deal with the ups and downs of a golf round and take everything in stride," is the golfer that Coach McGraw wants in his program. Obviously, they also must be technically superior in conjunction with their resilience.

THE PERFECT ATHLETE AND RECRUIT:

- Open to learning

- Team oriented /team player

- Positive mental attitude and outlook

- Self motivated

- Strong intrinsic values

MOST IMPORTANT ATHLETIC CHARACTERISTICS:

- Technique

- Core strength

- Flexibility

- Cardiovascular endurance

- Mental strength—strength of character

PSYCHOLOGICAL AND EMOTIONAL:

A positive interaction with everyone the prospect meets is important to Coach McGraw for his program. He is looking for young men that understand the tradition of golf—and golf at OSU—in addition to fostering a strong team spirit. When Coach McGraw and his team won the NCAA National Championship in 2006, Coach McGraw stated that the team continued to grow together throughout the year. "Not only was everyone playing great golf, they were doing it for each other, the golf program, and the university" he added.

BEST PIECE OF ADVICE:

"Learn discipline away from your support system," states Coach McGraw. "You need to be able to stand on your own two feet, away from your parents and your high school support system, and still be successful."

WOMEN'S LACROSSE

Michael Scerbo, Duquesne University

ACADEMICS:

When asked about the role of academics in his program, Coach Scerbo was quick to confirm that a well-qualified student-athlete is more attractive than one that is not. However, throughout his coaching career Coach Scerbo has been able to provide prospects opportunities to attain degrees though they might not have qualified for admissions were they not athletes. Due to a strong support network and well utilized academic resources, these student-athletes have been successful.

ATHLETICS:

First View: The first athletic attribute that draws Coach Scerbo to a recruit is the prospect's feet. He looks for the ability of a lacrosse player to change direction with fluid movements. An agile and balanced athlete can be a very strong women's lacrosse player. In addition, the prospect's speed and quickness is very important. Coach Scerbo defines "quickness" as the ability of a player to reach full speed in a short distance (5 yards) and maintain speed over a longer distance.

A recruit that works hard in "non-hard-working situations" will catch Coach Scerbo's eye as well. A young lacrosse player that is willing to get "dirty" and work hard off the ball (i.e. defensive recovery runs) will stand out during a game. Dual sport athletes, especially athletes that play sports that create "good feet," are those who have used a second sport to enhance their overall development. Prospects that play tennis, basketball and soccer add to the lacrosse field. There is a large transfer of ability from one sport to lacrosse, and Coach Scerbo prefers to have athletes that do not just play lacrosse throughout high school.

THE PERFECT ATHLETE AND RECRUIT:

- At least 5'8" tall
- Runs 40 yards in less than 5 seconds (goalkeepers are the exception)
- Skilled at the sport—mastered technique
- Good relationship with family
- Team Captain/Leadership positions—strong leadership qualities
- Competes on different athletic teams
- Part-time job—strong time management skills
- 3.5+ GPA and 1200+ SAT

THE MOST IMPORTANT ATHLETIC CHARACTERISTICS:

- Agility—most important
- Speed
- Balance
- Technique
- Endurance

PSYCHOLOGICAL AND EMOTIONAL:

During the recruitment process, Coach Scerbo is always assessing the prospect's "coachability." He discusses recruits with other coaches and listens for clues regarding the prospect's work ethic and leadership skills. He is looking for student-athletes that will be team players and he wants to know what that prospect will do to help her teammates, especially in times of adversity. If he does not believe that a prospect will help her teammates during these times, she may be dropped from his recruiting list.

Additionally, Coach Scerbo will look at a prospect's MySpace and Facebook pages to learn more about his recruits and to see if there are any unhealthy habits that he does not want to be a part of his program. Coach Scerbo also takes into consideration the way a prospect treats her teammates, opponents, coaches and parents. A PSA that has a strong respect for everyone around her will do very well in his program. Conversely, someone who does not develop a strong sense of respect for people will struggle as a lacrosse player at Duquesne University.

BEST PIECE OF ADVICE:

"Take advantage of your resources and develop good time management skills," advises Coach Scerbo. He encourages his student-athletes to take a class in time management during their first year in college. Coach Scerbo adds that student-athletes who regularly use their resources—strength coaches, tutors, medical staff and counselors—are the ones who most often experience success.

Coach Scerbo emphasizes summer training before college. He wishes his first year student-athletes understood the demands of college lacrosse and took their summer workout seriously. "Training during their high school years is not as demanding (intensity and frequency) as it is during college. If incoming freshmen were better prepared physically, they would have less overtraining injuries."

ROWING

Doug Wright, Southern Methodist University

ACADEMICS:

Coach Wright does not recruit prospective student-athletes that he knows will struggle within the competitive academic environment of SMU. A student-athlete that does not have the minimum required scores for admissions will not perform well in the classroom, and he feels that is not fair to that student-athlete. Coach Wright adds that there are many talented student-athletes that have high academic scores so he does not need to take a "risk" and upset the strong academic and athletic environment within his program.

ATHLETICS:

First View: During the recruitment process, the first physical characteristic that Coach Wright looks for is height. "A tall rower can provide more leverage," he notes. This leverage gives rowers more time to build speed through the drive phase of the stroke cycle, which in turn will provide a faster finish if executed properly. Second, Coach Wright looks at the rower's body composition and limb length—he is looking for athletes with obvious muscular tone to their composition—followed by a demonstrated strong physical endurance and flexibility.

Rowing is a sport that many athletes are attracted to after high school, and Coach Wright encourages both swimmers and cross country athletes to join his squad. He feels both those sports create athletes with a high level of endurance and dedication that will help them succeed as part of his rowing program.

In addition, Coach Wright and his staff will recruit a prospect based on pure athletic ability—the "raw" athlete—over a prospect that is technically proficient in the boat. He believes skills can be developed, and pure athletic talent can be a bigger benefit to his program. Taking various athletes who have proven themselves strong overall competitors in many different sports can develop a better program than simply a team of polished rowers.

THE PERFECT ATHLETE AND RECRUIT:

- At least 6' tall
- Erg test below 730 for 2000 meters
- Proven record on the race course and successful in head-to-head races
- Strong character
- Able to show empathy, discipline and respect
- Team oriented
- Self-starter who is intrinsically motivated

MOST IMPORTANT ATHLETIC CHARACTERISTICS:

- Power—combined with endurance
- Endurance

PSYCHOLOGICAL AND EMOTIONAL:

A strong sense of humility is an endearing characteristic of the "complete" athlete. Well known and highly respected rowing coach Jim Joy used to say, "To win humbly and lose graciously is the mark of good sportsman-ship." In addition to the physical and academic components of his pros-pects, Coach Wright looks for leaders. Prospects that are captains and show great leadership in high school are the student-athletes that will suc-ceed and, in turn, help the SMU rowing program succeed. Coach Wright always discusses the coachability and leadership qualities of his prospects with coaches that have worked with that athlete.

Coach Wright looks for prospects without large and disruptive egos that will enter his program with the ability to perform. Prospects who respect authority—whether it is their parents, captains or coaches—will be looked upon more favorably. A prospect that has a large ego, and may not know how to win humbly or lose graciously, will be left for another college coach to recruit. Additionally, Coach Wright looks for a rower that knows how to "train rather than simply exercise."

BEST PIECE OF ADVICE:

"Learn how to live a disciplined lifestyle! Become a good student and a good athlete, using discipline as a guideline," advises Coach Wright.

SOCCER

John Cossaboon, Gonzaga University

ACADEMICS:

In addition to recruiting qualified prospects, Coach Cossaboon feels that it is important to create academic opportunities for PSAs who may not reach normal admissions standards. He feels sometimes student-athletes that have not succeeded at a high standard during high school just need someone to believe in them. "As long as prospects or student-athletes want to succeed, they can." Setting high expectations and providing them with an appropriate academic support system, more often than not, enables these student-athletes to succeed.

ATHLETICS:

First View: When watching a youth soccer game, the first thing that Coach Cossaboon notices about potential prospects is their "athletic grace" or "athletic ease." He looks to see how "fluid and relaxed" the player moves, combined with overall balance. Additionally, Coach Cossaboon evaluates how well soccer players recover from bad situations. "It's important to see how well players regain balance and flow, as well as their mental approach to diverse situations."

Speed is an important component of a soccer player's make-up, but it can also be a liability if it is not developed appropriately. "Speed is very important when combined with knowledge and skill," notes Coach Cossaboon. Without the technical or tactical ability to be productive with speed, a fast player can be disruptive to the flow of their team or to the game itself. Along with speed, Coach Cossaboon looks for a "forward lean" of his prospects—athletes that are willing to aggressively use their quickness and speed.

Coach Cossaboon feels there are many collegiate programs that may not look to recruit the same players that he does. Some programs are looking for the biggest and strongest prospects they can find. A search for pure speed, strength and height may play into the soccer philosophy of some soccer programs, depending on how they play the game.

THE PERFECT ATHLETE AND RECRUIT:

- At least 5'8" or 5'9" tall

- Balanced

- Fluid runner and quick over 5-20 yards

- Understands the need for continued development

- Strong and confident and able to deal with adversity

- Accepts that everything is not always perfect

- Selfless and does not criticize others

- Technically and tactically proficient

MOST IMPORTANT ATHLETIC CHARACTERISTICS:

- Speed—when combined with knowledge and skill

- Agility—especially important when the student-athlete has control of the ball

- Power—essential in accelerating the ball and important for defending

- Jumping Ability—with proper heading technique

- Balance—controlled and graceful body movements

- Technique—most important when combined with knowledge of the game

- Endurance—a college soccer player is expected to be able to play for 90 minutes

PSYCHOLOGICAL AND EMOTIONAL:

When recruiting, Coach Cossaboon watches the prospects' body language to gauge their mental approach and attitude, and to determine whether they fit with the soccer program at Gonzaga. A mature, secure and confident prospect will succeed with Coach Cossaboon. In addition to talking with a prospect's coach, Coach Cossaboon likes to watch the PSA in training. He feels this allows an even better mental evaluation of that prospect.

Finally, the programs under the guidance of Coach Cossaboon always work within the mantra "no drama." Any prospect that is perceived to add unnecessary drama to a program will not be recruited. Coach Cossaboon advises students to make sure the university's environment is right for them. "Nothing is worse than seeing student-athletes feel like they don't fit in. They lose their confidence and it shows on the playing field."

BEST PIECE OF ADVICE:

"Never think that you have arrived." Coach Cossaboon believes a prospect needs to continue to develop and to be open to learning new skills, even after enrolling at a university and signing on to compete in an athletic program.

Coach Cossaboon has been fortunate to coach Olympic gold medal winners, World Cup winners and soccer players of the highest caliber. He attributes the success of these players to several key factors:

- A desire and need to get better at every aspect of the game

- An exceptional ability to ignore distractions and focus on the sport

- Strong self discipline and confidence

SOFTBALL

Glenn Moore, Baylor University

ACADEMICS:

The Baylor University Softball program is very proud of their academic record. As the only program ranked nationally both academically (Team GPA) and athletically in 2005 and 2006, it is no surprise that Coach Moore places academics as a high priority. There are times, however, when less academically qualified prospects are recruited to the university—and they succeed. Due to the high academic expectations placed on the student-athletes by their coaches and their teammates, a strong academic support system helps potentially weak or "struggling" students develop good habits and become high achievers—both on and off the field.

ATHLETICS:

First View: When first arriving on a softball field for recruiting purposes, Coach Moore notices the athleticism of the prospects. He looks for softball players that "look like athletes or look like they have formed strong healthy habits." Athletes that move with great ease, have coordination, and have long levers (both arms and legs), also catch Coach Moore's attention.

In addition, the prospect's attitude to the game is important. Coach Moore feels a prospect with a strong internal drive, intensity, and focus—the athlete that always wants to play—is someone that will succeed even when there is little talent.

Baylor Softball has recruited the "raw" athlete at times, but only when the talent pool did not have the complete student-athlete available. In more cases than not, the student-athletes succeed; however, the ones that fail typically do so because of their mental approach to the game. Failure can also be due to a lack of coachability or learning style issues that are not corrected early enough.

THE PERFECT ATHLETE AND RECRUIT:

- Talented—can play the game
- Has great natural speed
- Agile

- Attitude and Passion—a "fun" student-athlete

- Great student

MOST IMPORTANT ATHLETIC CHARACTERISTICS:

- Speed—helps steal bases and score runs

- Agility (lateral movement)—strong defensive quality

- Power

- Balance

- Technique—Coach Moore wishes freshmen were taught better throwing mechanics prior to college.

Coach Moore believes that part of the success of his program is due to the added time that student-athletes spend working on their agility. The strength and conditioning staff at Baylor places a great deal of emphasis on working with student athletes on agility as well as strength training and nutritional help.

PSYCHOLOGICAL AND EMOTIONAL:

During the recruiting process, Coach Moore contacts club and high school coaches to learn if their prospects are hard workers. His question is two-fold: "Do they have talent, but do they also condition hard?"

How the prospect deals with failure in a positive and constructive manner is another area that is important to Coach Moore. "Athletes that do not enjoy failing—and strive to change the factors that created the failure—are the student-athletes that will succeed and help our program succeed."

BEST PIECE OF ADVICE:

Coach Moore believes strong time management and organization skills are two things that help lead to success. A student-athlete that does not manage time wisely will get behind quickly, which can effect every part of that athlete's life. "When a student-athlete gets behind academically, the stress that this causes carries over to the softball field, causing a miserable time for that student-athlete."

A student-athlete's personal management of daily life is so important to Coach Moore that during the first week of school every year, he provides a workshop to help his student-athletes learn about time management and organization. He has found this has helped his athletes succeed.

Finally, Coach Moore believes in developing the physical and mental aspects of every student-athlete, but he feels there is more; and he has noticed that a neglected area for students can be the spiritual realm. He encourages student-athletes to nurture and strengthen all three areas of their lives (physical, mental, and spiritual) in order to become the "complete student- athlete".

SWIMMING

Steve Collins, Southern Methodist University

ACADEMICS:

Academics are important when it comes to recruiting prospective student-athletes to the swimming program at SMU. Not only does Coach Collins want great students, but he is looking for a diverse team/program to add to the successful academic and athletic environment.

ATHLETICS:

First View: A coach can use the posted race times of a prospect as an objective evaluation tool. When looking at the times of youth swimmers, Coach Collins relates these times to NCAA qualifying times. This helps him identify potential recruits at an early age.

From a physical and athletic standpoint, Coach Collins looks at a prospect's "natural speed"—including their kicking ability, stroke power, and development potential. However, knowing that a swimmer's technique and cardiovascular ability can develop, Coach Collins will recruit a prospect who has posted times that may not be at a high level.

Prospects can be recruited if they show a great deal of interest in SMU and if they show the correct characteristics to be a success within the program. Coach Collins believes a swimmer who has played other sports while in high school and did not train as a swimmer all year could develop in the right competitive swimming environment. He feels once those athletes focus on swimming, they will advance and become better swimmers.

THE PERFECT ATHLETE AND RECRUIT:

- Strong academics

- Team oriented

- Great attitude and work ethic

- Accomplished—ability to compete as a freshman

- Fast water speed

- Ability to build strength—strong kicker

- Tall

- Long reach—especially important for long axis strokes (freestyle and backstroke)

MOST IMPORTANT ATHLETIC CHARACTERISTICS:

- Water Speed

- Stroke Power

- Cardiovascular Endurance

- Agility—necessary for turns

PSYCHOLOGICAL AND EMOTIONAL:

Like most college coaches, Coach Collins does not want any behavioral problems within his program. During the recruitment process, he will ask other coaches about the behavioral profile of a prospect. He is looking for prospects that are coachable, and by that, he means student-athletes that are open to learning and developing their swimming ability in every way.

A positive team environment is the most important component of Coach Collins' swimming program. A prospect that shows respect for current teammates, future teammates, parents, coaches and opponents is the right fit for his program. He believes a positive influence within the program helps in all areas—academically, athletically and in the social components of the program.

Coach Collins has been fortunate to work with—and to develop— swimmers who compete and win on the international level, including the

Olympics and World Games. Coach Collins attributes the success of these swimmers to each athlete's mental approach to training and competition. The highest-level swimmers are able to stay focused on achieving success. On every occasion, those student-athletes were able to make the correct choices and chose not to become victims of negative peer pressure.

BEST PIECE OF ADVICE:

"Find a balance in your life." Coach Collins believes this will help a first year student-athlete succeed. "Realize that your primary goal is academic success as well as the ability to succeed in the pool. Eating properly and resting effectively will also help the student-athlete to be a success."

TENNIS

Debbie Southern, Furman University

ACADEMICS:

At Furman University, there is a strong academic environment created by the university's faculty. Therefore, academics play a very important role for Coach Southern during the recruitment process. It is important to the tennis program that each tennis student-athlete has a positive experience at the university. Coach Southern recruits student-athletes who do well academically in high school (for example, valedictorians) because she believes this demonstrates they will most likely do well in college.

On some occasions, however, Coach Southern has helped some students receive a "marginal admit" to the university and they have seen academic success. With small classes, a strong academic plan (including study hall hours and academic monitoring), marginal admits have been able to graduate from the academically rigorous institution.

ATHLETICS:

First View: The love for the game is the first thing that draws Coach Southern to a prospect. "I love to see the player that loves to play." The prospect's technique and her movement style are physical aspects that catch this coach's eye as well. "A tennis player with strong strokes, and one that can move fluidly—with ability to change directions— with balance and speed—will have the ability to use their 'weapons' and set up points."

Although Coach Southern looks for strong technical players, she has also recruited the less technical "raw" athlete to her program. As long as prospects are dedicated, have a hunger for development, have passion for the game and are enthusiastic about the sport (and university), they will add positively to the tennis program. Once these students are within the program, they will develop their game due to the competitive environment and strong athletic resources that are available.

THE PERFECT ATHLETE AND RECRUIT:

- Good student (qualified to receive academic money)

- Strong family support—well grounded

- Works hard every day

- Sets realistic goals—understands limitations and areas where improvement/development are needed

- Team Player—represents the program and university well

- Focused

- Strong and quick

- Makes good choices in critical situations

- Smart and strategic—can battle mentally during a match

MOST IMPORTANT ATHLETIC CHARACTERISTICS:

- Speed—can counter great shots

- Agility and Balance—allows quick and fluid transition during a point

- Power—important when coupled with strong technique and timing

- Endurance/Overall fitness—adds confidence to players, especially during long matches

PSYCHOLOGICAL AND EMOTIONAL:

Although tennis is an individual sport, the team dynamic for college tennis is important. During her coaching career, Coach Southern has noticed that after 8 to 10 years of playing individually, a prospect is usually excited about becoming a part of the team at Furman. "Prospects like being a part of a positive team environment, working under positive peer pressure, and developing their game."

Coach Southern believes confidence is important for a tennis player. "Having a strong belief in his or her ability will help a player win big points. When confident, a tennis player will stay relaxed and play more fluidly. This is also important in point construction. A confident player will be able to use great strategy and add pressure to opponents to win points."

Within Furman's tennis program, seniors are expected to help underclassmen adjust to college life. Purposefully designing a team environment without designated captains, Coach Southern believes everyone can be a leader, and can lead by performing well and working hard. In fact, "freshmen can be leaders if they play well and work hard," she allows.

During the recruiting process, Coach Southern talks to the prospect's local tennis professional to get further information. Does the player have a great work ethic? Does the prospect work hard on developing his or her game? Is the athlete the first to arrive and the last to leave a practice session?

BEST PIECE OF ADVICE:

The belief that you "get what you give" is an important message from Coach Southern. "Prospects that are excited, open-minded and prepared for diversity, who stay busy and make friends, will have a great chance of success in college athletics."

In preparation for college-level tennis, Coach Southern recommends freshmen improve their game of doubles. Often overlooked by tennis pros and coaches during high school, it is an important part of college tennis.

VOLLEYBALL

Chris Herron, Washburn University

ACADEMICS:

When recruiting athletes for his program, Coach Herron places a premium on academics. He recruits student-athletes that know the importance and value of a college education. Also, he wants young women who enjoy participating—and succeeding—in volleyball. If a student-athlete does not do well in the classroom, that player will not last long playing volleyball at Washburn University.

However, Coach Herron has taken chances on a few athletes that have not shown concern or dedication for their academics, with mixed returns. The student-athletes that have succeeded academically in the collegiate environment are the ones that have recognized the need for a positive academic experience and committed themselves to their academics.

ATHLETICS:

First View: Walking into a gymnasium for a volleyball game, the first thing that catches Coach Herron's eye is the athleticism of a potential prospect. Whether it is the height of the prospect, the ability to move laterally and quickly, or the technical ability of the athlete, each position is evaluated individually.

Coach Herron will recruit "raw" athletes for his program if he believes they will develop into technical players with appropriate training and hard work. However, the only time he will take that chance is if he knows there are older, more experienced student-athletes that will play during the year and allow the rawer athlete time to develop into a technically more proficient volleyball player.

Additionally, and equally important, what a prospect does between plays and after the game is evaluated. Coach Herron watches how prospects respond to plays in a game. The reactions of coaches, teammates and parents are all noted. These reactions can demonstrate the ability of the prospect to be coached and how well she will fit into the positive and competitive environment that the Washburn volleyball program creates.

THE PERFECT ATHLETE AND RECRUIT:

- Evidence of intent to become a better athlete/volleyball player
- Academically motivated and qualified
- Aversion to losing—*hates* to lose
- 6 foot plus in height—middle hitter
- Can jump to 9'9"—middle hitter
- Mentally tough
- Technically sound

MOST IMPORTANT ATHLETIC CHARACTERISTICS:

- Quickness
- Agility
- Power
- Jumping ability
- Technique

PSYCHOLOGICAL AND EMOTIONAL:

For Washburn College, volleyball players are recruited to start their freshman year, and returning student-athletes are expected to work hard to keep their starting roles and prevent the freshman from taking their places. With this mentality, Coach Herron is looking for student-athletes that are mentally strong, competitive, and want to work hard for their sport.

Additionally, prospects that are coachable and respond positively to adverse situations are more likely to succeed and therefore be recruited. One of the traits Coach Herron looks for in all his athletes is mental toughness and strength.

Finally, Coach Herron believes that most freshmen have trouble adjusting to the intensity associated with playing for a nationally ranked program. Recruits need to prepare to work harder—not relax after signing their NLI—to be able to contribute during their freshman year.

BEST PIECE OF ADVICE:

Prospective student-athletes should "go to as many college matches as possible" prior to attending college and participating in athletics. PSAs should understand the level they are aiming to participate in and what will be expected of them when they enroll in an institution of higher learning. Understanding the environment of college athletics is necessary for success.

Additionally, prospects should understand their needs when they are choosing a collegiate program. As well as appreciating the level of play at the college level, PSAs must seek out programs in which they can compete. Some athletes may find that they are more interested in going to an NCAA II program and competing for a national championship rather than becoming a role player for an NCAA I program where they may not win as many games or experience the intrinsic satisfaction associated with being part of a successful and competitive program.

CHAPTER FOUR

PHYSICALLY ... SMARTER

One of the hardest transitions from being a high school student-athlete to a college student-athlete is the physical demands of college athletics. Many athletes are training and practicing more than ever before—and with older, more experienced and better athletes. College freshmen may find that they are entering an environment where they are not the "best" player on the team as they were in high school and that they are playing in a team that has a stronger internal competitive spirit than they have ever experienced.

The will to win is important, but the will to prepare is vital.
—JOE PATERNO

With this transition in mind, it is important for high school athletes to prepare themselves properly for their step up to college athletics. The majority of college programs send all their athletes a summer workout, but the earlier that student-athletes can begin to ready themselves, the better. When high school-aged athletes start serious training early, their preparation will positively show during the recruitment process.

JULIE'S STORY

In Chapter One we followed Julie, a tennis player, during her recruitment to Tennis University. We listened in on her interaction with Coach Connors. Julie was very excited about her choice to join Tennis University and she desired success on the court. She was determined to justify the recruitment efforts of Coach Connors and the scholarship monies awarded to her.

Throughout her youth tennis career, Julie felt herself struggling near the end of long games. She did not understand whether it was a physical or a mental thing—or perhaps a combination of the two. Either way, Julie's endurance was not as strong as she wanted it to be, so she decided to change her training regimen and add long distance running to her practice. She thought running long distances would increase her endurance and therefore she would be better and stronger at the end of her long games.

As Julie increased her running mileage, she did not find an immediate benefit in her end-of-game endurance. Although she felt stronger and fitter in relation to her running mileage, Julie noticed a difference in her game—she was getting tired *earlier* in her matches. Her game stamina and endurance were actually getting worse! Julie was confused and wondered why her endurance had dropped.

The answer was simple: Julie was not training as a tennis player. She was training as a cross-country athlete who was playing tennis as an afterthought. A common problem among young athletes, and even some older ones, is that they are unsure how to train. Young athletes tend to train in one of two ways—either as a football player or as a cross-country runner. They do not understand that they should train specifically for their sport. Athletes believe that to get stronger, they should train like a football player and lift heavy weights *or* they need to run many miles for a long time, similar to a cross-country or long distance track runner.

THE SAID PRINCIPAL:
SPECIFIC ADAPTATION TO IMPOSED DEMANDS

An athlete's body will adapt relative to the demands placed on it by the training regimen. During the season, an athlete's workout should be very specific. In the off-season, an athlete can work out in a less specific way but must change the training program gradually, becoming more specific, the closer the athlete gets to being in-season.

Specificity in the training program will lead to stability and adaptation in the workout. However, the athlete cannot let a training program become too stable—there must be change in the training (volume, intensity, or exercises) to keep a constant development.

In short, athletes must train for their sport and the demands that their specific sport places on them. An endurance athlete must train as an endurance athlete. A power athlete must train as a power athlete. In Julie's situation—she needed to train as a tennis player. Julie had to elicit physiological responses in her training that would help her as a *tennis player*. The first thing she had to do was to understand the physical demands of her sport.

Julie spoke with two different coaches to determine a workout regimen that would work for her in attaining the strength and endurance she desired. Each coach told Julie to write down the demands of a tennis player and what areas she needed to improve the most.

Like all athletes, it was important for Julie to know the demands of her sport. Julie started with a generic list of physically demanding areas and determined if these areas related to tennis:

- Cardiovascular (aerobic) endurance: the ability to work at a relatively low intensity for a prolonged period of time

- Anaerobic endurance: the ability to produce short intense bursts of work/energy (with intermittent rest) for a prolonged period of time

- Upper Body Strength: the ability to produce large amounts of force

- Lower Body Strength: the ability to produce large amounts of force

- Core Strength/Power: the ability to use the body's core to produce force and remain balanced

- Upper Body Power: the ability to produce large amounts of force in a short time period

- Lower Body Power: the ability to produce large amounts of force in a short time period.

- Agility: the ability to change direction quickly while staying balanced

- Balance: the ability to keep the body in alignment when performing a physical or technical movement

- Speed: the ability to cover ground in a short period of time

- Quickness: the ability to gain top speed in a short period of time

First, the specificity of Julie's training needed to focus on anaerobic endurance (to carry Julie through the end of long matches) as well as her Core Power, Upper and Lower Body Power, Agility, Balance and Quickness.

Second, Julie had to know what exercises to do and how to perform them—including volume, intensity and rest periods. In addition, Julie needed to know how to train two or more areas at one time.

Although her focus was on anaerobic endurance, Julie needed to be able to perform tennis-like actions while increasing her ability to remain physically strong at the end of matches. In her training, Julie would need to remain focused on her main objective while working on her other needs: agility, quickness and power.

Third, Julie had to find a way to work on the technical aspects of her game while working on her physical side. Being able to perform the technical aspects of a sport when tired is important, especially against high-level competition. Many athletes and coaches focus on the physical development at the end of practice when they are already tired, which is less beneficial to the athlete.

Under the direction of her two coaches, Julie tried something different—she worked on her physical needs at the start of practice (low intensity agility and quickness) and again in the middle of her practice (higher intensity agility, speed, quickness and power). At the end of her practice, she continued to work on her technique while she was tired. After about three to four weeks of training like this, Julie felt—and her coaches saw in her—a vast improvement in her ability to perform at her usual high standards, even at the end of a long match.

PRINCIPAL OF OVERLOAD

An athlete must place stress on his or her body (muscles, tendons, bones, and ligaments) to cause development, improvement, and positive physical adaptations. The stress must be higher than what is considered "normal" for that specific movement. For example, if an athlete is capable of doing 10 squats with 200 pounds of weight, improvement comes by increasing the number of repetitions (volume) or by increasing the weight (intensity). This results in a positive adaptation for that exercise/movement.

Finally, Julie had to make sure she was taking enough time to recover so that she did not overtrain. She worked diligently and did not perform high intensity training on back-to-back days. Julie set a limit of training at high intensity three or four days a week in the off-season, and much less during times of competition.

CROSS-TRAINING

Cross-training is an effective way of reducing mental and physical burnout or boredom and consists of using another form of exercise, or sport, rather than a sport-specific workout. These workouts can be useful in low workload days, recovery days, or days prior to competition. For example, a long distance runner may swim; a football player may play basketball, etc. Julie played basketball as her cross-training sport because it mimicked the movement and intensity levels of tennis.

ROSS PARKER CSCS: COLLEGE SPEED, STRENGTH AND CONDITIONING COACH

What is the hardest transition for high school athletes as they become collegiate athletes?

In college, the demand placed on the athlete is much greater, where expectations are just as high in the classroom as on the field. Additionally, the training environment, especially in the weight-room, is more goal specific and may differ from what they were used to.

The student-athlete must be open-minded, like a "sponge," and must be trusting of the coaching staff. The goal of the staff is to make the students better athletes, which in turn, will help them excel on their field of play.

How can student-athletes better prepare for the transition from high school to college?

They should contact coaches (sport and strength coaches) and understand the demands that are going to be placed on them when they arrive on campus. In addition, following the summer training program closely and preparing for the team's fitness test will allow the athlete to be ready for training. However, it is important that student-athletes do not just focus on the fitness test; even though they will need to pass the test, the athlete needs to work on the overall program. Student-athletes that only focus on the fitness test will miss out—the test is only a small snapshot of the conditioning level required to be a success.

What is the most important message for prospects prior to their arrival at college?

Be mentally and physically prepared and open-minded. Arriving physically prepared will allow the athlete no room for doubt. Being open-minded will allow the athlete to learn "how" and "why" things are done the way they are.

What do you wish first year student-athletes were better at when they begin training with you?

Student-athletes need to arrive at college in "game shape"! They cannot use preseason to get ready for the season—they already need to be physically able to train at an elite level. Arriving in game-shape allows first year athletes to keep up or stay ahead of others. Then they can translate their training to their sport more easily.

Training is the easy part of being an athlete. The ability for a student-athlete to "work" at being a student-athlete outside of training is important. The student-athlete needs to prepare off the field—nutrition, rest and maintenance of a balanced lifestyle. In addition, the student-athlete should never be afraid to fail. If athletes want to grow, and to be successful, they are going to have to take chances and be prepared to do things they have never accomplished before. "I can't do it" never works in the college athletic arena.

From a strength and conditioning viewpoint, describe the perfect athlete.

- Open-minded
- Patient
- Has the ability to transfer workouts from the weight-room to the field/court
- Understands why athletes do what they do—enjoys the sport
- Recalls what they do with the team training and mimics it when training alone

What athletic attributes are important for every sport and should be trained consistently?

- Speed

- Strength/Power—has a large correlation to speed and jumping

- Skill development—including agility, balance and jumping ability

- Core strength

What additional training changes must a student-athlete prepare for?

A large variety of training, and training changes, should be expected. To decrease mental staleness and to increase athletic adaptations, a training program is changed every three weeks (approximately). To ensure being well prepared, a student-athlete needs to be flexible to change. The purpose of a training program is to increase strength and performance, to decrease rate of injury and to give student-athletes a mental edge by knowing that they are very well prepared.

WHAT IS A STRENGTH AND CONDITIONING COACH?

Most strength coaches hold a Certified Strength and Conditioning Specialist (CSCS) certificate—administered by the National Strength and Conditioning Association (NSCA). CSCS holders have a minimum of a Bachelor's degree. These trained and educated professionals create, administer and implement safe and effective strength and conditioning programs for athletes in a team setting.

BRYAN'S STORY

As an 800m and 1500m runner at Steeplechase University, Bryan was determined to train hard and to be a winner. Even though Bryan had enjoyed success at the national level during high school, he wanted to improve and continue that trend at the collegiate level. After a decent first season, Bryan wanted to increase his kick (increase in speed) at the end of his races. He wanted to accelerate past his competition with two or three hundred meters left in the race.

In preparation for his sophomore indoor track season, Bryan decided to add to his workout. Along with his normal endurance training with intermittent speed drills (twice weekly), Bryan added more speed work, and additional strength workouts four to five times a week. He thought the harder he trained, the better he would be. Bryan believed that increasing his total training load, especially the strength workouts and the speed work, would help him achieve a killer kick at the end of his races.

TRAINING LOAD: VOLUME AND INTENSITY

The training load of a workout is composed of two major components—volume and intensity. In simple terms, how hard is the workout? A general rule of a training program is that the higher the intensity, the lower the relative volume, and vice versa.

Volume is the total amount of work done in a training session. For example, the number of total repetitions done in a strength-training workout or the total distance covered in a running or swimming workout.

Intensity is the power output of a given exercise. Power is the amount of work performed in a given time. For an athlete performing a strength-training workout, the higher weights equate to a higher intensity workout. For endurance workouts, the percentage of the athlete's maximum aerobic volume or heart rate can determine the intensity of the workout.

LAW OF DIMINISHING RETURNS

The longer an athlete uses a training program, the harder it is for that athlete to see significant gains in the workout. At the beginning of a correctly designed training program, there will be initial and substantial gains. Over time, an athlete's body will adapt to that workout (SAID Principal and Principal of Overload) and the improvement will be less (plateau). When this occurs in an athlete's workout, it is time for a change.

A workout is re-stimulated by changing elements such as these:

- Intensity
- Volume
- Rest Periods (shorter or longer)
- Exercise
- Angles of movement

Initially, Bryan felt stronger and believed he was getting stronger at the end of his training runs and time trails. With this psychological boost, he continued to train harder and harder. Bryan pushed his body to limits that he had not yet experienced and for a while was achieving gains in everything he was doing—he was lifting more weight in his strength workouts and he was shortening his times during speed workouts.

During the first three to four weeks of a new strength and conditioning program, the majority of gains are due to muscles "learning" and not to actual gain in the strength of that muscle group.

As the indoor season approached, Bryan began to feel slower and his times reflected that. Bryan's answer was to train harder. Many inexperienced athletes believe that the harder they train, the better they will perform on the field, court, course or track. Bryan thought that his poor times were because he was not training hard enough. Unfortunately, Bryan again increased his training load and pulled his hamstring muscle.

At the start of Bryan's increased training load, he never discussed his program with anyone—not his strength coach, not the athletic trainer and definitely not his track coach. Now with a muscle injury, Bryan went to see the trainer and explained the muscle pull and how it happened.

Bryan's trainer and strength coach looked at his training regime and noted that he was overtraining. Bryan had never considered that as a possibility, and it was not until he realized that he had many of the signs of overtraining that he realized this had put undue strain on his hamstring.

COMMON SIGNS AND SYMPTOMS OF OVERTRAINING

- Unexpected drop in performance—or the athlete can perform at his or her usual standard but it feels harder for them

- Mood disturbance—depression, anxiety, anger

- General fatigue—muscle fatigue that can lead to strained muscles (pulled muscles)

- Increased muscle soreness after workouts

- Loss of coordination—decreased movement efficiency

- Loss of energy and vigor

- Sleep pattern changes

- Changes in appetite

- Loss or decreased menstrual cycle for female athletes

- Increase in morning resting heart rate

- Increased breathing frequency

- Additional medical symptoms that are harder for the athlete to notice

Agreeing that Brian had overtrained, the athletic staff developed a recovery plan for him, one which included rehabilitation for his hamstring strain. Bryan's approach to recovery included the following steps:

- Reduction in training (when overtraining is severe, the athlete may need total rest)

- Active recreation (this may be used for athletes that need rest from their sport—cross-training at low intensity and volume)

- Proper nutrition

- Proper hydration

- Professional psychological counseling

Additional approaches may be used under the direction of qualified medical personnel. Once Bryan was ready to resume training, he did so under the strict supervision of the coaching staff, the strength and conditioning staff, the team's athletic trainer and his physician. Bryan increased his training only under their direction—and it was a very slow build-up. In addition, Bryan took precautions to insure that his training did not lead to overtraining.

- He monitored and recorded his morning resting heart rate—If there was any increase in his morning heart rate, especially over multiple days, Bryan decreased his training load until his resting heart rate regained a normal value in the morning.

- He monitored his weight to assure no weight loss occurred due to decreased eating or decreased hydration.

- He added nutritious snacks between meals to his daily eating regimen.

- During times of high stress (test, projects, personal problems, decreased health) he decreased his training load.

- He *listened* carefully to his body and complied with all medical directions given to him

---

During times of high stress, athletes (both high school and college) may see or feel a decrease in performance, recovery or desire. Outside stress such as tests, projects, excessive travel and personal issues merit decreasing the training load to prevent an athlete from over-reaching and having to deal with the negative aspects of overtraining.

INDEPENDENT TRAINING

Will Lawrence is a certified strength and conditioning specialist (CSCS) who oversees the training programs at Velocity Sports Performance in Dallas, Texas. Velocity Sports Performance is a training company that uses scientifically designed training programs to develop athletes for competitive sports. They train with two goals in mind: to optimize athletic potential and to prevent athletic injuries.

A large part of a successful training program, whether under the direction of coaches or while training individually, is the ability to move properly. Athletes who play and train for more than one sport have the ability to pick up new training demands—for example, multi-directional movement and proper body alignment—quickly. Lawrence states that being "pigeon-holed" into certain sports at a young age, and only playing that one sport even in recreation, limits the development of a range of movements for that athlete.

CARDIOVASCULAR

Lawrence believes that a strong cardiovascular base for all training is essential as a proper foundation for optimal athletic performance. However, it is important for athletes to train their energy systems and to hone the skills needed for their specific sports. Most sports are anaerobic (physical activity that requires bursts of energy for periods shorter than two minutes). Even sports that have a large amount of running (soccer, lacrosse and basketball) are mainly anaerobic sports—but they still need a strong cardiovascular base.

Athletes that compete in anaerobic sports must develop a strong anaerobic endurance. *Fartlek* training is one way for an athlete to build that needed endurance. Also known as interval training, *Fartlek* training is comprised of slow recovery runs with bursts of high-energy output running of various lengths. Lawrence suggests distances of 300 meters be used on high energy days and much shorter distances during other days.

Lawrence states, "Although conditioning should be done daily, it is not beneficial to the athlete to have daily high-energy *Fartlek* or interval training. Not allowing an athlete's body to recover properly or having too many high-energy days can lead to injuries, mental fatigue and overtraining. Variety is important."

STRENGTH/POWER DEVELOPMENT

Prior to engaging in a strength-training program, an athlete must be able to perform the movements of the lifts properly. Many injuries occur in the weight room due to poor technique while lifting heavy weights. The coaches at Velocity Sports Performance focus on an athlete's technique using only their body weight. Then trainees are moved to light weights and later onto heavy, power-generating training.

Coach Lawrence recommends high school athletes train twice weekly with weights during their season, and three to four times a week during their off-season in addition to daily conditioning. In a typical training session, athletes should spend approximately one-third of their time with weights (the other two-thirds are equally broken into warming-up and movement training). For a high-school-aged athlete, this should be 20-30 minutes, depending on the length of the training session. A strength workout should not last longer than 45 minutes.

Strength training exercises are performed from hardest to simplest or multi-joint exercises to single-joint exercises. The multi-joint exercises are more functional and have a better carry-over to the athletic arena. Exercises such as the Olympic Lifts (The Snatch and the Clean and Jerk), squats, lunges and different forms of bench presses are all examples of multi-joint exercises.

These exercises, especially the Olympic Lifts, generate explosive power which can help in training for every sport—from jumping to running, acceleration and speed development. In order to generate power, high weight and low repetitions must be used during training once the athlete has mastered the technique of the lift. Coach Lawrence suggests to athletes that if they only have a short amount of time to strength-train (20 minutes or less), then they should focus completely on Olympic Lifts.

CORE STABILITY

Lawrence estimates approximately 95 percent of the youth athletes that he trains at Velocity Sports Performance have poor core strength and flexibility, which can lead to injuries and lower athletic performance. The athlete's core is located from the knees to the chest and it is important that each muscle group in that area be consistently trained. Core training is 360 degrees—front and back, left and right, and in all directions.

The core has an abundant blood supply and therefore recovers quickly. It is important for an athlete to work core muscles daily—3 or 4 days a week at a minimum. In addition to helping with athletic performance and injury prevention, a strong core will sustain better posture throughout the day, especially when sitting in front of a computer screen, at a desk in school, or in front of the TV like most teenagers do.

Swiss Balls (large balls filled with air) have become a welcome addition to core training. The large balls allow for a variety of exercises that move the body in all directions and help to stabilize and increase the strength of the athlete's core.

According to Coach Lawrence, there are three keys to good training:

- Use a variety of exercises.

- Make the exercise functional (specific) to the athlete's needs—train 360 degrees of movement.

- Use the athlete's body weight.

AGILITY AND BALANCE

Both agility (the ability to quickly change direction) and balance are important factors in most, if not all, sports. At Velocity Sports Performance, agility training occurs within every training session to increase fine motor control and to train the nervous system. The objective is to make the movements a part of the athlete's natural movements.

The best results from agility training are found when the training movements mimic the real movements of the sport(s) in which an athlete competes. The use of agility ladders and hurdles can play a large part in the development of these movements, but it is also important to continue what is learned in agility training on an individual basis. Continuation of the footwork or the addition of a sprint after the agility and balance work will create more carry-over to the sport.

Having worked with professional, collegiate, collegiate-bound, and high school athletes, Lawrence believes that the speed of the sport is always the biggest jump when moving up a level—whether from high school to college or even college to professional. Student-athletes in college have a higher workload and must be prepared physically and mentally for that jump. Lawrence believes any student-athlete who recognizes the need for an increase in intensity, and performs at that level prior to going to college, will be better prepared than his or her peers who do not ready themselves.

EXERCISE VS. TRAINING

There is a major difference in training for an event, competition, or contest and exercising for health and fitness benefits. An athlete utilizes the SAID Principal and the Principal of Overload when training. These training principals help attain athletic performance gains. For many, exercise is a way of maintaining or losing weight and/or for general health benefits. Someone who exercises is not competing with others and people who train are doing so in an effort to become a better athlete and succeed in the athletic arena.

According to a study published by the American College of Sports Medicine, there is only a 3 percent increase in strength gains when an adult performs 3 sets of an exercise compared to a similar adult that only does one set of the same exercise (at the same volume and intensity). For an athlete, that 3 percent increase in performance may be the difference between an Olympic gold medal and not winning a medal.

WARM-UP AND STRETCHING

On many occasions, athletes ignore the direction of the coaches to warm up properly, stretch well, and then cool down after an event. This is not wise, as a proper warm-up and stretching routine aligns the muscle fibers to help the athlete in movement—and stretching may prevent muscle and tendon injuries. In addition, a cool-down and stretch after training or competition allows the muscles the opportunity to relax and move toxins (lactic acid) out of the muscle tissue. This can prevent next day muscle soreness experienced by athletes after an intense athletic event.

For most sports, a quick jog and a stretch is not a well-designed warm-up. The warm-up should consist of sport-like movements: changing of direction, changing of speed, movement laterally, backwards and forwards, and jumping. The purpose of the warm-up is to raise the internal temperature of the body, thus making the muscles more conducive to stretching. The athlete's heart rate and breathing rate should be elevated prior to stretching. A simple indicator that the body is ready to stretch is sweat (unless the event is outside and the athlete is already sweating).

Coach Lawrence recommends that athletes perform "dynamic stretching" before doing any form of exercise. Dynamic stretching works through the athlete's natural range of motion—it increases as the core temperature increases from an appropriate warm-up. An example of dynamic stretching would be walking high-kicks, where an athlete kicks his or her feet up in the air as high as they will go while walking. This motion dynamically stretches the hamstrings.

TRAINING TECHNICALLY

In addition to training physically and mentally, it is important for athletes to work continually on their technique. Utilizing technical training during the warm-up, in the middle or even at the end of a conditioning session, is essential. Technical training after conditioning sessions helps the athlete mentally focus, understand what it is like to execute technique while tired (at the end of a game or tournament) and stimulates the nervous system.

Technical training is something that an athlete should do daily—and enjoy! Finding 20 minutes a day to work on throwing, running technique, shooting, passing, dribbling or hitting continues to teach the body biomechanical patterns that it will utilize during sports practice and competition.

SUMMARY

- Be prepared for higher physical demands as a collegiate student-athlete.

- Understand that you are entering a more competitive arena—even with your teammates.

- Prepare early for college athletics.

- Train specifically for your sport and/or position.

- Understand the SAID Principal.

- Change your training program often to prevent staleness.

- Know and understand the physical demands of your sport.

- Know what areas need your focus—and know how to train two or more areas at once.

- Vary your training—perform technical work after your physical workout.

- Understand the Principal of Overload.

- Take time to recover.

- Use cross-training in your training regimen to prevent boredom or staleness.

- Contact coaches and ask for summer strength and conditioning guidelines.

- Do not just focus on the fitness test—be ready to play.

- Be open minded to new ideas and approaches.

- Be flexible and prepared for change.

- Understand that increasing a training load does not always result in performance improvements.

- Re-stimulate your workout when your performance does not improve anymore.

- Know and understand the signs and symptoms of overtraining.

- Take into consideration outside stresses (tests, projects, etc.) when planning your training regime.

- Before training with weights, you must master the techniques of the lift—this will help with injury prevention.

- Perform multi-joint exercises at the start of your workout and progress to single-joint exercises.

- If you have little time to utilize weight training, focus on Olympic lifts.

- Core training is essential and must be from chest-to-knee and 360 degrees.

- Train for agility and balance daily to increase fine motor control.

- Understand the importance of warming up and cooling down.

- Understand the importance of stretching well for performance.

COMMON FITNESS TESTS

Testing is performed on athletes for two reasons:

- To assure that the athlete is performing his or her workout

- To assure that the training program is making adequate progress and allowing the athlete to develop properly

Prior to testing, the athlete will perform simulations of the test. This allows the athlete to become familiar with the test and therefore score better.

Each coach and/or program will have his or her own standards. You should ask about these standards prior to the summer before your senior year and make sure you can meet the minimum standards.

Coaches/programs may use different tests other than the ones detailed below. If you are required to perform different tests, ask for specific instructions and standards regarding each one.

In addition to fitness tests/standards, programs may administer the following:

- Technical Tests

- Body Composition (body fat percentage)

- Flexibility Tests

THE COOPER TEST (AEROBIC POWER)

The Cooper Test is a field test used to measure the aerobic capacity of an athlete. Conducted on a 400-meter track, the athlete is expected to travel a set distance in 12 minutes. Each sport and each coach will have their own standards for their athletes and their programs. Using a chart, the coaching staff can relate the distance traveled to a maximum aerobic capacity (VO2 max) of the athlete.

300-YARD SHUTTLE RUN (ANAEROBIC POWER)

The shuttle test can be performed in various shorter distances that are combined for a total distance of 300 yards. The most commonly used version consists of 25-yard laps. The athlete sprints 25 yards and returns to the starting point; then repeats for six trips (300-yards). Many programs repeat the run three times with breaks of 3-minutes between each test.

THE BEEP TEST (AEROBIC POWER)

The athlete runs intervals of 20 meters in length between beeps (on a pre-recorded CD) with given rest periods between each run. Each total run-rest period is 60 seconds with the test decreasing the running time during each of the 23 levels.

VERTICAL JUMP (ANAEROBIC POWER)

The vertical jump test measures an athlete's ability to jump. Athletes stand underneath testing arms and jump upwards, making marks on a wall or hitting specialized testing equipment to demonstrate the height of their jumps.

T-TEST (AGILITY)

Four markers are arranged in a "T" formation. Starting at the bottom of the "T", the athlete runs to the top, then shuffles left, shuffles right, and back to the middle. Then he or she turns and runs to the beginning point. The running of this test is timed.

40-YARD TIMED SPRINT (RUNNING/RAW SPEED)

The 40-yard sprint is a straightforward run of 40 yards. The athlete is timed over 40-yards, either from a standing or moving start.

MAXIMUM REPETITIONS (MUSCULAR STRENGTH/POWER)

The tester has the option of two different tests—one is finding the total weight with which the athlete can perform one repetition, and the second is allowing the athlete to perform the exercise with a lower weight for maximum repetitions. When administering the second test, a chart is utilized to allow the tester/athlete to see the corresponding one-repetition maximum.

WHAT TYPE OF SPORT IS YOURS?

Each sport is unique in its demands—both physically and mentally. For the specificity of training, it is important to know where to focus the training. The following is the recommended training per sport by the NSCA (National Strength & Conditioning Association):

Baseball: anaerobic, power sport—high intensity with long rest periods

Basketball: anaerobic, power sport—high intensity, short bursts of energy over a prolonged period

Cross-country: aerobic sport—lower intensity, higher volume with short intermittent bursts of energy

Diving: anaerobic, power sport—high intensity with long rest periods

Fencing: anaerobic sport—high intensity repetitions with short rest periods

Field Hockey: aerobic and anaerobic sport—high intensity with long periods of constant movement

Football: anaerobic, power sport—high intensity with long rest periods

Golf: anaerobic, power sport—high intensity with long rest periods

Gymnastics: anaerobic, power sport—high intensity with long rest periods

Ice Hockey: anaerobic, power sport—high intensity, short bursts of energy over a prolonged period

Lacrosse: aerobic and anaerobic sport—high intensity bursts of energy, long periods of constant movement

Rowing: aerobic and anaerobic sport—high intensity bursts of energy, long periods of constant movement

Cross Country Skiing: aerobic sport—lower intensity, higher volume with intermittent bursts of energy

Slalom Skiing: anaerobic, power sport—high intensity with long rest periods

Soccer: aerobic and anaerobic sport—high intensity bursts of energy, long periods of constant movement

50-100m Swimming: anaerobic, power sport—high intensity, short bursts of energy over a short period

200-1600m Swimming: aerobic sport—lower intensity, higher volume with intermittent bursts of energy

Tennis: aerobic and anaerobic sport—high intensity bursts of energy, long periods of constant movement

100-400m Track: anaerobic, power sport—high intensity, short bursts of energy over a short period

800m+ Track: aerobic sport—lower intensity, higher volume with short intermittent bursts of energy

Field Events: anaerobic, power sport—high intensity, short bursts of energy over a prolonged period

Volleyball: anaerobic, power sport—high intensity, short bursts of energy over a prolonged period

Wrestling: anaerobic, power sport—high intensity, short bursts of energy over a prolonged period

What Type of Sport is Yours? is reprinted from the *Essentials of Strength and Conditioning* which is published by the National Strength and Conditioning Association (www.nsca-lift.org).

CHAPTER FIVE

YOUR BODY
AS AN ATHLETIC
TEMPLE

Training hard and following the coach's instructions comprise only a part of being an athlete. Good training can help an athlete perform at a high standard on a consistent basis. However, what an athlete does in the other 20 to 22 hours away from training and competition can affect his or her performance in a positive or negative manner.

Every athlete and sport is different and it is essential that athletes learn what lifestyle works for them. Performing at a standard where they feel good and are happy with themselves is important for all athletes. Keeping a record of daily training, sleep, down time, eating habits and hydration as well as daily stresses can help athletes understand what really makes them tick—and what doesn't.

The battles that count aren't the ones for gold medals. The struggles within yourself—the invisible, inevitable battles inside all of us— that's where it's at.
—JESSE OWENS, FOUR-TIME OLYMPIC GOLD MEDAL WINNER

GARY'S STORY

As a 400-meter freestyle swimmer at Flipper University, Gary set ambitious goals for himself. Under the direction of Coach Goodhew, Gary hoped to win the Conference Championship as a sophomore and an NCAA Championship prior to the completion of his collegiate swimming career. In addition, Gary was aiming for an Olympic trial during his time at Flipper University.

At the beginning of his sophomore year, Gary received an invitation to become a member of a well-respected fraternity. Gary knew about the fraternity's reputation for inviting high-achieving students—students who were successful within the extracurricular areas such as student government, fine arts or athletics—to join their exclusive group. Gary was flattered.

Gary decided to go to a meeting of the fraternity to see if it was something that would be a positive addition to his college experience. He wanted to know if the fraternity would create an additional support system for him. Gary only wanted to be around positive and supportive people—people that would not disrupt his process to reach his goals.

At the meeting, Gary was introduced to everyone associated with the fraternity and he was encouraged to join their distinguished and accomplished membership. Initially, Gary was interested and felt at home among the very bright, energetic, giving and accomplished students. He thought he could be one of them—and have a positive support group around him. But those thoughts changed when he walked into another room in the fraternity house where students were drinking alcohol and smoking. Immediately, Gary knew it was *not* the place for him. Being in a fraternity, even one with a very positive reputation, would not be beneficial for his swimming career and goals.

After talking to the president of the fraternity who encouraged him to join, Gary declined this prestigious invitation. The rush leader told Gary that he was making a mistake and that he was going to miss out. He expressed to Gary that college was a time to party and have fun.

Gary explained to the fraternity leaders that he received satisfaction when he focused on being one of the best swimmers in the nation, which was his goal. Gary knew that this was a time in his life that he could never get back or relive. He could always "party" after his competitive swimming career was over. So, for the next three years, Gary focused on two things: college academics and swimming.

In the second half of the year, Gary, like his swimming teammates, was finely tuning himself for the conference meet. Fueled with good out-of-the-water habits and training sessions, Gary felt confident about his conditioning and ability to perform well in the upcoming conference finale.

During a school holiday, Gary was invited by his classmates to join them for a day of recreation—rock-climbing and paint balling. Gary agreed to go with his friends and spend time away from studying. He looked forward to a day of relaxation and down time, but Gary kept his swimming goals at the forefront of his thoughts. Although he was with his friends, he was not going to participate in the rock-climbing or paint ball competition. Gary did not want to expose himself to a potential horseplay injury. Even though he knew there was a very small chance that an injury could occur, he was not going to take any chances after working so hard all year. He was, after all, about to peak. Gary knew that a conference championship and the chance to compete at the NCAA Championship fast approached.

During the day, Gary hung out with his friends and just relaxed. He promised his friends that once the season was over, he would take time off from his stringent training regime and get back out with his buddies to play. Right then, however, Gary chose to sacrifice immediate pleasure for future success. His friends understood and looked forward to the next time they could get together.

College coaches are very quick to point out that successful athletes—especially the Olympic medal winners and athletes who turn professional—have two things in common:

- Successful athletes are willing to sacrifice a little bit of their personal life in order to succeed in their athletic careers.
- Successful athletes remain focused on their high goals no matter what outside influences try to distract them.

SETTING GOALS

Athletes should set high goals for themselves. However, the average goal-setter only sets one goal, or one set of goals—the ultimate goal. In order to reach the ultimate goal, the result of success, an athlete should create "process" goals—goals that are made before achieving *ultimate* goals.

Goals should be set in four stages:

1. *Daily Goals:* what does the athlete need to achieve every day? Daily goals can include working hard in training, eating and hydrating properly, getting the proper amount of sleep and/or achieving success in the classroom.

2. *Achievable but difficult goals:* smaller period goals that are attainable only if the daily goals are accomplished.

3. *Barrier-Breaking Goals*: these goals are attainable, but have not been achieved before. These goals need a lot of work but by achieving the first two levels of goals, the never-before-attained goals can be accomplished.

4. *Ultimate Goals:* What is the ultimate goal of the athlete/team? Winning an Olympic medal? Winning a national championship? Winning more games than losing? Starting for the team?

Goals need to be set based on the individual needs of the athlete. Having different levels of goals allows continued success relative to each level, which builds into higher, more difficult goals. Once athletes achieve their goals, it is important that they (individually or as a team) reset their goals to continually have something to work toward.

REST AND RECUPERATION

Many first-year collegiate student-athletes are away from home for the first time. This means being away from their parents, with no curfew, for the first time in their lives. Students can stay up all night hanging out with their friends, watching TV or playing games. No one is watching over them 24/7 to make sure that they are getting enough rest.

Sleep is a very important process in recovery and repair for everyone, especially athletes. A period of building for the body, sleep restores energy levels and repairs tissues. During the sleep cycle, the body releases Human Growth Hormone (HGH), which focuses on the repair of muscles and connective tissues. To perform at the highest standards, athletes must have fully functioning and energized muscles as well as strong connective tissues (tendons and ligaments).

Most adults need seven to eight hours of continuous sleep daily (some may need as much as ten hours) to feel and perform at their best. Sleep requirements vary, especially among athletes and students. Different stresses may cause the body to need more or less sleep, and not everyone needs the same amount. Changes in the student-athlete's academic load, training schedule and even personal issues may mean that the body needs more rest.

The Nap Trap: Many college students and student-athletes take advantage of the unstructured time between classes or time prior to (or after) training to get some sleep. Some student-athletes may be trying to catch up on sleep from the previous night. This is the nap trap!

When student-athletes take naps, this can disturb their sleeping patterns. At night, when the athletes should be going to bed to attain a continuous eight hours of sleep, they are not tired because they caught a few hours of sleep during the day. When they stay up late and have to get up early, the student-athletes don't complete their sleep cycles—and they don't get the physical and mental repairs their bodies need. This makes them feel sluggish and they want to take another nap. This disruptive sleeping pattern can decrease both academic and athletic performance.

Obviously, in addition to the quantity of sleep, the quality of sleep is very important, and naps do not provide the student-athlete with the appropriate quality of sleep.

Without the proper repair from the appropriate quality and quantity of sleep, an athlete will experience one or more of these symptoms:

- Irritability

- Decreased tolerance level

- Decrease in humor

- Slower brain function—slower thinking

- Decreased coordination

For the athletes who want to perform at high standards—run better, swim better, lift more weight and perform technical tasks more efficiently—sleep is critical in the rest and recovery process.

A study reported that college-aged male basketball players who sleep as much as they felt necessary performed better in sprint tests and had a higher free-throw percentage. Those student-athletes also felt more energized and were in a better overall mood.

In addition to sleep, the body needs to recover during the waking hours too. An increase in rest and recovery can lead to a greater increase in the physical performance when an athlete times workouts properly. After a workout, the body restores its energy level higher than its pre-workout level. When the athlete begins the next workout, the athlete can then theoretically work out harder and/or longer. Regarding rest, athletes need to follow their coach's instructions precisely.

Active Recovery: Rather than taking a day off and resting completely, it is better for an athlete to stay active. Low intensity exercise the day after intense training or competition allows the student-athlete to recover quicker and decreases the likelihood of any muscle soreness from fatigue. In addition, an active cool-down period after training or competition helps athletes in their physical and psychological recovery.

HYDRATION

An athlete's appropriate hydration level, or lack of, can change their level of athletic performance. Therefore, athletes must monitor their hydration level properly. A one-percent decrease in an athlete's hydration level results in a two-percent decrease in athletic performance—it is *that* important.

The common recommendation for the hydration of an average person is the consumption of a minimum of 64 fluid ounces daily; for an athlete, that amount needs to be higher. A simple formula can be used to determine suggested fluid intake. For active people, find the appropriate amount by dividing the person's body weight (in pounds) by two, and that is how much fluid ounces that person should consume daily. For example, a 160 lb. runner should consume a minimum of 80 fluid ounces daily. For athletes that are training or competing at a more intense level, the amount of consumed fluid must be higher.

Hydration recommendations for athletes:

- Consume 500 ml. (17 fluid oz.) of fluid approximately two hours prior to competition/training.

- Consume 8 ml. of fluid for every kilogram (6.5 fluid oz. per 10 pounds)of body weight approximately 5-10 minutes prior to competition/training.

- Consume 3 ml. for every kilogram (2.5 fluid oz. per 10 pounds) of body weight approximately every 15-20 minutes during competition/training (when possible).

- Consume enough fluid after competition/training to rehydrate completely.

To insure complete rehydration, athletes should weigh themselves prior to and after competition/training. When an athlete is properly hydrated again, he or she will weigh the same as prior to competition and/or training.

Another way to know if an athlete is hydrated properly is to notice whether the color of the urine is clear. The darker the urine, the more dehydrated the athlete is.

Athletes that are dehydrated will experience the following symptoms that can impair performance:

- Decreased cardiovascular efficiency—decrease in blood volume

- Increased blood pressure and heart-rate

- Decreased coordination

- Weakness and fatigue

- Decreased attention

- Decreased decision-making ability

Signs of dehydration include the following:

- Noticeable thirst

- Headache

- Nausea

- Dizziness

- Muscle cramps

SPORTS DRINKS

Competition or training that has a low intensity or is shorter than 60 minutes in length does not require a sports drink to help the athlete recover. However, sports drinks will help rehydrate in the following manner:

1. Sports drinks encourage the athlete to drink more fluids—flavors and the presence of sodium encourage consumption.

2. The solution of carbohydrates and electrolytes stimulates rapid absorption of fluids.

3. The solution of carbohydrates and electrolytes speeds recovery by refueling the muscles.

NUTRITION

To get ahead, and to out-perform the competition, a student-athlete must fuel his or her body properly for all aspects of athletics. Athletes who want to optimize their performance and recovery must educate themselves on the benefits of nutrition.

According to Ramsey Rodriguez, a sports nutrition expert and Director of Nutritional Ergogenic Systems in Dallas, Texas, most athletes believe that they *are* eating well, but really are not doing so. "Student-athletes choose their meals because of convenience and ease. A student-athlete chooses a bagel, fruit, or an energy bar and believes he or she is eating well, but these three food sources are high in carbohydrates, especially simple sugars, which can be detrimental to athletic performance and recovery," states Rodriguez.

Most student-athletes lack protein in their diet, and they consume too much carbohydrate and/or fat. The lack of protein, coupled with high carbohydrates, creates an inconsistency in energy levels. "Athletes have high days and low days," says Rodriguez, "which is due to the drop in blood sugar levels. A higher protein diet will stabilize the amount of energy released and allow for a more consistent performance." Rodriguez believes the optimum diet for athletes is *The Zone Diet*. It consists of 40 percent carbohydrates, 30 percent protein, and 30 percent fats—a higher percentage of protein than most other diet recommendations.

Knowing where to find protein is important for most athletes. Protein comes from animals—meat, eggs and dairy. For convenience, many student-athletes turn to supplements to get their protein. Shakes and bars that say they contain protein may be high in sugars and other carbohydrates, which the athlete does not need. Protein shakes tend to be better than bars, but they are not a substitute for animal proteins.

Calories: Most athletes do not consume enough calories on a daily basis. The consumable calories that are recommend for non-athletes are too few for athletes who must perform and recover properly. Rodriguez quotes a good caloric intake of 2500-3000 calories daily for athletes, depending on the sport and training load. "It is important to stay away from too many carbohydrates, too much fat and too many empty calories (alcohol)," he adds.

Pre-Workout and Post-Workout Meals: The meals for pre- and post-competition should be the same. An athlete should eat a small meal (300-500 calories) an hour before competition and within 90 minutes of the competition ending. These two meals can be in the form of solid foods or drinks. Ramsey Rodriguez suggests 3 ounces of meat and a cup (approximately 2 slices of bread) of carbohydrates.

The purpose of the pre-game meal is to assure that the athletes fuel themselves for their workload or competition. A small meal is digested quickly and the energy will be released to enhance athletic performance. The post-game meal will restore the athlete's body with carbohydrates and proteins that the body will then use for recovery. The recommended meal within 90 minutes of the workout/competition will take full advantage of substances in the blood (insulin) and increase muscle and brain recovery.

PRE-GAME FOODS TO AVOID

1. Sugary Foods—will cause a drop in blood sugar levels and the athlete will crash and have no energy

2. Fatty Foods—can slow the absorption of the meal and create a feeling of fullness which can hinder performance

3. Salty Foods— will cause the athlete to retain large amounts of water and to feel heavy and sluggish

4. High Fiber Foods—may cause bloating and the need to go to the bathroom during the competition

5. Gas Formers—will make the stomach feel uncomfortably bloated (beans, onions, etc.)

6. Untested/New Foods—not knowing how your body will react to food is a gamble that athletes do not need to take when preparing to perform

Supplements: Athletes should take daily supplements to help with their performance. The NCAA has strict policies regarding supplements, so before taking one, athletes should consult the NCAA banned substances list.

Rodriguez is the developer of *Tribustol*—a supplement used to enhance athletic recovery and development due to a unique blend of vitamins and minerals. Visit www.tribustol.com for more information.

Rodriguez suggests that most athletes take supplements with magnesium and potassium because these fuel muscle contractions and relaxations. Off-the-shelf complex multi-vitamin and mineral supplements are good, but they may not include enough minerals for athletes. In addition, Rodriguez advises athletes to increase their vitamin B and fish oils (fatty omega acids) intake to help their athletic performance.

Eating well, especially when dining in a cafeteria or when take out is the only option, can be a difficult process. However, an athlete that makes the right effort to eat with performance in mind will create an advantage over others. It can be helpful to keep a daily log of eating habits. If you performed well, you know what fueled your body properly. If you performed below your expectations and standards, you can ask yourself what you did or did not eat that caused the decrease in performance. Understanding the relationship between your athletic performance and what you eat on the day before and on the day of competition is important.

MESSAGE FROM AN EXPERT

Bill Currie MS, ATC, LAT, CSCS: Athletic Trainer, Southern Methodist University

What is the difference between high school and college athletics from an athletic training viewpoint?

In college, athletes are expected to work hard to get back onto the playing field. Unlike high school, rehabilitation and injury recovery is active. Before collegiate student-athletes are back in a competitive environment, they are expected to be 100 percent physically capable to participate in their sport.

Additionally, college freshman need to learn how to use the medical staff available to them. When student-athletes are injured, they need to talk to the athletic training staff and let them know what is going on. If the injury is treatable, the staff will treat it, rehabilitate the injury, and get them back on the field under the direction of the team physician. When the injury or illness is severe enough, the athletic training staff will arrange an appointment with a physician.

What common physical problems do you tend to see in freshmen student-athletes?

Most entering freshmen do not understand the increase in training load from high school to college. Even highly active club players may not prepare properly for the transition. In some cases, high school athletes have been the best at their school and have not had to excel in strength and conditioning programs and they believe that will continue in college.

A lack of proper conditioning will cause problems at the start of the year. Muscle soreness is the number one complaint of student-athletes, followed by tendonitis (swelling of the tendons), especially the patella (knee). Overuse injuries such as low back strains and hamstring problems are next on the list of student-athlete ailments. These injuries are all preventable with proper conditioning, heat acclimation for outside athletes and a sensible and balanced life-style.

How can high school student-athletes better prepare for college athletics?

Take time off! Too many high school student-athletes play all year at a competitive level. The body and mind need time to recover with time off or active rest. Playing and competing at a high level all the time leads to burn out and causes many recruits to enter college with chronic injuries that can hinder their development as collegiate athletes.

In addition, the students should change their training programs—not just a jog or lifting weights. Vary the training programs to condition properly for that specific sport. Finally, do not be afraid to ask for help from the athletic department staff. There are many well-qualified people within the department willing to help student-athletes—they just need to ask.

Are freshmen more susceptible to overtraining type injuries?

No. Any student-athlete that does not perform any amount of quality training during the off season/preseason is prone to injuries. Athletes should train for their sport. Training sessions should place demands on their muscles similar to what their sport does—this will help prevent injuries.

Also, athletes that do not stretch enough or stretch properly will find that this can lead to overuse injuries. It is important for athletes to stretch after warming up before practice and after a cool-down period at the end of a training session or game. Stretching allows the muscles to relax and recover quicker.

From an athletic training viewpoint, what makes a "perfect" student-athlete?

- Proactive about injuries—when an injury occurs, they get help immediately

- Sacrifice their time to heal—attend rehabilitation sessions regularly and on time

- Desire to get better

- Take treatment, injury prevention and rehabilitation seriously

- Be smart off the field—do not aggravate injury through horse-play

What off-field factors can hinder an athlete?

Coaches talk about eating right and staying hydrated but they rarely teach the athletes how to accomplish this. Some schools have psychological and nutritional support available to student-athletes and they should use those resources.

Nutritionally, athletes complain about the cafeteria and the choice of foods. It may be the choices of the student-athlete, however. They select chicken tenders rather than a grilled chicken breast or fries rather than a baked potato. These would be better.

Science has shown that a 1 percent decrease in hydration levels can reduce the potential athletic performance by 2 percent; therefore, it is important for an athlete to stay properly hydrated. More athletes are making better choices when it comes to rehydrating. Fewer athletes are drinking caffeinated drinks. The caffeine found in soft drinks, coffee and tea is a diuretic, which will lead to increased urination and decreased hydration levels. Approximately 60 percent of the American population functions in a state of dehydration and athletes are no different.

Additionally, alcohol can lead to injuries or physical problems. Alcohol can cause changes in sleep patterns, increases in caloric intake, dehydration issues and can lead to addiction. Alcohol has ruined athletes' careers. Although this is not common, it is still a concern that student-athletes need to consider.

What will help a student-athlete succeed?

On top of being physically prepared, the student-athlete must be open-minded. The athlete must be prepared to learn something new from everyone—coaches, support staff, teammates and other athletes.

What is your most important message to incoming student-athletes?

Learn to manage your time. There are many extra expectations for college athletes—on and off the field—and the student-athlete needs to manage his or her academics along with everything else. Additionally, do everything that is asked of you. Do everything to the best of your ability—if you are asked to shag balls, be the best ball shagger* you can be!

* A ball shagger is a term used in soccer for someone who collects the balls after they have been kicked all over the training facility.

About Bill Currie: *Bill Currie is a member of the Southern Methodist University Athletic Training Staff. He has been responsible for a variety of athletic teams at SMU during his tenure. Previously, Currie worked with the men's basketball team, the women's rowing team, the women's soccer team, the men's and women's golf teams, and the men's and women's swimming and diving teams. Currie will now be responsible for assisting the head athletic trainer with the football team. He received his Bachelor of Science degree in Kinesiology and Master of Science degree in Exercise Physiology from Texas Women's University.*

WHAT IS AN ATHLETIC TRAINER?

A Certified Athletic Trainer (ATC) is a board-certified allied health care provider that focuses on the assessment, treatment, rehabilitation and management of injuries and illness. All certified athletic trainers must complete 80 hours of continued education credits every three years to maintain their membership and certification through the National Athletic Trainers Association (NATA). Over 70 percent of certified athletic trainers hold a master's degree or higher.

DRUGS AND ALCOHOL

Most coaches, athletic programs and educational institutions, as well as the NCAA, have strict guidelines and policies regarding drugs and alcohol. The consumption of alcohol by someone under the age of 21 is illegal, and so is the use of many performance enhancing and recreational drugs.

Despite the legal implications of consuming alcohol, there are performance factors that athletes must consider if they choose to participate in the consumption of alcohol. First, alcohol of any kind (beer, wine or spirit) is a diuretic. A diuretic causes an increase in the need to go to the bathroom and can lead to dehydration. Second, alcohol disrupts the body's normal sleep pattern, which athletes need to help them recover properly from exercise.

Additionally, alcohol decreases an athlete's ability to perform at a high level. The following is a list of physical symptoms brought on by alcohol consumption:

- Decreased force of heart contractions—less blood flows through the heart

- Increased need for oxygen—breathing becomes harder and the athlete will tire sooner

- Increased sweat rate—will lead to hypohydration

- Increase in blood pressure

- Increased heart rate

- Decrease in endurance

● Decrease in potassium, magnesium, and zinc—can lead to muscle cramps

Athletes who enjoy a night out to celebrate after a game or use alcohol as a part of recreation should bear in mind that this does not help them recover properly since both alcohol and lack of sleep are involved. It is essential for an athlete to rehydrate after competition, and there is also the need to replenish carbohydrates and put protein back into the body. Additionally, athletes will recover quicker/better if they enjoy a night of quality sleep with few or no interruptions.

The NCAA strictly forbids the use of performance enhancing drugs (Ergogenic Aides) or recreational drugs. Every year, under the direction of the Compliance Department, every student-athlete signs a form allowing the institution and the NCAA to drug test them at any time during the academic year. An institution can administer a drug test on a random basis or by the request of the coaching staff or the student-athlete.

It is important for a student-athlete taking medication to let the athletic trainers and the team physicians know what drugs have been prescribed to them. Even when an athlete is taking medication under the direction of a licensed physician, that medication, or part of the medication, may be on the *List of Banned Substances* published by the NCAA.

The athletic training staff stays up to date with all banned substances. They will be able to advise a student-athlete regarding their medication and any drug interaction or legalities with the medication—it is better to know than to guess, and the medical staff will help their student-athletes with relevant information.

The following is the list of banned-drug classes from the NCAA:

Stimulants
amiphenazole
amphetamine
bemigride
benzphetamine
bromantan
caffeine
chlorphentermine
cocaine
cropropamide
crothetamide
diethylpropion
dimethylamphetamine
doxapram
ephedrine
ethamivan
ethylamphetamine
fencamfamine
meclofenoxate
methamphetamine
methylene-dioxymethamphetamine
    (MDMA) (Ecstasy)
methylphenidate
nikethamide
pemoline
pentetrazol
phendimetrazine
phenmetrazine
phentermine
picrotoxine
pipradol
prolintane
strychnine

Anabolic Agents
anabolic steroids
androstenediol
androstenedione
boldenone
clostebol
dehydrochlormethyl-testosterone
dehydroepiandrosterone (DHEA)
dihydrotestosterone (DHT)
dromostanolone
fluoxymesterone

mesterolone
methandienone
methenolone
methyltestosterone
nandrolone
norandrostenediol
norandrostenedione
norethandrolone
oxandrolone
oxymesterone
oxymetholone
stanozolol
testosterone

Other Anabolic Agents
clenbuterolacetazolamide
bendroflumethiazide
benzthiazide
bumetanide
chlorothiazide
chlorthalidone
ethacrynic acid
flumethiazide
furosemide
hydrochlorothiazide
hydroflumethiazide
methyclothiazide
metolazone
polythiazide
quinethazone
spironolactone
triamterene
trichlormethiazide

Street Drugs
heroin
marijuana
THC (tetrahydrocannabinol)

Peptide Hormones and Analogues
chorionic gonadotrophin (HCG—
    human chorionic gonadotrophin)
corticotrophin (ACTH)
growth hormone (HGH,
    somatotrophin)

The above list is taken from the NCAA official Web site.

SUMMARY

LIFESTYLE, REST AND RECOVERY

- Understand that what you do away from training can effect your athletic performance positively and negatively.

- Do not be part of something that does not provide a positive environment for you.

- Do not open yourself up to potential injury by "playing around."

- Set aside time out of season to be a kid and/or college student.

- Set more than one goal—create goals that are steps to your ultimate goal.

- Remain focused on your goals and ignore outside influences that attempt to sabotage them.

- Create time in your schedule to get enough sleep.

- Do not get caught in the "nap trap."

- Use active recovery when taking a day off from competition and training.

HYDRATION

- Consume the proper amount of water (and other quality fluids) daily.

- Follow hydration recommendations for athletes.

- Understand the signs and symptoms of dehydration and its effects on competition.

- Use sports drinks for recovery—if you believe they help you.

- Nutrition

- Make sure you are consuming enough protein in your diet.

- Consume enough "good" calories throughout the day.

- Understand what pre-game and post-game foods work for you.

- Take nutritional supplements to help with your performance—if you believe they help you.

INJURIES AND HEALTH

- In college you are expected to be active in your injury recovery process—and you need to take it seriously.

- Utilize all medical staff when needed—they are there to help you be a success.

- Take time off to recover.

- Understand how to stretch properly—effectively and efficiently.

- Be proactive with your injuries.

- Be open-minded to all new ideas from coaches and support staff.

DRUGS AND ALCOHOL

- Respect the legal implications of consuming alcohol under the legal age.

- Understand the problems alcohol can cause on an athlete's performance.

- Know that you can be drug tested at any time as a college athlete.

- Inform the athletic training staff and/or team physician if you are taking any medication.

CHAPTER SIX

TUCK IN YOUR SHIRT AND PULL UP YOUR SOCKS

Every impression counts on the long and tricky road through college recruitment. College coaches evaluate prospective student-athletes at every opportunity, whether in a text message, email, letter, resume, on the field or while on campus. The recruiting process is an opportunity for the PSA to paint a self-portrait as a student, as an athlete and as a young adult. The first impression will occur mostly in an arena of competition. Every time a prospect steps foot on the field, court or course, he or she is likely under a coach's microscope. During the game, pre-game and post-game, college coaches are looking to see if the prospect is good enough for their program. How a prospective student-athlete reacts to his or her teammates, coaches, parents and opponents makes an impression.

> *"We are what we do repeatedly.*
> *Excellence then, is not an act but a habit."*
>
> —ARISTOTLE

Great habits make great athletes! College coaches want to see athletes' positive life choices every time they see them play, train or socialize. Presenting yourself properly is of utmost importance. Every situation can be a good—or bad—sign of your ability to succeed in the collegiate athletic arena. Through the recruiting attempts and mistakes of Abbey, Carrie, Shannon, Jessica, Liz and Jonathan, you will learn successful recruiting conduct.

COACH MCNEIL'S STORY

Coach McNeil had just completed her third year of coaching at a nationally ranked NCAA II school. Realizing the right PSA can make or break a team, she needed to recruit players that would help champion her women's soccer program to the final four.

As the youth state championship approached, Coach McNeil received multiple phone calls from club coaches regarding several players. Four prospects seemed to fit the profile she was looking for and she decided to watch them play in the championship. All four players would play in the final game, two on each team, and Coach McNeil wanted to see every minute. The four players—Shannon, Abbey, Carrie and Jessica—could possibly be great additions to her program. Coach McNeil also knew she had limited scholarship funds and she needed to make sure she spent the money wisely.

How these players handled this very important game was going to be key insight for Coach McNeil. She knew the 10:00 a.m. game would require a 9:00 a.m. warm-up, so Coach McNeil planned to arrive early. She felt attitudes were more honest during the warm-up, and she liked to see how the players handled pre-game stress.

In addition to evaluating the players, Coach McNeil wanted to see how the parents behaved during the game. She often found parents provided insight into a player's emotional stability. She was curious to see how they reacted to the game as she sat amongst the parents and prepared to watch the team's warm-up.

As 9:00 a.m. approached, Coach McNeil was surprised to notice only three of the four prospects had arrived. Jessica was not with her team and she wondered if she was sick or injured.

Fifteen minutes later, as Jessica's team was well into their warm-up, Coach McNeil noticed they were motioning toward the parking lot. It was

Jessica, eating her McMuffin, sipping her Coke and wearing the wrong uniform. As her teammates yelled at her to hurry up, Jessica ignored them. It was obvious she knew she was a star player and did things on her own time. Even her coach motioned for her to hurry, but she continued her casual stroll over to the field.

This prima donna behavior from Jessica was enough for Coach McNeil to scratch a big line through her name. It would not matter how well she played, Coach McNeil would never consider her a team player and would never recruit Jessica for her program.

If she had only been late, Coach McNeil might have given her a chance. She would have asked Jessica's club coach if her tardiness was a regular occurrence and if not, she could have marked it as an unfortunate situation. Jessica's lateness was not the only problem, however. Her casual stroll from the parking lot showed she did not care about the game or her team. Even worse, Jessica had on the wrong uniform. She was a mess! Clearly, Jessica did not warrant the prestigious title of a collegiate student-athlete.

As 10:00 a.m. approached, the starting players took the field without Jessica. Parents found their places around the field along with the college coaches and anticipated the kick-off. Some parents sat quietly while others yelled encouragement to their daughters and teammates. Overall, it was a positive sideline as everyone looked forward to a tough game between two of the best club teams in the nation. A state championship was on the line, and everyone felt it. Coach McNeil was happy to see Abbey, Carrie and Shannon all playing with great enthusiasm.

Shannon was very high on Coach McNeil's recruiting list along with several other coaches. As the leading scorer on her team, she was the key player her teammates counted on to win games. Unfortunately, this morning was not going well. Every time she went forward, she gave the ball away and her frustrations mounted. Shannon felt she was not getting the appropriate support from her teammates and started to yell. It seemed the more frustrated and vocal Shannon became, the more frustrated and vocal Shannon's parents became. Constantly yelling at Shannon and her teammates, they stirred up everyone observing the game—especially Shannon. This finally came to a crashing halt near the end of the half. Shannon made a mistake, gave the ball away again, and there was an exchange of words between parent and player.

"You are playing like crap, Shannon! Get your act together," screamed Shannon's mom.

Shannon turned and snapped, "Mom, just shut-up! Leave me alone."

"Don't you yell at me, young lady! You need to go score a goal. That team sucks! You should be winning. Get your act together and score a *%! goal."

"*%! you, Mom. Shut the *%! up! Leave me alone."

Coach McNeil was shocked and disgusted by the vulgarity. She looked at the other parents on the sidelines and was even more surprised at their lack of shock at the verbiage. Obviously, this was not the first conversation of this type.

Needless to say, this exchange between Shannon and her mother turned away many, if not all, college coaches that morning. Not too many coaches have the patience for that kind of negative temperament.

NOTE TO PARENTS

Susie walked into the kitchen as her mom started breakfast and yelled, "Mom, get the eggs! Quick, turn the eggs over! Make sure you flip them right! Don't break the yolk! Quick, Mom! What about the toast? The toast is burning! You need to get the toast! Quick, Mom! We're all hungry! What about the bacon? The sausages? Don't burn them! You need to turn them over. TURN OVER THE BACON! Hey, what about the grits? Mix the grits, add the butter, add the pepper, add the salt! Mom, HURRY UP! You need to butter the toast before it gets too cold! You know how we love it all melted. MOM, YOU HAD BETTER NOT RUIN BREAKFAST FOR US! DON'T RUIN OUR DAY BECAUSE YOU ARE LAZY AND SLOW!"

Susie's mom finally had enough and turned to Susie waving her spatula. "What on earth is wrong with you? I've cooked breakfast a million times! I think I know how to cook breakfast! When have you ever cooked breakfast?"

Susie replied, "Well, Mom, now you know how I feel every time I play soccer!"

Parents, let your kids enjoy the game without your sideline commentary.

Disappointed, Coach McNeil was now down to two recruits. Meanwhile, Shannon's mother sensed that Coach McNeil had lost interest in Shannon. Although she knew an NCAA rule forbade parent and coach to communicate during the game, she persisted anyway. Coach McNeil patiently explained communication was strictly forbidden during the game. Not surprisingly, the mother insisted on a response. Coach McNeil stood up, "Feel free to give me a call at a more appropriate time." She picked up her notebook and chair, and she walked away to another area of the field where she could observe her remaining two recruits.

> **MIND THE RULES:** NCAA rules forbid communication between coach and parent/PSA during competition.

When the game hit halftime, the referee blew his whistle and both teams ran to their coaches. Coach McNeil noticed Carrie ran and talked to her dad. Carrie's dad was more than willing to express his opinions on how she and her teammates were playing. Carrie's dad was quick to point out everyone's flaws from the players to the coaches to the officials.

Remember! Players, give respect and attention to your coach first. Save time for your parents after the game has ended.

Eventually Carrie made her way over to her coach and his halftime talk. Unfortunately, Carrie's head was full of her dad's opinions, and she told her coach what he thought. Obviously, the coach, in the middle of an important game, did not want to hear sideline commentary from Carrie's dad and told Carrie to keep her opinions to herself. Carrie stormed off to the bench and sat down alone. After seeing the exchange, Carrie's dad started to bad-mouth the coach to all the parents who would listen.

A central midfield player, tall and intelligent, Carrie was not the quickest soccer player in the world but was technically proficient and tactically better than anyone on the field. However, Coach McNeil was disenchanted after seeing this behavior. She did not like the fact that Carrie disrespected her coach or her temperamental reaction.

This was not the first time Coach McNeil had seen a little rebelliousness in Carrie. In previous evaluations, she always seemed to have her shirt untucked, her long soccer socks around her ankles, and her shoes dirty and unpolished. On occasion, Carrie had shown up to games in non-team issued equipment, just because she wanted to.

Although Carrie had created quite a reputation for herself, she was a talented young soccer player and Coach McNeil predicted she would straighten up within her disciplined program. She was willing to take the gamble if those were the only things that created reservations regarding her temperament as a prospective student-athlete. However, the exchange with her dad and coach created a bigger concern.

As the second half began, and Carrie remained on the bench, second thoughts ran through Coach McNeil's mind.

- A reservation about the way Carrie presented herself before and during games bothered her. The way she was always untucked and messy showed a lack of self-respect for herself and her teammates.

- Carrie's dad was a greater concern. The coach knew that he might not relinquish control even when Carrie went to college. She could see Carrie's dad working behind the scenes and starting trouble.

- Carrie listened to her father over her coach and even challenged her coach with her dad's comments. This upset and unfocused her teammates and created unnecessary tension.

- Carrie took herself out of the game mentally by responding negatively toward her coach. She unnecessarily wasted her time and talent.

Remember! Coaches notice the care and attention players put toward their team uniform. Tuck in your shirt and pull up your socks! Show your respect to the team and sport.

Carrie did not get back onto the field until late in the second half when her team was one goal down with ten minutes to play. The team had played the whole game without Jessica and the second half without Carrie. Shannon had turned her game around and scored the only goal of the game but was still arguing with her mother on the sideline. Abbey had done brilliantly however, with consistent game-winning saves.

Abbey was the kind of player Coach McNeil was looking for. She was a strong athlete, talented and confident. She had produced some very fine saves during the game. Just as important, Abbey remained emotionally in control throughout the game and her teammates showed great confidence in her ability. Coach McNeil thought Abbey was not only a great athlete and goalkeeper, but her attitude was a perfect fit for her program.

- Abbey showed up on time (early).

- Abbey wore the appropriate equipment.

- Abbey looked refreshed and energetic during the warm-up.

- Abbey warmed up with intensity and focus.

- Abbey played well and with confidence.

- Abbey's teammates showed confidence in her and respected her (they also liked her).

- Abbey's parents were positive toward all the players on the field and supportive of the coach.

- Abbey was a team player and a positive influence on her team.

- Even the opposing team respected Abbey.

At the conclusion of the game, Abbey's team celebrated their win thanks to Shannon's only goal. Everyone ran toward Shannon and Abbey, hugging and patting each other on the back. Abbey broke from her group and went to shake hands with the opposing team. As Abbey approached Carrie, Carrie pushed her and stomped off toward her dad and the parking lot. Carrie was a poor loser and did not think about going to her teammates or coach. Jessica was despondent, as she knew her early morning antics had let down her team. She knew she could have made a difference on the field that day. Shannon ran toward her mom with a huge *"I told you so!"*

Overall, Coach McNeil was disappointed with what she saw that day. Carrie and her dad's poor attitude were too much for Coach McNeil and her program, even though she believed Carrie to be a very talented soccer player. Shannon was also a great soccer player with great potential. However, if she could not respect her mom appropriately, what chance was there that she would respect her college soccer coach? Jessica was just a mess; her tardiness and unorganized and uncommitted behavior was not a student-athlete that Coach McNeil wanted in her program. Abbey was the only one who presented herself well. She played well and respected her teammates and opponents. Most importantly, Abbey was a team player and a leader. Coach McNeil decided to continue to recruit Abbey.

Even after a quality first impression on the playing field, college coaches do not stop monitoring PSAs. There are many more steps to take before the recruiting process is complete. PSAs must continually make positive impressions every step of the way.

CARE ABOUT YOUR CORRESPONDENCE

LIZ'S STORY

Liz scored goals. She was fast and strong and could get past any defender in her way. She was explosive over a short distance, especially in a crowd. As a dynamic athlete with great stick skills, Liz could be a great college field hockey player. During her junior year, Liz developed further as an athlete and started to gain a lot of attention from many nationally ranked collegiate programs.

Liz's athletic talents, coupled with her outstanding academic record, resulted in a mailbox full of letters from college coaches after September 1st of her junior year. With every letter that arrived, Liz emailed the coach in return, sharing her feelings regarding the school or program. Liz told each coach that she was either very interested in the program, curious about the program and wanted to learn more, or that she was not interested in the program but would keep them in mind if circumstances changed.

Wisely, Liz was honest with recruiters up front. She did not want to waste time with programs that she was not interested in, but she wanted to be polite as well.

Remember! Always be courteous and respectful to coaches, regardless of your interest level in their program. The college coach network is small and they talk. You do not want to be considered rude and disrespectful by any one of them.

As part of the emails to the coaches that interested her, Liz included her profile and resume, a copy of her grades and a list of upcoming competitions. Liz made sure to CC every coach in the program (not just the head coach) in an effort to open communications with the entire coaching staff for that sport. Liz believed she had done everything correctly to keep college programs interested in her, and she had. She waited and waited for replies to her emails, but responses from coaches never came. Confused, Liz called one of the coaches she had been waiting to hear from. Liz wanted to know why coaches were not responding.

It turned out that coaches had lost interest in Liz for one very simple reason—her email address LIZ420@email.com had a drug reference in it. After seeing this, the coaches stopped recruiting her immediately. Liz was horrified and very embarrassed. She did not know about the drug reference in her email address and had chosen it because it was her birth date! She immediately changed her email address to LizLastname@email.com.

After creating a new email account, Liz emailed every coach that had shown interest in her and tried to rectify her mistake.

TO: CoachStevens@email.fhu.edu

FROM:LizLastname@email.com

SUBJECT: Recruiting Mix-up

Dear Coach Stevens,

I would like to continue the recruiting process with you and your program. Since our last email exchange, I have learned that my previous email address had a drug reference attached to it, and that this may have been the reason that I have not heard from you again. I am extremely embarrassed by this and did not know that this was a drug reference when I created that email name and account. I do not endorse the use of recreational drugs and have never used drugs at any time. "420" is the month and date of my birth.

I have attached a copy of my profile, my resume and my upcoming game schedule. I am very interested in Field Hockey University and would like to reopen our recruiting communications and set up an unofficial visit in the very near future.

I look forward to hearing from you soon,

Liz Lastname

Every college coach was impressed that Liz had been mature enough to admit a mistake, even an unknown one. It said a lot about Liz's character. After her email explanation, many college coaches regained interest in her and replied to her email to continue the recruitment process.

Remember! A simple email address is best. Use your name and, if needed, a jersey number and/or sport. Do not get too fancy!

● firstname.lastname@email.com

● lastname.firstname@email.com

● firstname_lastname@email.com

● lastname_firstname@email.com

Using your name as your email address is a simple form of advertising yourself, plus...

1. When coaches open their email inboxes, they recognize your name and know immediately that the email is from you. This eliminates the need for coaches to guess who sent the email.

2. You have less chance of creating a controversial email name that could show you in an unfavorable light.

Do not use the name of a college or university in your email address. Seeing another university referenced in the email can put off coaches.

Although Liz had created a very bad first impression, she managed to rescue the recruiting process once she changed her email address and admitted her mistake. Not every mistake is "fixable" however.

In addition to having an easily recognizable email address, it is a good idea to create an email signature with relevant information about you—contact information that is readily available for the coaches to use and utilize. In your signature, you should list the following:

● High School and graduation year

● Club team/High school and jersey number

● Home- and cell-phone numbers

● Link to your—or your team's—Web page

You do not need your email address in the signature.

Example:

Liz Lastname
Field Hockey High 2010

Wing Bangers Hockey Club #5
Home 111-222-3333 Cell 111-444-5555
www.WingBangersHockeyClub.net/LizLastname

JONATHAN'S STORY

Jonathan was an exceptional student, ranked in the top 3 percent of his senior class. His SAT scores qualified him for an academic scholarship at every institution to which he had applied, and his Advanced Placement (AP) classes allowed him to enter his collegiate freshman year with close to sophomore year status. Although Jonathon was only an average cross-country runner at his high school, he was the type of student that college coaches want in their programs. Smart students create less eligibility worries for the coaches and with great team spirit, they can help foster a stronger academic environment for the program.

Although Jonathan did not receive any recruiting interest from the universities he was applying to, he desperately wanted to be a part of a collegiate cross-country team. Jonathan started sending letters with his athletic and academic resume to the coaches of academic institutions where he was applying, offering to be a walk-on. Look for the problems in his letter.

Coach Clinton
Cross Country Coach
Running University
Running, TX 75555

Dear Coach Mack,

I would like to take this opportunity to introduce myself to you. I am currently applying to various universities and Cross Country College is one of my top choices. CCC fits my needs academically and I hope to fit in with your cross-country program.

As you can see by my enclosed transcripts, I am a very good student. I will be receiving an academic scholarship from your school and would like to walk on to your program.

I am a huge Running University supporter and both my parents graduated from RU in the early 80's. I hope to follow their example and be a Road Runner! I have enclosed my recent official times from our current cross-country season where I normally finish fourth on our state championship team. My 5K personal best as a junior was 19:35 and as a senior this year, I have improved that to 19:04.

I know my limitations as an athlete but believe I will be a great addition to your program, especially from academic and team spirit standpoints. My work ethic is exceptional in everything that I do, and cross-country is no different! Please feel free to contact my high school coach, Coach Martin, at 898-898-889 for a reference.

I hope there is a position for me within your program. You can reach me via email at RunJonathan@email or by calling my cell phone number which is 222-555-6666. I look forward to hearing from you soon.

Sincerely,

Jonathan

Walk-On Athletes seek to be a part of the athletic program of the school they are attending. Some programs are more open to this than others.

Recruited Walk-On Athletes are PSAs that are asked to join the program but receive no financial or admission assistance from the school's athletic department.

Jonathan sent this letter to Coach Clinton and hoped to hear from him relatively soon in order to finalize his college selection. He was very excited about the prospect of being a collegiate student-athlete, especially at his parents' Alma Mater! Jonathan eagerly awaited a response from Coach Clinton but it never came.

Not one to give up easily, Jonathan followed up with another email to Coach Clinton:

TO: CoachClinton@email.RunningU.edu

FROM: RunJonathan@email.com

SUBJECT: Well???

Dear Coach,

I sent you a letter the other week and have not heard back from you. Would you, or would you not, like me to be part of your program??

Jonathan

Again, Jonathan heard nothing from the coach or any of his staff. Confused, Jonathan spoke with an admissions representative who told him that the cross-country program *was* looking for a few walk-ons for the fall. Even more confused, Jonathan pulled out a copy of the letter he had sent to Coach Clinton. That is when he realized his mistakes.

- The letter was addressed to Coach Clinton at Running University, while the introduction of the letter was addressed to Coach Mack at Cross Country College—another school to which he was applying. Most college coaches would throw the letter away with this mistake.

- The use of "school" in the second paragraph is lazy. The use of "university" for Running University and "college" for Cross Country College is more appropriate.

- Making the presumption in the first paragraph that he would receive an academic scholarship is just that: presumptuous!

- In the fourth paragraph, Coach Martin's telephone number is incomplete, one number short.

- Jonathan's email address is incomplete. He should not have assumed that the coach would know the domain extension of his email address.

It is vitally important to proofread your letters and emails and address the letter and/or email to the correct person. Coaches do not like having their names misspelled or having the wrong name on the letter. Check the spelling especially when there has been a recent change in coaching staff. There is nothing a coach dislikes more than a letter addressed to the coach that they have just replaced. All coaches have egos—do not play against them!

The second email was another problem for Jonathan. He addressed the email *"Dear Coach"* rather than *"Dear Coach Clinton."* Some coaches feel it is a sign of laziness if the email is not personalized. These coaches would press the delete button before they reached the first paragraph. The second problem with Jonathan's email was the informal and demanding tone he used. College coaches want to be treated with respect in all forms of communications, on and off the field. Using email for the recruiting process can be very smart, but only if used correctly.

- Be careful when sending emails to a group of coaches at the same time. Do not ever group their names together in the "To" field. Email each one independently. CoachA@University1.com does not want to see CoachB@University2.com next to his name.

- Do not set up BCC lists to a group of "College Coaches." That is just lazy.

- Start each email with a personal touch. *Dear Coach Clinton* or *Dear Coach Mack* is more appropriate than *"Dear Coach."*

- Include the assistant coaches in the CC line. Sometimes they do more recruiting than the head coach does.

- Within the body of the email, place some significant statement that can only relate to that particular coach or program. This extra touch shows your genuine interest in their program.

- Put your name and incoming class year on the subject line of your first email. Farther along into the recruiting process, you can be more specific such as "Housing Question" or "Upcoming Campus Visit."

TO: CoachClinton@email.RunningU.edu

FROM: RunJonathan@email.com

SUBJECT: Jonathan Lastname Class of 2008

Dear Coach Clinton,

I am still interested in being part of your program next year by walking on. I have been very impressed with your team's placements this fall, especially Jimmy Fast and his three first place finishes. I would also like to congratulate your being named Conference Coach of the Year for the second time in three years.

It is my desire to be part of Running University and I look forward to hearing from you soon,

Jonathan Runner
Hilly High School, Class of 2008

Varsity Cross-Country
Home 222-333-4444 Cell 222-555-6666
www.hillyHS.org/crosscountry

Like Jonathan, there are many high school student-athletes that do not get recruited by colleges for one reason or another. Sometimes the coaches overlook them, other times they do not fit the immediate needs of the program, and most times the coaches do not know of the prospect's interest in their program or institution.

If by the winter of the junior year, a high school athlete is not receiving an adequate amount of recruiting interest, it becomes important that the high school athlete gain the attention of the college coaches. Sending emails, letters, profiles and even a recruiting video are all effective ways to grab the attention of coaches. Again, it is vitally important that everything is proofread and appropriate.

CREATING AN ATHLETIC RESUME/PROFILE

A recruiting resume, or profile, should be easy to read (plenty of white space and reader-friendly font such as Arial or Times New Roman), specific and to the point. It should contain all relevant academic and athletic information and provide the coach with information he or she requires to contact you.

The layout of the information should include these items:

- **Personal Information**: Name, address, phone number(s), email address, date of birth, and if you have registered with the NCAA Eligibility Center you should state that in this section.

- Do not include your social security number on your profile, in case it is thrown away inappropriately—coaches may need your social security number later in the recruitment process (signing of NLI) and you can relay that information if, and when, it is appropriate.

- **Academic Information:** Include high school, year of graduation (not your grade when you send the resume/profile), grade point average (GPA), class rank (if known), standardized test scores, any academic awards and AP classes/scores.

- **Athletic Information:** Position, club (if applicable), any significant athletic awards since high school age (include team awards if significant; i.e. National Championship) and any objective athletic information (i.e. game statistics, times for tests, etc.)

- **Extracurricular activities:** Work, volunteer work and/or additional school activities (i.e. newspaper, year book, choir, band, plays, etc.)
- **References:** These should be athletically related to your sport. Include coaches, trainers, past coaches and athletic directors. Include their contact information, including email addresses and phone numbers.

If you have a personal Web page or a team site, you should post your resume/profile on the Web page. If you choose to do this, you will need to edit your profile so that you do not include your contact information, social security number or date of birth. Under contact information, write "Please contact Coach *(name of your coach)* for additional information."

CREATING AN ATHLETIC RECRUITMENT VIDEO

Recruiting videos can be a good way of either introducing yourself to a coach or giving coaches a look at you as a potential recruit. They are especially beneficial if the coaches have not been able to see you play or compete in person, or if you have not performed up to your usual standard when they have seen you play. However, these recruiting videos should be short and to the point—a resume in motion.

If you have had correspondence with the coach for whom you are making the video, ask them for input concerning the video and tailor it to suit their needs. If the video is being sent to gain the attention of a coach that has not returned correspondence to you, or if you are sending it as part of your first correspondence, follow the procedure below:

- Start with an **introduction** (1 minute)—Face the camera and state your name, position, club/high school team and any relevant academic and athletic information. Even though this may be uncomfortable for you, it is important that you are energetic, professional and confident. For example, you might say, "Hello, Coach Stevens. I am Liz Lastname and I am a forward and captain for Wing Bangers Hockey Club where I scored 37 goals in 32 games last season. I have an SAT score of 1290 and a grade-point average of 3.7 from Hockey High School. I run 40 yards in 4.3 seconds and have a vertical jump of 22 inches. Please enjoy the next 6 minutes of me in action."

- Next, show footage of you **practicing** (3 minutes)—Emphasize technique that is specific to your position (when applicable) and physical ability similar to game situations, i.e. technique, running, agility, jumping ability, etc.

- Then show **highlighted game footage** (3 minutes)—Make sure the highlights focus on you and your movement. Start with a great clip (for example, a goal, touchdown, dunk, save, etc.) and finish on a great clip.

- **Closure** (30 seconds)—Speak into the camera and explain how the coach may contact you. Thank the coach for taking the time to view the video and offer them the opportunity for a longer video if they cannot see you in person.

Do not send video of complete games—it takes too long and there will not be enough focused footage of you. The video is only an introduction to you as a prospective student-athlete and should not take more than 10 minutes. Anything longer and a coach will switch it off quickly. The purpose of the video is to grab the attention of coaches so that they will come and see you for themselves or they will ask you for a longer video or full game tape.

Include a profile/resume with the video.

If you have the capability to email the video and profile/resume to the coaches, this is recommended because it will make it easier for them to view.

Videos are only effective for sports that require a subjective evaluation from the recruiting coaches. For sports that have scores and times, the coaches will use these numbers to begin their evaluation process.

SENDING ADDITIONAL MATERIALS

Coaches are busy people and do not want to spend hours reading through newspaper articles where you are mentioned. If you have had an article where you are the main feature, send that *one* article only.

PHOTOGRAPHS, FACEBOOK AND MYSPACE

Under the instruction of their high school coaches and guidance counselors, both Liz and Jonathan created athletic resumes with photographs.

Liz included two photographs on her resume, one on the first page at the top right hand corner and one near the bottom. The first one was an action shot of her running past a couple of athletic-looking defenders, getting her shirt pulled, but continuing on with a look of great determination on her face. The photograph showed Liz as a serious field hockey player committed to success. (Note, if the opposition players in the photograph had not looked athletic, it would not have been as strong a photograph.

Running past a bunch of defenders who are not athletic will not impress coaches.)

Photograph Rules: Some coaches like to see photographs of recruits only if it helps their recruiting process. Use a well-taken, recent *action* photograph, never a glamour shot. A coach will see nothing from a yearbook or prom photograph. Looking good in a tuxedo or dress does not make you a good athlete! ■

Liz's second photograph was one of her and her teammates celebrating a goal. Liz is the center of attention and all her teammates surround her. Looking exhilarated and satisfied, Liz and her teammates are obviously extremely excited about what she just accomplished. This photo illustrates what college coaches want in their programs: happy, enthusiastic, respected and successful athletes.

Jonathan's first photograph was one from his yearbook. It was a very nice photograph that both his mom and his grandmother liked, and it showed that he looked like a very nice young man, but it showed nothing about his athleticism. Why include a photograph if it is not going to tell a good athletic story? He would have been better off sending a photograph of himself studying in the library or in a laboratory class wearing goggles and a white lab coat! Jonathan's coaches, who proofread his resume, suggested he replace the yearbook photograph with one of him competing in a cross-country meet. Jonathan found a photo that showed him waiting for the gun to go off at the start of a race. He looked ready, he looked focused, but he was standing there doing nothing. Jonathan's coaches suggested that he use a different shot, one where he was fighting to get to the front of the pack early in the race. His coaches explained to Jonathan that any movement—any action—shows much more to coaches than a photograph in which the subject is stationary.

Coach Stevens from Field Hockey University was once again interested in Liz as a prospect for her field hockey program. Coach Stevens continued her research to make sure Liz was indeed telling the truth about her lifestyle and commitment to becoming a collegiate student-athlete. She made some follow-up phone calls to other coaches: high school, club and even a few of her close friends in the college coaching community. Finally, Coach Stevens came to a point where she was near the end of her research.

She had only two more places to check before offering Liz a scholarship to the program at FHU.

Remember! College coaches do talk to one another! They often use their multi-level network (high school, club and college) to check, double check and triple check on recruits.

Many high school students have created their own identities on Internet sites like MySpace and Facebook. It is common practice for parents, prospective employers, admissions staff, as well as collegiate coaches to monitor these sites for questionable behavior. What students put on their pages reveals a lot about their lifestyle and personality.

Coach Stevens logged on to look at Liz's MySpace and Facebook pages to see if there were any warning signs that might make the coach rethink offering Liz a scholarship. Any photograph of her partying, with or without drugs or alcohol, would be a red flag. In addition, any negative comments within her written statements regarding her parents, her teachers, her coaches or her teammates would be yet another red flag.

Remember! Photographs say a lot! Remove any photographs from your MySpace or Facebook pages if you are acting unsuitably. Coaches want healthy athletes and could even drop recruits if they see too many photos of the recruit eating fast food! Any detrimental behavior, true or perceived, will cause a college coach to reconsider his or her choice to recruit a prospect.

Fortunately, for Liz, she was a very positive and clean-living high school student-athlete. She had nothing to hide. In one of her pages, she discussed games and tactics with her teammates and showed many photographs of her teammates enjoying themselves at training, in games and off the playing field. What the network of coaches and teachers had told Coach Stevens confirmed what she saw on the Web sites. Liz was a model student-athlete, and she would be a great addition to her program.

BE ON YOUR BEST BEHAVIOR

When coaches recruit a prospective student-athlete, they are looking at these young men and women as people who will represent the university, the athletic department, their program and their team at all times. Everything a student-athlete does is a reflection of the institution. Continually under the microscope, one mistake can undo many great things that a student-athlete has done previously. Most coaches cannot afford to take a gamble on student-athletes that may cause problems, create headaches or diminish a positive environment within their program.

Not all of these issues will turn every college coach away and some coaches may not care about any of these issues. Every coach sets his or her own standards. As a prospective student-athlete, it is always better to demonstrate high standards of ethics, morality and politeness throughout the recruiting process. You cannot go wrong if you present yourself in the best possible way.

Remember! No coach wants a headache. Present yourself in a positive way and it will be easy for the coach to pursue you with vigor and excitement. Simple things such as tucking your shirt in, pulling your socks up and arriving on time tells a great deal about your respect for the game. Shaking hands with your opponents and teammates after the game tells a lot about your character.

It is easy to read a coach's mind. Most coaches need to insert student-athletes into their programs that bring good habits and values. Are you a team player? Are you going to represent the university well? If you are, then college coaches will want you in their programs.

SUMMARY

PROSPECTIVE STUDENT-ATHLETES

- Be on time/early for all recruiting events.

- Be organized: wear appropriate attire.

- Be respectful to your teammates, coaches, opponents, parents and fans.

- Be positive with all communication during games: teammates, coaches, opponents, parents and fans.

- Ignore negative comments from everyone on the sidelines or in the stands.

- Stay with your team at all times until dismissed by coaches.
- Dress team-appropriate: have your shirt tucked in, etc.
- Show good sportsmanship.
- Be honest in all correspondence with college coaches.
- Aggressively recruit yourself to the institutions of your choice.
- CC assistant coaches in your correspondence to head coaches.
- Create and use a simple email address.
- Proofread all correspondence to college coaches and admissions offices.
- Address all correspondence, email and letters, personally and appropriately.
- Use "college" or "university" appropriately.
- Be humble in all communication—verbal and written—with college coaches.
- Present full and correct contact information for yourself and all references.
- Use an action photograph, not a glamour shot.
- Have G-rated MySpace and FaceBook pages if you have them.

PARENTS OF PROSPECTIVE STUDENT-ATHLETES

- Please don't yell negatively at games, not at your child or other athletes.
- Don't publicly question your child's coaches and their choices.
- Refrain from talking to college coaches during games.
- Be respectful to everyone at the games.
- Proofread all correspondence.
- Help your child create good first impressions.

SAMPLE PROFILE

Personal Information

Jonathan Runner
7506 Northwest Hill • Hilly, ST 00000 • C 222-555-6666 • H 222-333-4444
RunJonathan@email.com

Academics

Hilly High School
Class of 2010

- GPA: 3.39
- SAT: 1290 (Old), 1910 (New); 630 Math, 660 Critical Reading, 620 Writing
- ACT: 28; 31 English, 27 Math, 31 Reading, 23 Science
- AP Tests: 4 English, 4 US History

Advanced Placement Courses

- World Geography Pre-AP, World History AP, U.S. History AP, Economics AP, Government AP
- English I Pre-AP, English II Pre-AP, English III AP, English IV AP
- Environmental Science AP
- Pre-Calculus Pre-AP

Electives & Extracurricular Activities

- School Newspaper, *The Hill Times*—Asst. Section Editor & Reporter
  - Journalism I (NP), Adv. Journalism I (NP), Adv. Journalism III (NP), Adv. Journalism IV (NP)/Desktop Publishing
  - Staff received Gold Crown Award for Excellence in Journalism (2008)
  - Staff received NSPA Pacemaker; 1 of 15 given throughout nation (2008)
  - Staff named National Gold Medalist Newspaper by the Columbia Scholastic Press Association at Columbia University, NY
- Literary Magazine, *Lit On The Hill*—Editor & Writer

Athletics & Training

Varsity Letterman Cross Country (Junior–Senior)

- Personal Best: 19:02 (Senior); 19:35 (Junior)
- Award for "Core. Cut and Ripped" (Junior)
- Thanksgiving Turkey Trot Placed in the top 1/13th (295/4054)

Varsity Letterman Track (Junior–Senior)

- 800m, 1600m

Running Club: Chairman (Senior)

Navy SEALs Specialized pre-BUD/S personal training (2008–2010):
SEAL PFT (personally recorded):

- 500 yd Swim: 8'45" sidestroke
- 2 min. Pushup Max: 130
- 2 min. Sit-up Max: 120   Pull-Up Max: 23
- 1.5 mi. Run: 8'27"
- Breath Holding: 3'02"

Lifeguard Training

- Certified in Lifeguard Training & First Aid, CPR/AED for the Professional Rescuer, and Blood-borne Pathogens Training

Work Experience

Lifeguard, Hilly Towne Park Pool (2008 and 2009)

- Worked in a team of eight, supervising approximately 300 swimmers per day

Cashier, Hilly Grocery and Boutique (2008)

- Responsible for customer checkout and payment processing

Child Care Provider & Pet Sitter (2005–2008)

- Supervised children and pets consistently for select neighbors

Personal & Memberships

Red Cross: Volunteer (2006–Present)

Guitar: Self-taught, performances at Guitar Club and Open-Mic nights (2001–2007)

French I, French II, French III

Independent Studies: Health-science, kinesiology and personal training

References

Coach Jog Martin
Varsity Cross Country Coach
Hilly High School
Tel: 898-898-8898
Email: coachmartin@email.com

Mr. I. M. Jolly
Counselor

Hilly High School
Tel: 898-898-8899
Email: imjolly@email.com

Ms. Bonnie MacDougall
Lifeguard Supervisor
Hilly Towne Park Pool
Tel: 898-898-8889
Email: bonniemac@email.com

CHAPTER SEVEN

NOT A 48-HOUR VACATION: COLLEGE VISITS

Chapter One introduced unofficial and official visits to the recruiting process. Visits are opportunities for prospective student-athletes to see campus, to meet the coaching staff and student-athletes and to get a general feel for the institution academically, athletically and socially. For some, it is the final step to committing to an institution; for others, it is an opportunity to impress the coaching staff and hopefully pique their interest. Visits can be the most important aspect of college recruitment for the prospective student-athlete. They can make or break recruiting opportunities, so treat each visit with respect. Many coaches have stopped the recruitment of a prospect because of the way his or her visit played out.

Approach each visit with intelligence and vigor. It is up to you to make a great impression!

SIMON'S STORY

Coach Montgomery and the golf program at Small Golf University had recruited Simon, an avid and successful youth golfer. Simon and his parents wanted to visit the campus during a busy time so that they could see the golf program, its coaches and its student-athletes, in the usual environment of their season. Simon arranged a visit to SGU early in the morning before the coach and his team left to compete in a very important regional event.

Prior to this date, all recruiting correspondence had been very positive and reassuring to both Simon and his family. Everyone liked the wholesome atmosphere at SGU, and especially the golf program. Simon and his family knew that it was a perfect environment for him to succeed. His parents wanted Simon to enjoy his visit to the university and more importantly, to enjoy his experience with the coach and the golfers of the institution.

Simon arranged a 9:00 a.m. office meeting with Coach Montgomery the week prior to the visit. During the confirmation call, Coach Montgomery explained to Simon that it was going to be a busy day, but he promised to do his best to show him what SGU had to offer and to answer questions that Simon and his family might have.

Every morning prior to travel, Coach Montgomery usually spent time with his family before being away for four days. They got up early and had a family breakfast before taking the children to school. Then, he and his wife went for a long walk and relaxed before he left for the office. It was a custom that he and his family enjoyed. In only a couple of instances had they ever interrupted that routine. Because Simon was a very important prospect for the small NCAA II institution, his visit was to be one of those few occasions.

That morning, Coach Montgomery got to his office early to prepare for the trip and to confirm all the plans. It was important to him that he reserve plenty of time to spend with Simon and his family. Nine a.m. came and went and there was still no sign of Simon. It was not until 9:30 that Simon strolled into the office with his parents. By this time, Coach Montgomery was not happy. Even worse, Simon's dad was wearing a baseball cap from the big state university across town, and Simon was wearing a sweatshirt from a competing institution. No one was wearing the colors of Small Golf University!

Coach Montgomery was a hands-on recruiter and normally spent all his time, whenever possible, with prospective student-athletes and their families. He enjoyed the discussions and learning about every one of his recruits while showing off his beautiful campus. Coach Montgomery believed in the family atmosphere that he had created within the program. He believed that his program worked because it all boiled down to respect—respect for the institution, respect for the program, and respect for all the components that made up the Small Golf University environment. Coach Montgomery felt the lateness—and lack of an apology—together with wearing another institution's colors was a slap in the face. It showed disrespect for him, his program and the university. Needless to say, the meeting did not start well.

As Coach Montgomery and his graduate assistant coach started their discussion, Simon's dad Jim began to dominate the conversation. He asked questions and added his opinions. He continually compared the institution and athletic program negatively to other schools and Coach Montgomery to other coaches.

- "Okay, my kid is a great golfer, even though he doesn't putt as well as I do. He is obviously better than most of your players here. I assume that he will be one of your 'go-to' guys and he will be captain."

- "I know Simon is good enough to get money at every school he is looking at. How much are you offering?"

- "Being a small school, your academics are not as good as State's… so it will be easier for Simon…he is not the brightest kid!"

- "So it is just you and a grad assistant…does the AD not think too highly of the program? Over at State they have a great coach, an assistant, and a graduate assistant… not to mention a full-time trainer and strength coach!"

- "Why should Simon be with you? You have never had a professional come through your ranks at this school or at that other school where you used to work."

At every opportunity, Coach Montgomery attempted to turn the conversation to Simon. Every coach wants the prospective student-athlete to talk, ask the questions, show initiative and have a strong interest in the institution and program. Coach Montgomery was no different. He wanted to engage Simon and get his thoughts and his feelings regarding SGU and its golf program. Coach Montgomery wanted to know how and why SGU fit Simon's plans. Some parent interaction is good but not a conversation dominated by the parent.

There are three fundamental recruiting blunders that parents should avoid:

1. Answering for their child

2. Interrupting the coach

3. Contradicting and/or arguing with the coach

Simon's dad committed all three while his mom continually rolled her eyes when Coach Montgomery tried to get the conversation back on track to Simon. Jim went wrong in the following ways:

- A parent should never comment on how good his or her child is in any area: academically, athletically or other. When it comes to analyzing your child's athletic ability, that is the coach's job; he/she is the professional.

- Parents should not compare themselves to their child in any way. This shows egocentric behavior that turn coaches off. The assumption is that your child will develop the same behavior and not be a team player or contribute to a positive environment. The apple never falls far from the tree!

- Money is a touchy subject. Parents should not initiate finances in the beginning of a conversation. Allow coaches to bring up the subject—and on their terms. If coaches do not discuss the cost of the education and the available athletic and academic scholarships, then they are unlikely to do so. When a coaching staff is willing to offer scholarship money, they will do so at the appropriate time. However, it is okay for parents to discuss finances when…

  1. They are sure that the institution is where their son or daughter wants to attend, or

  2. When money is a deciding factor and they need to respond to another offer that has already been made.

Never assume that your child will receive a scholarship worth 100 percent of the education's cost, especially if your child competes in an
equivalency sport.

- Don't assume that larger schools and NCAA I schools provide a
  better academic environment for every student. Each academic
  institution should be evaluated individually, and in all areas of the
  higher educational experience. In addition, making the assumption that an NCAA I athletic program is better (and receives more
  funding) than either an NCAA II or III program is a mistake.
  There are many smaller institutions that can provide academic and
  athletic packages for students and student-athletes that are perfectly suited for those young persons and their families. The secondary part of Simon's dad's comment was unnecessary. Ultimately,
  the best judge of how well a student-athlete will do in any given
  academic environment is the Admissions Office and the coaching
  staff who have experience recruiting for the institution.

- Simon's dad put an emphasis on the development of his son as a
  golfer and not as a student or a young man. He should have asked
  the coach about his program's Athletic Progress Rate (APR), graduation rate, GPA and retention rate. He should have also asked how
  many student-athletes were on academic probation or arrest, even
  how many incident rates of the athletic department and the individual sports programs there were.

- Passing judgment on other programs and coaches is not appreciated by the coach you are talking to. Coaches within a department
  are normally supportive of each other, especially at smaller institutions. Unsolicited criticism is never well received. Again, remember
  that coaches talk! One bad experience can be passed along to other
  institutions and the PSA could easily be put on a "bad recruit" list.

With the way the conversation went between Coach Montgomery
and Simon's family, coupled with his negative first impression, Coach
Montgomery had seen and heard enough regarding Simon. He was not
interested in pursuing Simon as a recruit, and his staff seconded that.

PHILIP'S STORY

During his junior year, Philip decided on two large schools in his home state. Both schools were far enough away from home that his parents could not pop in for a visit but close enough that he could get home easily for a weekend visit and be back for classes on Monday. He had his heart set on one of these two schools, even though he was not getting much interest from the institutions regarding his athletic ability.

Philip was a golfer—a very dedicated golfer. He practiced at the driving range every day after school and spent hours hitting balls and perfecting his putting. His best competitive score was a 74 and he knew he was just beginning to develop the mental aspects of his game that would allow him the opportunity to become more competitive. Philip believed the environment at either State University or the University of State would help him blossom into a talented and successful collegiate golfer. Essentially, he believed he was a student-athlete that any coach would be proud to have in his program.

In an effort to get more attention from both schools prior to the beginning of the spring golf season, Philip arranged to go on unofficial visits to both institutions. He wanted to see the team practice, view the practice facility and watch the conditioning program. Most importantly, he did not want to impose on the coach during the season, when travel or tournaments would make the coach extremely busy. This was a smart policy and one that he had learned from his older brother Simon. A few years earlier, Simon had visited a coach when he was preparing to travel with his team for a tournament, and the visit had not gone well.

Philip arranged a time with Coach Faldo at State University on Wednesday morning. He anticipated staying throughout the day and possibly into the evening, depending on what the visit warranted. Philip arranged a meeting with the admissions staff first so that he could start the visit with an information session about the university and a walking tour of the campus. He wanted to see the campus from a student's perspective first and then as an athlete.

The coach was very grateful to Philip for taking into consideration his busy schedule, especially considering that Coach Faldo was not actively recruiting Philip. Coach Faldo agreed that seeing campus first and hearing about the institution should be Philip's priority. In reality, Coach Faldo was unconvinced that Philip was the right person for his program. After all, Philip's brother and family came with quite a reputation!

After the campus tour, it was time for Philip to meet Coach Faldo and Assistant Coach Harrington to learn more about their golf program, the Athletic Department and the support systems for their student-athletes. Philip had arranged an 11:00 a.m. meeting with the coaches, a time that was convenient for the coach and his staff. At 10:50, the family arrived at Coach Faldo's office for their meeting and waited patiently until the coach was ready. However, the coach was caught in a meeting with his two captains, so Coach Harrington came out of the meeting and explained there was a delay. In an effort to keep everything on time for the remainder of the day, Coach Harrington took Philip and his family on a tour of the Athletic Department, including the weight room, locker room and medical facilities before heading back to meet with Coach Faldo.

Once in the office, Philip's parents sat to the side and allowed Philip to sit in front of Coach Faldo's desk so they could have a one-on-one conversation with each other. Philip's parents understood that they were there for support and could ask questions but only at the end of the meeting. Philip was prepared, had a list of questions for the coach, and took the initiative after Coach Faldo's introduction and overview.

- "I am interested in your communications program, especially broadcast journalism. The school advisor said I had the appropriate educational background for the program but questioned the likelihood of doing well in the program *and* of also being an athlete. Do you have students from the program in the communications school, and if so, how well do they do? If not, do you see it being a problem academically or athletically to do both?"

- "How well does your program do academically? What is your team's GPA, and its graduation rate? What are the most popular majors for your athletes? Do they do better academically during the on- or off-season? What extra academic support, if any, do the athletes receive?"

- "What is a typical weekly and daily schedule for your athletes?"

- "Outside of team practice, is there an opportunity for individual instruction with you or Coach Harrington?"

- "How do you perceive the support of the Athletic Department from the students and faculty? From the local community? Your program alumni?"

- "Can you please explain your program philosophy? Do you have a team mission statement? If so, can I see a copy?"

- "This program has achieved much through the years that you have been here. What do you believe is your biggest accomplishment as head coach at State?"

- "Why did you decide to come/stay at State?"

- "Have you seen me compete? If so, how do you see me fitting into your program as a golfer? If you haven't seen me play, I will be happy to send you my upcoming schedule, recent results and statistics."

- "I see your program is graduating four student-athletes for my recruiting year. How many are you looking to bring in to the team and how many places have you already filled?"

- "Is there any other information you would like to tell me?"

STATE UNIVERSITY MEN'S GOLF MISSION STATEMENT

The men's golf program, within the educational institution of State University and the Department of Athletics, will reflect the university's mission of integrity, academic excellence, leadership, diversity and success. The men's golf program will add to the overall educational experience of the student-athletes by creating an environment where the student-athlete becomes a successful young man, developing leadership qualities within the University, within the men's golf program and within the local golf community.

Each student-athlete will show the highest degree of dedication, commitment, selflessness and respect, as well as living by the Five P's: Pride, Passion, Patience, Positive Attitude and Proactive Participation. This will be performed in all aspects of the student's collegiate life—academically and athletically.

It is the responsibility of every member of the program to live up to these high standards and to hold everyone else to these high demands. Yearly academic and athletic goals will be set and attained, knowing that everyone's full cooperation and drive will make the men's golf program an asset to State University and the Department of Athletics.

These questions opened the door to many others; and while the coach talked, Philip and his family listened intently. Only when Coach Faldo asked Philip's parents if they had any questions did they ask a few questions regarding the academics and the golf program.

Due to the professional manner that Philip and his parents treated Coach Faldo and his staff, the visit piqued further interest in Philip. The coaches had heard he was a talented and developing golfer, but they had been turned off previously by rumors and reports of the recruiting process that Philip's brother Simon had gone through. However, it looked as if the family had learned its lesson from their eldest child, and it was going to benefit Philip in the recruiting process.

Coach Harrington invited Philip to attend practice with the team that afternoon, and he arranged for him to spend time with the student-athletes after practice and through dinner. Based on Philip's visit, Coach Faldo decided to further research Philip as a prospective student-athlete for State University and its golf program. Philip had impressed him, and he now considered him a possible recruit.

SONIA'S STORY

As a lifelong gymnast, Sonia had focused all her life on her sport. Being an elite gymnast was a life choice. Daily hours of training and a strict control of her dietary intake along with sufficient rest made Sonia the gymnastic blue-chipper she was today. Sonia assumed that everyone was as dedicated as she was, but soon found out otherwise—and on her official visit no less.

VERBAL COMMITMENTS

Some coaches have created a trend that encourages high school students to verbally commit as juniors to certain programs. Each sport has its own timeline, and each coach places pressure on recruits at different levels and at different times. However, when high school students verbally commit to college programs as juniors, they still have to wait until the appropriate date during their senior year to complete the process by signing an NLI and an athletic scholarship agreement.

A verbal commitment is not binding by either party. A college coach can change his or her mind at any time prior to signing day for any reason, or for no reason at all. Additionally, a prospect can change his or her mind for any reason. It is very uncommon for either of these situations to occur, but it can happen. It is important for high school students to receive written clarification of a scholarship offer when they commit at any grade level.

There is a positive side to an early verbal commitment:

● It alleviates recruitment pressure from the student-athlete so that he or she can focus on the sport (rather than recruitment) during the remainder of high school.

● Students can prepare themselves better for a specific program by understanding what is expected of them by the beginning of their freshman year.

● Parents of the student-athlete can know earlier what to expect financially during the student's years and how they can best prepare for their child's college education.

Likewise, there is a negative side to an early verbal commitment:

● The commitment is not legally binding.

● A student-athlete can take the situation for granted and deteriorate academically or athletically.

● The student does not make the choice of the university, college or program with the benefit of official visits.

● Coaching and/or other personnel changes can occur.

● Student-athletes may change their wants/needs over the two-year period between verbally committing and actually enrolling in college.

Sonia had committed to her first-choice university as a junior. Early in the fall of her senior year, she flew to Gymnastic University for an official visit. As expected, one of the coaches picked her up at the airport and transported her to the university where she was to spend two days (no longer than 48 hours) at the university. During the trip from the airport to the university, Coach Retton outlined the weekend to Sonia and gave her insight into her student-host, the person who would look after her for the weekend.

The student-host is the person primarily responsible for the prospect during an official visit. The student-host has $30 a day for expenses during the visit, which can only be used for food and entertainment within a 30-mile radius of the university. The money cannot be used to buy souvenirs or memorabilia. At the end of the visit, the student-host returns any unused monies to the Athletic Department. Some institutions have additional rules for the use of the money. In these situations, the Athletic Department staff explains these rules to the student-host and the prospective student-athlete before the visit. A student-host may also house the prospect during the visit when the prospect stays on campus rather than at a hotel or other lodging.

Sonia's host was Suzanne, a gymnastic student-athlete who was also participating that weekend in a competition against Gymnast State University.

Everything was going well during the first few hours of the visit. With arrangements that seemed to be quite suitable, everyone was comfortable—especially in light of Sonia's commitment to enroll at Gymnastic University the next fall. The atmosphere was relaxed and the visit was a great opportunity for Sonia to become better acquainted with the institution, the program, its coaches and its athletes. Sonia planned to meet a couple of other prospective student-athletes that would be part of her freshman class the following year.

Sonia expected a very restful night since Suzanne had a competition the next day. She looked forward to having dinner with the team per her visit itinerary and then perhaps spending the rest of the evening getting to know her future teammates. Dinner was great, and the team hung out for a while before breaking away for the evening. Then a couple of athletes left to do homework and a few went to ice down before bed. After the remaining gymnasts left, Suzanne suggested the she and Sonia meet some of the other students on campus. Suzanne wanted Sonia to meet her boyfriend and his friends, so they walked over to a fraternity house. Sonia assumed it would be a quiet and quick get-together before heading back to Suzanne's room.

When Sonia and Suzanne entered the frat house, however, Suzanne went straight to the kitchen to collect a beer for both her and Sonia. Surprised, Sonia explained to Suzanne that she did not drink and certainly would not drink the night before an event. Sonia wondered if Suzanne was testing her to see how dedicated she really was as an athlete. Maybe they test all recruits like that, she thought.

Sonia stood by Suzanne for an hour, watching her drink at what Sonia could only classify as binge rate. She asked Suzanne to leave, but Suzanne rationalized that as long as she was asleep by 2:00 a.m. she could still get 8 hours of sleep before the 11:00 a.m. start of the event. Suzanne continued to make excuses about her behavior and eventually Sonia left. With Suzanne's keys in hand, she headed back to the room where she stayed the remainder of the night by herself.

The following day, Coach Retton checked on all her recruits. She could tell that there was something on Sonia's mind. Unfortunately, Coach Retton had to focus on the competition, but she promised Sonia she would spend time with her at the end of the event and discuss any of her concerns. After a strong win by those in her program (even though Suzanne injured herself), Coach Retton sat with Sonia in the large and now empty arena.

Sonia explained to Coach Retton that she loved the school. She loved the coaching staff and the support staff and thought the girls were very friendly and welcoming to her and the other recruits. There was just one thing, a very important thing to Sonia, and she explained what happened the previous night. Sonia told the coach that she was disappointed and wondered if that was a common occurrence within the program. If they expected that behavior of her, then she could not remain committed to Gymnastic University.

Coach Retton was furious! She explained that Suzanne had broken team and Athletic Department rules and that there would be consequences for Suzanne's actions, as there would be for any other member of her program that broke the rules. Coach Retton further explained that anyone who even *knew* about that behavior could potentially be in trouble according to the rules of the program. She promised Sonia that there would be an investigation into the matter and that she would do whatever it took to solidify Sonia's commitment to GU and the gymnastic program. She also thanked Sonia for her honesty.

Like the coaches at most schools, Coach Retton had explained the rules to her student-hosts and all the visiting prospective student-athletes prior to the scheduled visits. Each athlete had signed paperwork stating that she knew the rules and would follow them. Coach Retton had explained to both sets of athletes that if anything went wrong during the visit, they should call her and she would clear up any issues at that time. However, it is unrealistic to expect a prospective student-athlete to call the coach on a visit and *sell out* her future teammates. Only after discussing the situation with the other recruits did Sonia feel that she should talk to the coach. The other recruits wisely advised her that it could get back to the coach that it was Sonia's idea to go to that party rather than Suzanne's. Sonia did not want to risk her position on the team.

When Coach Retton addressed Suzanne, the athlete admitted her mistake and agreed to a suspension. She wrote an apology to Sonia and her teammates, admitting she had jeopardized the program and her own health in an effort to please her boyfriend. Her teammates rallied around her and reminded Suzanne that as a college athlete, she needed to make sacrifices. Suzanne was lucky. She was only temporarily suspended. She knew, however, that one more mistake would result in her dismissal from the team and the revoking of her scholarship.

Although the visit was not what Sonia had expected, she was able to keep her commitment to GU through the coach's support. She asked Coach Retton to give her a written promise that if that behavior continued to be a part of the program, then Sonia would be allowed to transfer. Both parties agreed, and Sonia enrolled the following fall.

JASMINE'S STORY

As a mid-level basketball player, Jasmine was considered a good addition to the squad at Basketball Tech. She was happy with the honesty of Coach O'Neal regarding her role within the basketball program at BT. Coach O'Neal had told Jasmine early in the recruiting process that she would be a scholarship athlete but would most likely not be a starter, at least early in her collegiate basketball career. Jasmine was happy with this. She loved basketball, but it was not her whole life. Jasmine had more social interests than just playing ball. She loved going to parties and hanging out with her friends.

Jasmine had chosen Basketball Tech because of its reputation as a great "party" school. She thought it was a great fit—she could play basketball, get a decent education, and have fun at the same time! Jasmine wanted the large social environment to be part of her collegiate experience and could not wait to enroll. Although she had made her final decision to go to BT, she still wanted to go on one more visit to take in the social scene of the school.

As Jasmine unpacked her bag in the hotel room she was sharing with another recruit, she explained her plans for the night. She told her weekend roommate and her student-host that she had been talking with some guys on FaceBook earlier that week and they were coming to pick her up and take her to a frat party. Jasmine was really excited! She had never been to a frat party before. She invited the girls to join her at the party, but they both declined.

The team rules regarding alcohol consumption at BT were clear:

1. Basketball student-athletes would not drink during pre-season and during the season if they were over 21 years old.

2. If they were younger than 21 years old, per law, they could not drink at any time.

Although Jasmine had signed the Athletic Department's paperwork that stated no alcohol or drug use would be tolerated, she was not worried about it. It was college, after all!

After grabbing a bottle of tequila from her bag, Jasmine text-messaged the guys she had met on FaceBook to come pick her up. Tracey, the student-host, knew that she was responsible for the welfare of each of her prospective student-athletes. She repeatedly explained the team rules and risks involved to Jasmine, but it fell on deaf ears. Jasmine was determined to go to the party. Jasmine failed to realize that she was putting her host and the other recruit in a very bad situation. Her actions could cost them their entire academic and athletic careers at Basketball Tech. Nevertheless, Jasmine was on a mission. She wished the girls a good night and happily ran out the door.

Tracey knew that she had to protect herself and the other recruit first and foremost. She called Coach O'Neal and explained the situation. Coach O'Neal drove over to the hotel to meet with Tracey and her other prospective student-athlete. As she heard their story, she knew that she had to protect these young women, herself and her program. Coach O'Neal called Jasmine on her cell phone and told her to come back to the hotel right away and pack her bags.

Once Jasmine returned, Coach O'Neal explained to her that she would not be offered a place on the team or a scholarship at Basketball Tech. Jasmine had violated the law, the rules of the Athletic Department and the program. She would be sent home immediately the following morning.

Dreading the call to her parents, Jasmine realized her need to party had destroyed any hopes of going to Basketball Tech. She also remembered that coaches talk and that she probably ruined her chances for other programs as well.

Use your head! Although college visits can be tempting in many ways, think through the choices that present themselves to you. One fun night is not worth throwing your future away. Even if other people around you are doing something wrong, put yourself in a safe position at all times.

TONY'S STORY

A three-year starting quarterback at his high school, and a two-time State 100 meter champion, it was no surprise that Tony was being recruited by many winning football programs. He was multi-talented and could cover ground with the ball in his hands or by throwing it. Many institutions had taken notice of his talent, and they wanted to get Tony committed to their programs.

During the summer prior to his senior year, Tony began to arrange official visits to his top choice universities with the help of his parents and high school coach. Tony arranged the visits around his HS game schedule, as well as the schedule of the recruiting institutions. He wanted to watch the college teams at close range and thoroughly experience the program by evaluating the coaches and the student-athletes, as well as the support staff. Tony wanted a comprehensive look into the program so that he could evaluate how he could be a successful part of one of them.

Tony was particularly impressed with the head coach and quarterback coach at Football University. They had been exceptionally nice to him via email and over the phone during the correspondence phase of the recruiting process. Tony scheduled a visit to FU, as he was leaning heavily to committing to the institution and their football program. It was not the best academic fit for Tony; however, he liked the coaches better than any of the others that were recruiting him. He liked it when they told him how great he was, and how great he was going to make Football University. They even told him that playing for FU could get him drafted by the pros. Like any committed athlete, Tony was optimistic about his future.

During the visit, Tony spent a lot of time with the starting and number two quarterbacks. Wanting to get the inside scoop from the current student-athletes, Tony asked them significant questions, many of the questions he had asked the coaches previously on the phone and in person. Tony wanted to confirm that the answers from Coach Washington and Coach Jackson were the same as the answers from the student-athletes that were a part of the program. If the perception of the program varied, then that could indicate a problem between the coaches and the athletes. Although Tony had stars in his eyes, he was smart. He wanted to make sure the coaches were not just courting him to sign with their program.

Tony was careful with his probing questions about the program, the school and the coaches. He knew that it was important to get these questions answered from both sets of student-athletes, the starters and the non-starters. Tony kept in mind though that the starter might be the happier of the two athletes, and therefore the answers could be skewed.

Tony started with simple, open questions that he dropped into general conversation. Formally running through a list of questions might be unsettling for the student-athlete and student-hosts. They may feel pressure to answer in a way that they thought the coaches would want them to answer. It was very important for Tony to get candid answers in a low-key situation. Tony started with these basic questions over lunch:

- "How do you think the other students perceive the football program?"

- "Is the local community supportive of the school and football programs? What about other sports?"

- "How helpful are the professors? Do they help when you travel?"

- "What is a typical day and week for you?"

- "What about the coach? What is he *really* like?"

- "Do you think you are treated well—and fair—by the coach and his staff?"

- "Are you happy here? Are you happy you made the choice to come here?"

- "Did what the coach tell you about the program and institution become fact when you enrolled?"

In addition to these questions, Tony was able to ask both quarterbacks about the social part of the school and how the football program fit into the campus environment of the institution.

As Tony spent his 48 hours on campus, he questioned athletes at different stages of their college lives so that he could get the "big picture." As the answers unfolded, Tony became concerned regarding the reaction from the student-athletes toward their coaches. Several student-athletes expressed that they were not told the truth during the recruitment process. They felt they were given false promises about their education, the development of the program, and how they were going to fit into the program. Both quarterbacks shared this feeling as well.

The general consensus from the student-athletes was that during the recruiting process, and during time in the coach's office, he was very nice, enthusiastic and charismatic. During times of high pressure, however—such as during games—the coach was prone to acting unprofessionally toward the student-athletes, almost "abusive," as one student-athlete claimed.

Tony had chosen a weekend visit for a reason: he could watch the team in action from pre-game to post-game and get a feel for the athletic environment. It was during the pre-game meeting that Tony first saw the true Coach Washington. His negative and pessimistic pre-game talk about the failings of the team really surprised Tony. The coach emphasized that if they failed, they would be bad athletes and bad people. It was as if the coaching staff had already lined up their excuses for the failure of the team (a team that they had recruited and trained) and that it was full of losers. Coach Washington and Coach Jackson were very quick to point out the mistakes made by the quarterbacks in previous games and continued to blame them for every failing of the team.

Tony picked up a few odd comments during his visit. First, during conversations with the coaches, they told Tony he was a great quarterback—a much better option than these "failures." That bothered Tony. Obviously, these quarterbacks were good players during their high-school careers or they would not have been highly recruited by Football University or any other institution. In addition, the coaching staff had helped develop them to where they were today! Second, the negative pre-game "motivational" talk was a detriment to the team, and especially to the student-athletes that Coach Washington singled out. Tony could tell by the body language of the players that their drive to succeed was gone. They were told too many times that they were bad athletes and weak young men. Unfortunately, they began to believe what they heard. Coach Washington and his staff had made a season out of self-fulfilling prophecies of failure.

Sometimes the coaching staff makes a recruiting mistake. It does happen occasionally. Respectable coaches however will work with the athletes as best they can. Most important, decent coaches accept it as their own error, not the athlete's. A good coach always wants what is best for his or her student-athletes and will work with them and find a way to help the student-athletes attain their goals. ▮

As the game started and the clock ticked down, Tony watched the quarterback, the quarterback coach and the head coach. Tony saw the constant emotional abuse of the student-athletes, and that was all he needed to see to help him make his decision. Tony knew he needed to find another institution. Seeing the student-athletes demoralized, Tony knew FU was not the program he wanted to enter. It was not the kind of environment that would help Tony succeed academically, athletically and definitely not emotionally. Tony decided that he would approach each college visit as thoroughly as he had this one. It was important for him to find a completely positive environment in which to spend the next four years.

SUMMARY

VISITS

- Visits can make or break a decision by either the prospective student-athlete or the college coach.

- It is an opportunity for both parties to impress and show their true colors. Be observant!

- The more prepared prospective student-athletes are for all situations, the more successful they are likely to be during the visits, and the more likely they will be able to make the correct choices.

- It is important for prospective student-athletes and their parents to read each and every situation on an individual basis. Every program is different. What is standard during a visit for one college coach is not necessarily the way other coaches arrange their visits.

YOU CAN READ THE COACH'S MIND

- Spending significant time with the head coach rather than the assistant coach will show a great deal of interest on the school's part. If the head coach does not make time for a prospect, that coach may not regard the prospective student-athlete highly.

- Exceptions:

  ○ Where the assistant coach is primarily responsible for recruiting.

  ○ When the prospective student-athlete has already committed to the institution and the primary reason for the visit is to spend time with future teammates.

- The head coach should be open to all questions and answer candidly. If the coach tends to ramble and/or skirt around the questions, be cautious and follow up your questions with other coaches and/or players.

- If a coach does not know the answer to a question, he or she should admit it but offer to find a way to get the answer before the visit ends, or soon after. If the question is never answered, do not be afraid to ask again as the coach may have forgotten about it.

- Visiting the facilities with the coaching staff is important. If coaches are not willing to show prospects the facilities, they either do not hold the prospect in high regard as a recruit and/or they are embarrassed by the facilities.

- When discussing athletically related financial aid, a coach will be straightforward with the prospect and the parents. If a coach talks around the subject and talks in ballpark figures for an equivalency sport, then again, be cautious.

- Honest coaches will not guarantee playing time or a starting position—if the prospect is guaranteed playing time, you should question the program and the coaches' motives.

- Any discussion with the coach and prospective student-athlete should be a two-way dialog. A one-way conversation with the prospect asking questions and the coach answering while showing little interest in the prospective student-athlete is a sign that the coach has limited interest. An interested coach will ask questions to the prospective student-athlete in an attempt to learn more about him or her as a future athlete.

- A coach should know about you when you arrive for your visit/ meeting. If a coach does not know what year you are, where you are from, or what position you play, it is unlikely you are strong prospect for their program.

BE PREPARED TO IMPRESS

- Show up on time and be respectful of the coach's time. If you are running late (caught in traffic, airport delays, etc.) call the coach and explain the situation.

- Dress appropriately for the situation: treat it like a job interview. Do not wear any attire from other universities.

- Have opening-ended questions that are important to you and your family. It is okay to read from a list and take notes. Do not be afraid to improvise your questions based on previous answers from the coach.

- Do not interrupt or give unwanted opinions when talking to anyone in the program—especially the coaches.

- Act with good judgment in all situations. Do not do anything that you would not like to have to tell your parents. You are there to make a positive impression.

- Interact with current student-athletes appropriately. Ask candid and open-ended questions. You need to prepare for all answers. Do not judge the answers.

- Comment positively on aspects of the visit, including the campus, the facilities, the program and the people you meet.

- Show initiative during the visit. Do not let your parents take control.

SAMPLE OFFICIAL VISIT GUIDELINES

Student-Athlete Hosts Guidelines

Student-Athlete Host_____

Sport_____

Prospect _____Date(s) of official visit _____

Your Coach must **personally review** these guidelines with you before participating in any official visit activities. **You** and **your** coach must sign below, attesting that this review was completed as required.

Financial Responsibilities

- You will receive **$30 for each day** to spend only during the prospect's official visit to cover all entertainment expenses for the prospect, his/her parents or legal guardians, or spouse.

- Neither you nor the prospect may spend expense money on other people, including the prospect's siblings or other student-athletes.

- You may receive an **additional $15 per day** from the athletic office for each additional prospect you entertain.

- You **must spend only the amount** of money you receive from the athletic office to pay for official visit expenses.

- You **may not** use **additional money from a coach** or anyone else to spend during the prospect's official visit.

- You are **required** to return any remaining cash from the advance money to the athletic office on Monday following the recruiting weekend. Failure to comply may result in withholding future advance money for hosting purposes.

- You **may not** use host money to buy souvenirs for a prospect such as T-shirts, hats or other items.

Social Responsibilities

- Do not put yourself or your prospect in any situations or go to any places where there could be the appearance of sexual impropriety Athletes are held to higher standards than non-athletes.

- Use good judgment at all times and do not force your prospect to do anything that he or she is not comfortable doing.

- You **may not** provide the prospect with alcoholic beverages or drugs of any kind at any time.

- You **may not** use host money for admission to any adult establishment with alcohol. Avoid these places at all times.

- You may pay only for yourself, the prospect, his/her parents or guardians, or spouse.

- You **may not** use host money to buy any other student-athletes a meal when you take a prospect to a restaurant.

- Neither you nor the prospect may accept a meal discount unless the same deal is available to everyone.

Travel Responsibilities

- You **MAY NOT** transport the prospect, or anyone accompanying him/her, more than 30 miles from the main campus.

- You **MAY NOT** use a motor vehicle provided by athletic coaches/staff, alumni or boosters at any time.

COACH certifies having reviewed and discussed these guidelines with the HOST.

Head or Assistant Coach Signature _____

Date _____

HOST certifies that he/she has reviewed the guidelines with the COACH listed above.

Student-Athlete Host Signature _____

Date _____

CHAPTER EIGHT

I'M IN . . . NOW WHAT?

For most high school graduates, the summer after graduation means relaxing and hanging out with friends before they venture off to college. They deserve a break from all their hard work and are ready to chill out and have some fun. Unfortunately, for future student-athletes, the summer before they begin college is the most important summer of their athletic career…if they want to enjoy success as college athletes.

Once a prospective student-athlete finishes the application process and is accepted into an institution, there are still steps remaining before the student can enroll in the university and become a student-athlete. Students must secure housing, make arrangements for freshman orientation, and attend preseason camp if they are fall sport athletes. In addition, they need to follow up with their high school counselors and insure a final transcript stating that graduating requirements have been met has been sent to their future academic institution as well as the NCAA Eligibility Center. Finally, future college athletes must make sure that they are in top physical condition so they are ready for any fitness test that awaits them.

JOSE'S STORY

Jose is an entering freshman soccer athlete at Upper Ninety University where the coaching staff is anticipating a successful first year from him. Heavily recruited by the coaching staff from the start of his junior year, Jose is very excited about his college future at UNU. Realistically, recruiting Jose was not too hard. In fact, his decision to play at UNU was easy. Coach Ferguson and Jose recruited each other very well and the combination of academics, athletics, size and location was a perfect fit for Jose. He can hardly wait to play his first game for Upper Ninety University.

At the end of his junior year, Jose completed all the paperwork for the NCAA Eligibility Center and made sure he had the correct institutional codes for his high school and UNU. Jose made sure his SAT and ACT scores were sent to the Eligibility Center from the College Board and made certain that his transcripts were sent from his high school. Jose thought he had taken care of everything.

Reminder: The code for the NCAA Eligibility Center is 9999. Standardized test scores (ACT or SAT) must be sent directly from the testing agency.

By the completion of his junior year, Jose was almost ready for his NCAA eligibility. With the exception of an English class, Jose had everything that would deem him eligible once he graduated from high school. He had the test scores and the GPA that would allow him to play college soccer. All he had to do was complete his senior year, pass his English class, and graduate…and have his final and complete transcript sent to the NCAA Eligibility Center from his school.

Under the direction of Coach Ferguson, Jose explained to his counselor how important it was for the school to send the transcripts to the Eligibility Center as soon as graduation was complete. As the end of his senior year approached, Jose met with his counselor.

During the summer, the Eligibility Center works with over 100,000 prospective student-athletes in an attempt to get them eligible for the coming fall. In many situations, they have only two months to process all the information they receive. The NCAA looks at each athlete's core classes, GPA, and standardized test scores to assure that no one is deemed ineligible when he or she should be able to compete, and vice-versa.

Considering the summer is a high demand period, it is critically important that Jose have his final transcript sent as soon as possible after graduation to insure a timely handling of his paperwork. It becomes a first-come-first-serve situation and the sooner the NCAA Eligibility Center has the final paperwork from his school and standardized testing agency, the sooner Jose can be processed and the official results sent to UNU. Obviously, the more time the NCAA Eligibility Center has with his transcript, the better off Jose will be.

In addition to having his final transcript sent to the Eligibility Center, Jose requested that a copy of his transcript be sent to Upper Ninety University's Department of Admissions. Like all higher education institutions, UNU requires proof of high school graduation, and for many students, a finalization of any academic scholarships that they have applied for. Without a final transcript, Jose would not be able to enroll for the fall semester even though he had confirmation of his acceptance.

A week after graduation, Jose followed up with his high school counselor to assure that his final transcript was sent to both UNU and the NCAA. The counselor assured Jose that his requests had been taken care of and to enjoy his summer. Jose left the counselor's office with full confidence that it would just be a matter of time until the NCAA told him he was eligible for his freshman season.

Throughout the summer, Coach Ferguson and Jose were in contact regarding all the freshman issues that needed to be taken care of, such as his deposit for his housing arrangement, his summer workout schedule and his eligibility from the NCAA. Coach Ferguson spoke with Jose on many occasions to ask about his final transcript. The weekly reports that came to Coach Ferguson from the Compliance Department still showed that Jose's file was missing his final English class and lacked confirmation of his graduation. Jose assured his future coach that it had been taken care of and that he had even followed up personally with his guidance counselor.

However, a month before pre-season started, Coach Ferguson contacted Jose to explain his concern that everyone had been processed through the Eligibility Center except for Jose. Coach Ferguson urged Jose to go to his high school and have another copy of the transcript sent to the NCAA. However, Jose was in the middle of vacationing with his friends at the beach, so he decided to call his counselor instead of personally going into the office. Not knowing his counselor was on vacation, Jose left a voicemail and resumed his summer activities. He assumed it would be taken care of and he certainly was not going to let some paperwork interrupt his fun!

The day to report for preseason training was soon upon Jose and he headed to his introductory team meeting with the coaching staff and the Compliance Department. During the meeting, one of the compliance officers told Jose that he was not eligible to compete. They had called and spoken with the NCAA Eligibility Center and they said they had not received Jose's final transcript. Jose would remain ineligible until the transcript arrived at the Eligibility Center and was evaluated along with all the other late submissions.

The compliance officer explained to Jose that he could train with the team for fifteen days while his eligibility was pending. However, Jose could not partake in the preseason scrimmage that was scheduled within that fifteen-day window. After the fifteen days had passed, and if Jose was still not eligible, then he would need to stop training with the team until the NCAA had deemed him eligible.

Shocked at the seriousness of the situation, Jose was excused from the meeting so he could call his high school counselor. His counselor apologized and said it was probably lost in the mail. He would be happy to send another transcript but Jose or his parents would need to fill out the appropriate paperwork first. Jose could not believe that his first day of training was going like this and all because of a piece of paper! A strong feeling of shame swept over him as he realized that he should have followed Coach Ferguson's directions earlier in the summer and made a physical trip to his high school to ask that another copy of his final grades be sent to the NCAA.

Jose called his mom at work and asked her to leave her job and go to his high school to complete the appropriate paperwork and have his transcript sent to the Eligibility Center. Obviously, Jose's summer procrastination became a huge inconvenience for his mother as she left her office to meet with the counselor.

At the high school, Jose's mom met with the counselor, filled out the paper work and gave the counselor the correct mailing address of the Eligibility Center. She reluctantly paid the express mail fee and stayed to make sure the counselor processed the paperwork, signed it and placed in the out-going mail. Jose's mom also had a copy faxed to the Compliance Office of UNU to show them that Jose would be eligible once the NCAA received and evaluated his transcript.

Mailing Address:
NCAA Eligibility Center
301 ACT Drive
Box 4043
Iowa City, Iowa 52243-4043

Jose began preseason with his teammates but he knew he was not off to a stellar start in his collegiate soccer career. He realized that he let Coach Ferguson down and made extra work for his support staff, not to mention inconveniencing his mom. All this together certainly culminated in a lousy first impression to his teammates! These factors weighed heavily on Jose and hindered his training.

The Eligibility Center received Jose's transcripts two days later, but it still took a few days for them to evaluate the data to decide if he had completed all the steps to become eligible. The day before the preseason scrimmage, the Compliance Department called the NCAA Eligibility Center and asked if Jose's transcript could be evaluated in an urgent manner. Even with the request, it was still a long shot that the transcript would be handled quickly. The Athletic Department of UNU was only one of hundreds that had similar situations, and the requests for expedient handling of athletes' paperwork are made almost every day throughout the late summer/early fall by one university or another. During that time of year, the Eligibility Center is inundated by requests for priority and urgent help.

Unfortunately, the Eligibility Center could not deliver in time, so Jose had to sit and watch his teammates as they played their only preseason scrimmage in preparation for their season. Coach Ferguson had made it clear during the scrimmage that everyone had a chance to stake a claim for a starting role or playing time; but since Jose could not play the scrimmage, he did not get that opportunity. Jose knew that his failure to follow up during the summer had prevented him from being where he should be—on the soccer field.

A few days later, the Eligibility Center declared Jose eligible. Jose was now ready to play for UNU, but he did not have a starting position on the team or any guarantee of getting any playing time. Jose threw himself into the training leading up to the first weekend of competition. As he gave his all, he became frustrated when things went wrong. Unfortunately for Jose, it seemed that the harder he tried, the harder it was for him to succeed. He could not allow himself to relax, enjoy his soccer and play to the best of his abilities. Jose always felt he had to make up for his Eligibility Center mix-up.

Jose could have easily avoided the situation and had a strong start to his college athletic career if he had ...

- Expressed to the high school counselor the importance of the NCAA Eligibility Center and then followed up two weeks later.

- Understood and fully appreciated that Coach Ferguson could not take care of the paperwork for him and he had to follow up with the NCAA himself.

- Monitored his eligibility on the NCAA Eligibility Center Web site to make sure it had been received and was being processed.

- Called the NCAA Eligibility Center (877-262-1492) and asked if there had been a problem with his transcript since he had sent it, but it was not showing up on their posted information.

- Realized the seriousness of the situation when his eligibility was still not declared a week before preseason and made a request that another transcript be sent to the NCAA immediately, in person, and not simply left a voicemail message for his counselor.

It is vitally important for the soon-to-be student-athletes to stay on top of their eligibility requirements. From the classes they take, to the registration with the NCAA and the completion of the process, students need to check regularly on the status of their eligibility. Transcripts can be lost and damaged during the journey from the high school counselor to the Eligibility Center. On many occasions, it is no one's fault, but just an array of bad circumstances. Unfortunately, there is only one person that can truly suffer in the situation, and that is the first-year athlete.

WHAT IS A REDSHIRT?

The NCAA defines a *redshirt* season as one in which a student-athlete does not participate against outside competition for the institution in which they are enrolled. This season does not count toward the four seasons of competition each student-athlete is initially granted once they are deemed eligible by the NCAA Eligibility Center and enroll in college.

Each student has five years (10 semesters) to complete four seasons. A college student-athlete may redshirt for one of the following reasons:

- The program has decided to use an athlete's first year to develop him or her physically. This is a common practice in football.

- The program has decided to protect a player's eligibility of four seasons because they have a starter that is older and unlikely to allow the younger athlete any playing opportunities.

- The student-athlete is deemed academically ineligible by the NCAA Eligibility Center or has not made the appropriate academic progression.

- The student-athlete has decided to take time away from athletics for personal or academic reasons.

- The student-athlete is unable to participate because of a medical issue.

- The student-athlete has transferred and is required to have one year of residency before he or she can compete for the new institution.

Just one second of participation counts as a season of competition. However, there are medical exceptions: if student-athletes have participated in less than 20 percent of their team's regular season competition because of medical reasons, they can apply to the NCAA for a *medical redshirt* to regain an additional year of competition. If student-athletes are in their fifth year of eligibility when they are injured, a sixth year can be granted by the NCAA.

During a redshirt season, student-athletes can receive athletically related financial aid and are still under all NCAA rules and directives.

MESSAGE FROM AN EXPERT

Jon Mamula, Academic Counselor, NCAA Coordinator, and Military Coordinator, Highland Park High School, Dallas, Texas

As a high school counselor, can you suggest when students should start talking to you about college—and what do they need to know?

It is important for high school athletes to work with their HS counselors in their junior year. If students wait until their senior year, it may be too late to make any positive changes to their schedules. Juniors should work with their counselors to assure that they have the correct courses and course load.

College Admissions look at the student's junior year course load to determine if he or she is a strong candidate for that college or university. Students working closely with their HS counselor will be able to develop a more appropriate schedule. Some students could have been accepted to an institution, had they just made a little extra effort to assure a proper and challenging schedule.

Students should not rely on college coaches to get them through the admissions process. Each student should gain acceptance to a college by his or her own merit. Being accepted on personal achievement will prove that a student is able to succeed well in the collegiate classroom and will probably remain eligible at the school once there.

What can students do to help you help them regarding college admissions?

Even as student-athletes, it is important they work with their high school counselor through the recruitment and admissions process. Student-athletes tend to bypass their counselors and they should not do that. Working with a counselor will help the student gain acceptance by his or her own merit.

Additionally, highly recruited athletes should sign an athletic release form for their high school counselor. Once a student has signed the release, the high school counselor can send unofficial transcripts to college coaches that request a copy of the student's classes and grades.

High school students are notorious for waiting to the last minute to get stuff done. Do high school counselors do a better job with more time, and how much preparation time would you like for rec. letters, etc?

A period of one month is ideal to let the counselors write a strong letter of recommendation. This allows the counselor time to write a personal and appropriate letter. It also gives the student an opportunity to verify application materials and know it is complete.

A second advantage of doing things in a timely manner is that the application arrives at the college Admissions Office before the rush of a deadline. What does it tell the Admissions Department if you are rushing at the last minute to turn in your application materials?

What is the key to being accepted to your dream college?

The admissions counselors at your dream college! The admissions counselor can turn an electronic application into a real person. Getting to know your college admissions counselors, having face time with them, and continually communicating with them (not harassing) can help your application process.

If there are two students applying to the same college—one communicated regularly, and one did not—the student that communicated would likely be accepted first. Consistent communication with the College Admissions representatives shows a desire to be at that institution.

What common misconceptions regarding college admissions and athletics would you like to clear up?

Regarding athletics, you cannot be part of a top program unless you are a top player/athlete. Additionally, if athletics is an important part of your college choice, there is a program for everyone.

Regarding academics, there is also a school for everyone. Just because a school is not ranked as "competitive" does not mean it is not a good school. There are many great smaller schools out there for everyone.

Finally, two-year schools are a fantastic stepping stone for some students. They allow the students to prove themselves athletically and academically.

About Jon Mamula: *Highland Park High School is one of the top ranked high schools in the nation and Mr. Mamula has been a high school counselor there for 11 years. In addition to counseling his students and helping them with their college admissions and NCAA Eligibility issues, Mr. Mamula was the boys' soccer coach at HPHS. Mr. Mamula received a B.A. and M.A. from Southern Methodist University and an M.S. from Texas A&M Commerce.*

MARLO'S STORY

Due to a change in academic interests, Marlo transferred from Volleyball College to Volleyball University. As a junior, Marlo decided that the end of her sophomore year was the best time for her to make that academic change. With a little bit of research, she concluded that most of her credits would transfer and that she would still be able to graduate on time from Volleyball University.

Marlo went through the correct transferring procedures. At the end of her fall semester, she notified her coaches she wanted to transfer because of academic reasons and asked for their support. Marlo explained to the coaches that her decision had nothing to do with the athletic side of her collegiate life, but was purely academic. Marlo's coaches notified the Compliance Department and gave her a full release to contact any university, and they assured her that she would leave the college in good standing.

With the coach's permission and recommendations, the Compliance Office released Marlo to talk with the coaches at Volleyball University. Once Volleyball University received the release from Volleyball College, Marlo opened up a dialog with the coaching staff. It was not long before Marlo secured her spot on the volleyball program roster and further arrangements were made regarding her academic needs and scholarships.

Marlo duly applied to VU and requested that transcripts of her first three semesters be sent to the Admissions Department from Volleyball College. Before long, Marlo was accepted as a transfer student for the following fall and all scholarship arrangements were made through the coaches. Marlo and her new coaches were excited about the situation and both parties looked forward to the fall. Marlo also looked forward to moving forward with her academic career at VU.

At the end of her sophomore year, Marlo had to have her transcripts sent to her new school. Marlo made the appropriate requests, filled out the correct forms, and paid the applicable fees so that her transcripts would be sent. Believing the forms were just a formality, Marlo said goodbye to everyone at VC and looked forward to her summer of preparation for VU.

When she showed up for the beginning of preseason, both Marlo and her new coaches believed that everything was in order. Assuming that Marlo's application and acceptance were enough for her to be eligible and ready to compete, everyone was shocked when the Compliance Department came to pull her out of the team's first preseason practice. Marlo was told that VU only had three semester's worth of grades on file for her; therefore, the Registrar and Compliance Department could not deem her eligible for collegiate competition. With only three semesters of classes, Marlo had not shown sufficient progression in her academic career or toward her major.

Even though Marlo explained to the Compliance Department that she had completed four semesters, made good grades and had progressed toward a degree, she could not be cleared for NCAA competition. Marlo even showed her grades to the Registrar via the Internet, but Volleyball University needed official copies of her transcript from Volleyball College. Marlo was also informed that her scholarship could not be awarded until she was eligible, and that she had a significant bill at the business office that she needed to pay before classes started the following week.

Marlo called the Registrar's Office at Volleyball College and explained her frustration and dilemma. The Registrar at VC informed Marlo that it is not the policy of VC to rush transcripts to another university, even though she had paid for the service three months prior. Marlo asked the Registrar at VC to expedite the transcripts to Volleyball University, explaining her dilemma with scholarship monies, class registration and her inability to compete until the Registrar declared her eligible.

Despite Marlo's polite requests, it was still a week before the Admissions Department at VU received the transcripts. They then had to work their way to the Registrar's Office, to the Compliance Office, and then back to the Registrar before Marlo was deemed eligible. The Registrar had to complete paperwork declaring the number of total hours that transferred and determine where the classes counted toward a general education core and where they applied directly to her major.

After the Registrar's Office completed their process, the Athletic Department was informed of Marlo's status so the Compliance Department could do a review. They ensured that Marlo had collected the appropriate number of hours over her four semesters at Volleyball College and that she had made a progression toward a degree and graduation. Once completed, the Compliance Office declared Marlo eligible.

In the meantime, the slow delivery of Marlo's fourth semester grades created many problems for Marlo, her family and her coaches.

- Marlo's family had to apply for loans to pay her tuition to keep her in school.

- Marlo missed preseason games.

- Due to not playing in preseason games, it took her longer to get significant playing time.

Even though Marlo had filled out the appropriate paperwork, it was important for her to follow up on her transcript request from her first educational institution. In hindsight, Marlo should have asked for a copy of her official transcript, sealed in an envelope, which she could have taken with her to Volleyball University. She could have hand-delivered it herself just to be safe.

Even though it was not directly her fault that Volleyball College did not send the transcripts, Marlo created a lot of tension between these entities:

- Athlete and Coaching Staff

- Athlete and Compliance Department

- Athlete and Registrar's Office

- Coaches and Compliance Department

- Coaches and Registrar's Office

- Compliance Department and Registrar's Office

- Athlete's parents and university

All this could have been avoided had Marlo been more proactive—and persistent—in the movement of her transcripts. Just like Jose, it would have been better for both of them to have stayed on top of all these situations earlier on. Being proactive can save everyone a lot of problems and may even prevent a potentially great season going in the wrong direction.

The last part of Marlo's transfer was to insure that her classes were transferred in and counted at Volleyball University. Under the direction of her coaches, Marlo brought a course catalog from Volleyball College with her to Volleyball University. That allowed her to take the book to the Registrar and show the Registrar that certain classes were the same as classes offered at VU despite a different name. This saved Marlo from having to retake classes at VU.

Being proactive and responsible extends beyond the paperwork. Future student-athletes also need to stay in peak physical shape and on top of their game as well. There is a big difference between high school and college athletics; and to do well, athletes need to be mentally and physically prepared.

ARTHUR'S STORY

A highly recruited high school basketball center, Arthur had expectations of an outstanding collegiate basketball career. Many coaches told him he would carry their team further than they had ever gone before. Arthur himself expected success would be easy, just like it had been throughout his high school career. He had worked really hard to get where he was, receiving glowing credits after every game, and he certainly deserved the recruiting chase that was set upon him his junior and senior years.

In the fall of his senior year, Arthur chose to sign a National Letter of Intent (NLI) for Slam Dunk University. Signing the NLI relieved a great deal of pressure from Arthur and his family. He could now relax, enjoy his basketball and make sure he was prepared to lead SDU to a conference title and a run at the NCAA Championship. After all, Arthur was a blue-chipper—a full-ride athlete that had always been a huge success. Why would it be any different when he attended Slam Dunk University?

Similar to many future college student-athletes, Arthur's whole focus in high school was gaining a scholarship and signing the NLI. That was his goal and he had accomplished it. Unfortunately, not knowing there was more, he let his internal drive ease up since he thought he had accomplished everything he needed to do. Arthur did not feel the need to realign his athletic goals for a successful collegiate career. Essentially, he put himself on cruise control.

Arthur understood that he had work to do in the classroom to insure his eligibility. Remaining focused on finalizing all his core classes, assuring his high school graduation and passing his standardized tests, Arthur's academic discipline was right where it needed to be. Arthur focused on his academics because that was the factor he was worried about most.

While making good grades was a good thing, Arthur erred in letting his basketball skills deteriorate due to a lack of practice and self-discipline. During basketball season, he had practiced daily with his team and played games twice a week. But when basketball season ended, Arthur really began to slip from his elite standards.

When Arthur signed with Slam Dunk University, they explained to him the areas of his game and physical make-up that needed to be tailored for SDU. It is a common practice for college coaches to talk to their future student-athletes about what to develop for their freshman year.

Unfortunately, Arthur believed he was already perfect and did not need to further develop his game or his athletic ability.

Ignoring the coaching staff's advice and expertly arranged workout program, Arthur sat back and enjoyed a rest. He believed that he had earned time off after all those years of hard work. After all, Arthur mused, I'm a full-scholarship athlete. He was a star and he did not need to work hard any more—at least that is what he thought.

During Arthur's rest period, he ate too much. In fact, he consumed fast food on a regular basis. Eating too much, too often and with little or no exercise to compensate for his new habits, Arthur began to put on weight. With his lack of conditioning and training, he lost muscle mass and replaced it with fat.

When Arthur did get motivated to work out (probably immediately after his high school or future college coach asked him about his work-outs) he did the minimum he needed to do to break a sweat. Arthur never got into a regular routine. He created excuses for why he was putting on weight, or not working out or both. Arthur's bank of one-liners included some just like these: "This time of year I add a couple of pounds," or "I'm sore after yesterday's workout so I'll just take today off."

Despite many warnings from his high school and future collegiate coaches, Arthur continued to ignore the necessity of getting himself physically ready for college athletics. His high school coach explained to him that it was a big jump up from high school to the collegiate game, a jump he would be ready to handle only if he prepared himself properly. Arthur was warned that he needed to be on the basketball court, working on his game, following the directions of his future coaches and working on his anaerobic conditioning. Keeping in shape also required that he spend time in the weight-room working on his agility, his balance, his power and his strength.

Developing these areas of his portfolio could have helped Arthur get ahead of his freshmen teammates because he would have been able to play significant minutes. Arthur forgot that he might have all the "natural" ability in the world, but he needed to continue to develop it. Despite all the warnings, Arthur continued to develop bad habits throughout the summer and did not follow any of the summer workout plans that the strength coaches sent to him.

Fall arrived and Arthur moved to Slam Dunk University. During the second week of school, the basketball team began their individual workouts, strength training and conditioning. Included within the workout was the basketball team's first battery of physical tests. Every basketball player was expected to be in minimum shape and pass the tests as the semester started. Administering further fitness tests throughout the year, the coaching staff could continually gauge everyone's fitness level.

Unfortunately for Arthur, he failed every fitness test—from the agility tests to the strength tests and everything in-between. Arthur was significantly below the minimum standards set by Coach Jordan and his staff. Arthur, in the opinion of the SDU basketball staff, was in no condition physically to contribute positively to the team.

Coach Jordan arranged a meeting with Arthur, the conditioning coaches and the athletic training staff in an effort to get Arthur back on track with the rest of his teammates. During the meeting, all the staff expressed their disappointment in Arthur's lack of desire to improve himself as a SDU basketball player. His internal drive was questioned, and a further appointment was arranged where Arthur would reset all his goals—academic, athletic and social—and align them with the mission statement of the basketball program and the Athletic Department.

The staff placed Arthur on a strict training regimen which included monitoring his eating. Under the direction of the athletic training staff, everyone was confident that Arthur would be ready for the first tip-off. To further get him fit and ready for the start of basketball season, Arthur would increase his workouts with the strength and conditioning coaches. Arthur also agreed that he would have to meet all minimum standards before he would be considered for any playing time.

Arthur's extra training, early in the morning before class, was soon to make a bad situation worse. Due to his poor initial condition, coupled with the increase in his workload, Arthur's body started to break down. Arthur showed signs of overtraining syndrome—increased recovery time, increased morning heart rate, increased muscle soreness and finally a break down of his muscle tissue that led to muscle pulls and strains.

It was not that the conditioning staff was overtraining Arthur; it was that Arthur was in such poor initial shape that the workload was too much for his fitness level. For a college athlete, the level of conditioning should have been beneficial, not detrimental. However, Arthur was not in the *typ-*

ical condition expected of student-athletes where he could easily handle the levels of exercise scheduled for him.

Additionally, Arthur was not getting the proper amount of rest his body needed to recover. Due to his early morning conditioning sessions, he was tired all day. For the first time in his life, Arthur had the luxury of having freedom in the afternoons; so he took advantage of this and napped. Arthur was soon caught in the nap-trap. Arthur's napping habit became a vicious cycle. He slept all afternoon and then studied late into the night. He could not sleep long at night because he had to get up early for his additional training, and then he was tired again in the afternoon. It was a bad cycle to break. The longer it went on, the more difficult it became for Arthur to break. He was not getting the appropriate rest.

Arthur's physical problems were worsening rather than improving. The more he tried to rectify them, the more things seems to fall apart. Arthur was constantly injured! Just as he was recovering from one muscle pull, another one crept up on him. Arthur never managed to attain the physical shape that was expected of him during his freshman year at Slam Dunk University.

Limping through his first year at SDU, Arthur did not live up to expectations. The mounting frustration of everyone—coaches, teammates, and Arthur himself—did not create a positive environment. Arthur's pre-college actions had prevented him from being a freshman success at SDU.

After a very rough first year, Arthur re-focused on everything that had allowed him to be successful during his high school years. He started to work hard both on and off the court. Although Arthur was a year behind, his sophomore year became an important developmental year for him—and he eventually caught up to everyone else. However, it was not until Arthur's junior year that he managed to live up to his own previous expectations. Arthur turned things around and was ready to make an impact for Slam Dunk University. Fortunately for Arthur, Coach Jordan was a very patient person and helped Arthur with every step. Many coaches would have given up on Arthur and replaced him. However, Arthur realized his mistakes and vowed never to repeat them.

JENNA'S STORY

As a freshman softball player, Jenna was overwhelmed for much of her first year at Big Bat College. During high school, Jenna never needed to develop a strong self-discipline or to manage her time appropriately. She had been a strong student and a talented athlete, and her parents and coaches had micro-managed her life.

As midterm of Jenna's first semester approached, her grades were not what they should have been—or needed to be. Jenna's roommate was not an athlete, did not have early morning classes and kept Jenna up late at night, which threw off her sleep schedule. Jenna's biggest problem became climbing out of bed for an 8:00 a.m. philosophy class. Philosophy was not a class she was interested in, and she was only taking it because it counted toward her core classes; it was easy for Jenna to blow it off.

Some coaches and programs may request, or even strongly suggest, that your roommate is a teammate. It helps if you are both on the same training schedule and have a similar class schedule. Having a non-athlete roommate with a different schedule can cause problems.

Because she missed too many of her philosophy classes, Professor Aristotle dropped Jenna from his class. At first, it was a relief for Jenna because she did not have to worry about trying to get up early anymore. However, the NCAA requires student-athletes to take a minimum of twelve hours each semester. Jenna was now at the minimum. Additionally, she needed to average 15 hours per semester to graduate from Big Bat College in four years. Jenna was at the end of her first semester, and she was already behind.

Later in the semester, Jenna found that she was in danger of failing her biology class. As the final date to drop classes approached, Jenna told her coach she needed to drop the class rather than fail. Jenna believed that she would simply take it again the following year. However, Coach Bonds told Jenna that she could not drop the class. If she dropped the class and fell below the required 12 semester hours, then she would be ineligible to play the remaining games of her fall season. Even more importantly, she would have to repay any scholarship money for that semester.

Coach Bonds encouraged Jenna to keep the class and talk with the professor to see if there was anything she could do to save her grade. In a bid to show Professor Darwin that she cared about the class, Jenna asked him for extra help. Thankfully, the professor gave her some extra credit work to help her raise her average. Jenna was relieved at having a second chance and finally decided to make classes a priority. She worked hard through the remainder of the semester and managed to scrape by with a passing grade in biology. She also requested a roommate change to one of her teammates at the end of the semester. Jenna was determined to begin her spring semester correctly.

A student-athlete is a student first and an athlete second. The NCAA places manageable academic standards on all athletes. They must reach these standards every year in order to compete. Further, the NCAA evaluates and grades each athletic program and department yearly to obtain data which they use to report the Athletic Progress Rate (APR). Using a scoring system of one out of one thousand (100 percent), this report publishes the number of student-athletes that complete their degrees in five years or less. If the score is below standard, an athletic program will lose scholarship monies until the program has maintained the minimum acceptable level.

Ask coaches about their program's APR, transfer rates, graduation rates and team grade point averages during the recruiting process. This will tell you the importance of academics to that individual program as well as to the overall athletic department of that school.

Coach Bonds told Jenna that she had to get her grades back up and set a goal of graduation in four years, even if she had to take summer school classes. The coach also directed Jenna to the appropriate resources to help her, such as the Academic Support Center. Jenna assured Coach Bonds that she would maintain at least the minimum standards expected of her, which meant that she had to . . .

- Maintain a minimum GPA that kept her in good academic standing at her institution.

- Complete a minimum 24-semester hours or 36-quarter hours prior to enrollment the following year.

- Complete 18 hours of academic credit since the previous fall.

- Complete 6 hours of academic credit from the previous semester.

Each student should know about the Academic Support Center available at his or her campus. Each institution has different uses for the ASC, but all are supportive in helping students succeed in all aspects of their college life. Many Academic Support Centers provide these services:

- Study skills
- Technology help
- Time management
- Academic tutoring
- Additional academic resources
- Reading/writing support
- Life skills
- Resume building
- Internships
- Post-graduation education
- Study abroad programs
- Safe and quiet study environment

Jenna learned that by the beginning of her fifth semester (the start of her junior year), she needed to declare a course of academic study and a major. To officially declare her major, Jenna would have to be formally enrolled within that degree program *and* receive approval from the appropriate academic official(s).

Finally, Jenna would need to show proper academic progress toward her degree. At the beginning of her junior year (fifth semester), Jenna would need to have completed 40 percent of her academic class work toward her degree. By the beginning of her senior year (7th semester), Jenna should have completed 60 percent. At the beginning of her fifth year, if needed (9th semester), Jenna would need to have completed a minimum of 80 percent of her degree work.

If Jenna were not to maintain the minimum standards set forth by the NCAA, she would be deemed ineligible for competition against other colleges or universities. Coach Bonds would have to withdraw Jenna's scholarship and dismiss her from the softball program because of the change in her eligibility.

Under the threat of not being able to compete in athletics anymore, Jenna took the steps to gain help from the Academic Support Center and to find a new roommate. With hard work, Jenna regained her positive academic standing and managed to pass an average of 15 hours every semester to graduate in four years. In fact, upon completion of her four-year degree, Jenna was accepted to graduate school!

> Even if Jenna had been ineligible for a year, she still could have completed her eligibility and her degree if she had managed to achieve appropriate academic hours and acceptable GPA. A student-athlete has five years to use his or her four years of athletic eligibility. Jenna could have used her fifth year to complete her four years of eligibility.

SUMMARY

HIGH SCHOOL TO-DO LIST

- Recruit yourself to the academic institution.

- Complete NCAA Eligibility Center paperwork at the end of your junior year.

- Make sure you use all the correct institutional codes with the SAT and ACT.

- Have your ACT/SAT scores sent directly to the NCAA Eligibility Center (Code: 9999).

- Send transcripts from your high school to the NCAA Eligibility Center at the end of your junior year.

- Meet with your high school counselor to create a plan of study that will allow you to complete the minimum required core classes.

- Immediately at the conclusion of your senior year, have official transcripts sent to both the NCAA Eligibility Center and the academic institution you are planning to attend.

- Follow and track your status on the NCAA Eligibility Center Web site (www.ncaaclearinghouse.net).

- If you have requested paperwork to be sent and you are told that it has not arrived, follow up immediately with the sending institution and the NCAA Eligibility Center.

- Call the NCAA Eligibility Center if you have any questions (877-262-1492) and utilize the NCAA Eligibility Center Web site.

TRANSFER TO-DO LIST

- Explain thoroughly to coaches why you want to transfer.

- Ask for a release to talk with other institutions.

- Apply, and have an official transcript sent to the institution you are transferring to—there is no need to have your SAT/ACT scores sent to most institutions as a transfer.

- Follow up with Admissions to make sure transcripts were sent and received.

- Keep a copy of the course catalog from the institution you are transferring from, as this can help you with transferring course credits.

- Research an institution and the amount of transferable hours you will have.

ATHLETIC TO-DO LIST

- Reset all academic and athletic goals after signing an NLI or accepting a scholarship (or place on a collegiate team) to an institution.

- Follow directions of the coaching staff in preparation for your freshman year.

- Be prepared for fitness tests and evaluations on a regular basis—with high standards.

- Do not let yourself go—physically or mentally.

- Do not make excuses.

- Be prepared, mentally and physically, for higher intensity, more volume and higher physical demands.

ACADEMIC TO-DO LIST

- Go to ALL classes.

- Take more than 12 hours per semester.

- Find a roommate that understands your schedule and the demands of being an athlete.

- Ask for help and advice in a proactive manner.

- Understand all NCAA eligibility requirements and how they relate to you and your academic career path.

- Remain in good academic standing at all times.

- Utilize any academic support systems that the university provides.

- Declare a major by the start of your junior year.

Developmental Challenges for First-Year Student-Athletes

Dr. Robert Hynes: Director of Counseling Services and Assistant Dean for Student Support Services, Fitchburg State College (Fitchburg, MA)

I'm careful about the title I use to this section; specifically, the use of the term "developmental challenges." I choose my words here very much intentionally: first, to highlight that the transition from high school student-athlete to college student-athlete is, indeed, a developmental process, and like any developmental process, involves significant change and adaptation...Second, I use "challenges," as opposed to "problems," "issues," "obstacles" or any other language that implies that the processes involved in this important developmental step in the student-athlete's life should be viewed negatively. Growth and adaptation is simply that which it is: another of life's challenges. Thus, the following discussion works from the assumption that a healthy and positive outcome will be the end result of these new challenges presented to the college student-athlete.

One of the basic rules of human nature I've come to discover after a number of years of doing psychotherapy with college students is that change, itself, is challenging. And "challenging" here should be taken to mean that significant life changes press our ability to find new attitudes and behaviors that will enable us to adapt to new life circumstances. The *really* good news here is that student-athletes, taken as a group, have shown that they tend to embrace challenge with significant hard work and persistence, evidenced by the academic and athletic success that have allowed them to proceed to this "next level." This latter point notwithstanding, it is realistic to expect that like most human beings, the new college student-athlete is likely to find this significant change in their life's routine disruptive, and probably somewhat stressful. This "stress" is most often the catalyst behind struggles that may emerge early in the new student-athlete's collegiate career, and some common difficulties such as impaired academic or athletic functioning and social or emotional difficulties may catch the student-athlete (and those close to him or her) somewhat off-guard.

Sometimes it seems that parents, coaches and college faculty and administrators either underestimate (or have long since forgotten) just how much of an adjustment going to college is. The majority of college student-athletes are residential; many have traveled a significant distance from home to pursue their education and continue to compete in their sport. Most (barring the occasional junior college transfer) have had little or no exposure to college-level academic demands. Most have had little or no experience in the degree of independence and personal accountability now expected (and required) of a collegiate student-athlete. Many, while likely having excelled in their sport(s) as a high school student, will be surprised at just how significant the jump is in the expectations (athletic and otherwise) that college coaches have for them. In addition, on a practical note, the large majority of today's college freshmen have never had the experience of sharing a bedroom with another person (chalk this up to smaller families, wealth, etc.); now, most will have to negotiate living peaceably with a roommate(s).

Against the above backdrop, we continue to tell incoming freshmen that they should expect to "experience the best four years of their life," effectively increasing, for many, the pressure to excel academically, socially, romantically and athletically. When the student-athlete has predictable bumps-in-the-road (and most certainly, every student-athlete will, during their college career), the continuing echo of our prediction of "the best four years…" may serve to increase the sense of failure and/or isolation that a student has perhaps begun to feel (e.g., "College is going pretty poorly for me right now, and yet everyone keeps telling me that this is the best time of my life. Something must *really* be wrong with me.").

I'd like to be able to confidently report that today's college freshman has preparation in place that is at least equal to the demands (e.g., independence, academic and athletic success, social pressures and expectations) of being a new college student-athlete. Unfortunately, though, (and please don't take this as personal criticism) there is reason to believe that the opposite just might be the case. As an example, "helicopter parents" has become a buzz-term among college administrators in the past couple of years. For the uninitiated, the so-called "helicopter parent" is the mom or dad who has meticulously managed their son or daughter's life to this point in their development and will continue to try to do so during their child's college career. Faculty will bemoan the phone calls they get from home asking whether or not their son or daughter came to class that morning. Judicial officers will struggle through hearings in which mom or dad has retained pricy legal counsel to help defend against a minor on-campus conduct charge. Administrators will lament whether or not today's college student can ever realize a sense of maturity with his or her parents (still) so intimately involved in their everyday affairs. And if we are to give any credence to the "helicopter parent" phenomenon, the logical concern becomes that fewer college students have had the experience of self-advocacy, the opportunity to practice appropriate assertiveness skills, or occasion to independently address concerns with authority figures in their life (e.g., scheduling a private meeting with Coach to discuss playing time). Thus, when placed in remarkably common challenging situations on campus (e.g., roommate conflict, difficulty with advisement and registration, conflict with teammates or coaches), many students find themselves in uncharted waters, and are likely to either regress (e.g., call the mom and/or dad to fix the problem for them ASAP), or panic (e.g., consider withdrawing from the institution, quitting the team, moving out of the residence hall, etc.).

So with respect to such "normative" developmental challenges associated with being a first-year student-athlete, the good news (again) is that the average student-athlete, assuming no other complicating factors, will find the courage and strength to rise up and meet these challenges head-on. After all, we are talking about a group of people who have already demonstrated they are pretty resilient and remarkably tough. This is NOT to say that there won't be doubts, tears, arguments and utter panic along the way (any college counselor or coach can attest to this); it is to say, however, that all things held equal, the new student-athlete, given the opportunity to struggle with new life challenges, will find a way to make this new environment work for them.

I occasionally get concerned with "adults" in this process (e.g., parents, coaches), who, well-meaning as they are, impede normal development. I've seen many times some variant of the following scenario: Freshman A is dissatisfied that his or her roommate's alarm clock goes off at 7AM every morning. Rather than address the concern promptly and appropriately, Freshman A calls home to Dad, who in turn angrily calls Freshman A's Coach, demanding action. Coach calls the Residence Life Office, gets some information, and calls Dad back. Not satisfied with the answers he has received to this point, Dad then calls the Dean's Office, and eventually the President. Eventually some sort of "resolution" to the matter occurs, for better or worse, with Freshman A having had little opportunity to exercise any independence, assertiveness or communication skills. Sadly, another "learning moment" passes, and we've simply reinforced the message to Freshman A that he or she is not capable, on their own, of struggling through a problem and arriving at a solution, and that the first choice of action should always be to call a "helpful adult" in their life. I absolutely respect how difficult it is for a parent to sit by and watch their child struggle with some challenge, and I absolutely recognize that, on occasion, it may be appropriate for a parent or coach to intervene in some matter occurring on-campus. I caution, however, against depriving the young student-athlete of the very developmental challenges that will result in the sort of growth and confidence we expect to see, eventually, in our college graduates.

As I've stated, it is my experience that the large majority of new student-athletes end up transitioning remarkably well to college, even in the face of fairly significant developmental challenges. Each year, however, I do come in contact with some students who begin to manifest signs of more serious psychological concerns. Most often, it's a case of a student bringing some pre-existing condition to campus with them, or, on occasion, the stress associated with this major developmental step pushes the student past some threshold where a normal developmental struggle becomes a significant emotional or psychological problem. Some of the more typical (more serious) psychological concerns that we tend to see in college students would include:

- **Anxiety problems.** Students may find that they have strong anxiety experiences, sometimes rising to the level of "panic," either in specific situations or more generally. Anxiety may manifest itself as intense fear, physical symptoms (e.g., headaches, gastrointestinal disturbance) and/or avoidance of certain situations. Anxiety is notorious for creating a "vicious circle" with some college students; strong negative emotional responses may tie themselves to a specific activity (e.g., football practice). Students may avoid the situation that causes such emotional upset (occasionally coming up with plausible reasons why they skipped the activity), with the goal of avoiding the anxiety associated with it. Often, this avoidance makes it increasingly difficult to return to the activity, effectively removing the student from this part of their life which had (prior) been a source of accomplishment and pride and opening the student up to additional problems. In the general population, anxiety disorders are the most commonly-diagnosed of any psychological disorders, and this is likely the case in college, as well.

- **Mood problems.** It is not uncommon for students to have a first serious episode of depression during their college years. It should be noted that while *every* college student-athlete will have moments of sadness, less-than-usual motivation and doubt; depression is a far less common (and far more serious) disorder that seriously impacts a student's functioning and should be addressed professionally as soon as possible.

- **Eating disorders.** Research indicates that just *being* a college student-athlete serves as a "protective factor" against most psychological disorders (i.e., all things held equal, the college student-athlete is at less risk than other, same-age peers). Eating disorders are the significant exception to the above rule. While disorders like anorexia nervosa and bulimia nervosa are still more common in females, prevalence rates in males are increasing at a higher rate. Perhaps because of the emphasis on fitness that is critical to most successful student-athletes, and exacerbated in those particular sports where weight and/or body image is such a critical component (e.g., wrestling, gymnastics), college mental health professionals are particularly attuned to the potential for eating disorders in our student-athlete populations.

- **Substance abuse/dependence.** I recently appeared on a local television program to discuss alcohol use among college students. The host of the show, a man likely in his fifties or so, remarked something along the lines of, "So what's the big deal? Experimenting with alcohol has always been part of the college experience." What I tried then to explain to him, and similarly try to explain to every new group of first-year college students I meet with each fall, is that the way in which college students are using alcohol these days is quite different from the "experimentation" of generations ago. Sadly, "drinking" to many college students does *not* look like the picture we may have in our mind of happy, healthy students having a beer with their pizza while watching the Red Sox game. Colleges today (rightfully) are expending tremendous resources in an attempt to curb what is termed "high-risk" or "binge" drinking among students.

- **Colleagues of mine in the field work from the following mind-set with respect to students and alcohol:** "If they drink, they binge." Binge-drinking (defined in the field as males consuming five or more standard "drinks" in a sitting, or females consuming four or more) dramatically increases a number of risks for students, including sexual or other victimization, assault, legal and/or campus judicial problems, health problems, and, of particular concern to student-athletes, performance problems (both athletic and academic). Further, high-risk drinking in college will, for some, evolve into lifelong difficulties with alcohol. The same "rules," so to speak, apply for illicit drugs as well, excepting perhaps that U.S. colleges are far less likely to take an educational or "developmental" approach to dealing with drug violations, preferring instead to turn such issues over to law enforcement. New college student-athletes should know *before* they show up on campus that most institutions are now confronting issues around substance use head-on, and not simply winking and looking the other way, as was perhaps common in years past. The additional problem that the student-athlete faces in this area, of course, is the increased scrutiny that he or she is likely to receive if, indeed, found to be in violation of campus alcohol and/or drug use policies (i.e., the local news is far more interested in problems experienced by the star wide receiver on campus than they are the chemistry major who doesn't wear the college's uniform). Institutions themselves have proven that they are more than willing to limit athletic participation as a judicial sanction for conduct concerns. Wrong or right, in this particular area, the rules *are* different for the student-athlete.

In many respects, as a mental health professional on a college campus, I "worry less" about student-athletes. As stated earlier, they tend to be a remarkably healthy, well-adjusted, motivated, and goal-oriented group of young people. They typically arrive at our institutions with an impressive "safety net" in place, including parents, friends, teammates, coaches, and professionals on campus who have experience in helping students navigate the challenge that is college life. The struggles they will face, in most cases, are developmental in nature, and with appropriate guidance and support, they will arrive at resolutions that are healthy and adaptive. For the more serious concerns that may emerge, most institutions have the resources available (e.g., counseling and health services) to effectively help our student-athletes stay on track. Though not without challenge, sacrifice and struggle, today's college student-athletes should prepare themselves for an experience that is incredibly exciting and rewarding; one which will help provide them the tools to live a rich and rewarding life when their playing days have come to an end.

About Robert Hynes: *Dr. Robert Hynes is Director of Counseling Services and Assistant Dean for Student Support Services at Fitchburg State College in Massachusetts. He earned his Ph.D. in Clinical and School Psychology from Hofstra University in 1996 and now works closely with college student-athletes in a clinical and educational capacity.*

CHAPTER NINE

WHEN DO I GET A DAY OFF?

A s student-athletes quickly discover, life as a college student and college athlete is very different from life in high school. Many live in a sort of two-way zone: a non-structured academic and private life away from their parents *and* a very structured, even micromanaged life as an athlete.

The omnipresent approach from an athletic program's head coach and his or her staff can make some student-athletes feel stifled, while others enjoy and grow very well within a regimented environment. Every prospective student-athlete should take time during the recruiting process to ask current players about their daily environment. Keep an open mind, however—what one athlete considers smothering might be caring to another. Ask for opinions from different people and then decide if you will succeed in that environment.

Once in a program, there are many rules that protect the student-athlete from an overzealous coach—or protect the workaholic athlete from himself. The following real-life examples from Rita, the certified athletic trainer, and Gavin, a student-athlete, demonstrate the need for proper time management, as well as complete understanding of what to expect as a student-athlete and the rules that protect their time.

RITA'S STORY

Rita, a certified athletic trainer at Super University, a small division two school, also functioned as the Senior Women's Administrator. She worked closely with the coaching staff to make sure they did not overwork the student-athletes and train too much. Even though it is the coach's choice when and where the team practices, works out or meets, Rita was the eyes and ears for both the coaches and the student-athletes when it came to preventing burnout and making sure the student-athletes had enough time to focus on their class work.

All the coaches at Super University gave their student-athletes a schedule for the season that included meetings, training sessions, conditioning times, study hall hours and travel dates. Rita's attention to detail helped the coaches understand the benefits of giving their athletes a schedule to work with. Creating an athletic schedule allows everyone—students, faculty and staff members—the opportunity to help balance the life of the student-athlete. The more organized a student-athlete can be, the better the grades will be and the less overwhelmed and stressed he or she will be. Not knowing a schedule from one day to the next does not allow students to prepare adequately for academics or athletics.

Not all coaches like to give athletes a schedule. Some coaches like to keep their athletes on their toes so they cannot schedule social activities. A prospect needs to ask the coaches and the players about their scheduling policies during the recruiting process.

Although Rita encountered changes to the schedule because of inclement weather, academic changes or other conflicts, she and her staff were always prepared to be flexible. The most important thing for Rita was that the student-athletes had a well structured (but flexible) plan that allowed them plenty of time to study and succeed in the classroom. The second most important part of her job was from an athletic standpoint—Rita needed to make sure the student-athletes were getting enough rest between games, training and conditioning sessions.

In one instance, the captains from the women's basketball program were concerned about the number of days they were constantly involved with their sport. They had been traveling across the country playing in games and tournaments in preparation for their conference season and were feeling burnt out. The captains approached Rita and asked for help. The captains believed they did not have a day off for over three weeks, but the coach considered their travel day an off day. Rita met with the coach and made sure that no athletic activity occurred during that day.

Upon meeting with the coach and her staff, Rita determined that the coach did, in fact, use a travel day as an off day. However, a team meeting and film breakdown were also added to that same day. This meant that, no matter how brief the meetings, the day was "countable" and was not an off day. In reality, the student-athletes had not received a day off from all athletically related activities. The coach acknowledged her mistake, apologized to the team and athletic administration. She then created two days off the following week in an effort to let her team catch up on all missed work due to their tough travel schedule.

The NCAA regulates time off for each sport. Each NCAA sport has a traditional season and a non-traditional season. The traditional season is the time of year when their national championship occurs. For example, the traditional season for volleyball, soccer and football is the fall. The traditional season for baseball, softball and lacrosse is the spring. However, some sports play through the winter. These sports begin their season in the fall but conclude in the spring—examples are basketball and swimming.

The NCAA mandates that a coach can only require student-athletes to work on their sport a maximum of 20 hours per week. Each sport also has a maximum total number of days throughout the academic year that they can train. (A list is provided at the end of this chapter.) During the traditional season, Rita worked with the staff in the Compliance Department to insure student-athletes did not spend more than 20 hours a week and a maximum of four hours per day on their athletic duties.

By NCAA regulations, it is okay to divide the maximum four hours a day into different sessions and different countable activities. For example, a student-athlete may practice for two hours, work with a strength coach for one hour, and be involved with a team meeting for an hour—four hours total. Some sports have exceptions to the four-hour rule. A round of golf may take more than four hours but it is recorded as four hours.

Each head coach, or designated assistant, is required to complete a form on a weekly basis stating the time that each athlete spends on all countable activities. The form, known as a CARA (Countable Athletic Related Activities), documents all weekly hours that a coach mandates for their student-athletes.

Countable Athletic Related Activities are all activities that the coach has control over. Under the guidance of the NCAA, these include the following:

- Practice

- Weight Training/Conditioning

- Team Meetings

- Individual Meetings required by the coaching staff

- Film/Video analysis

- Competition

Activities that are not included in the 20-hour-a-week schedule include these times:

- Travel to and from competition

- Travel to and from practice

- Voluntary strength and conditioning workouts without a coach's supervision

- Team meals

- Coach mandated study hall/study hours/academic support

A day of travel, even during a regular training or practice day, can be counted as an "off" day by the coach as long as no countable athletic related activities occur during the travel day.

Use your travel day wisely—study and seek academic help during this time.

According to the 20-hour-a-week rule, student-athletes are required to have one full day off from athletic related activities every week. Each sport has a designated work week—a seven-day period in which the student-athlete must have one day off to rest and study. Most work weeks run

Monday thru Sunday and the day off will depend on their game schedule. For example, many football coaches take Sunday off after a Saturday game. Soccer programs that play on Fridays and Sundays will take either Saturday or Monday off, depending on travel schedules. Sometimes the day off will change from work week to work week.

It is possible for student-athletes to have practice, conditioning and games for 12 days in a row without getting a day off. For example, if the student-athletes are off on Monday of week number one, they are not required to have a day off until the following Sunday. This is a very uncommon situation as most coaches and their support staff recognize the need for rest and recuperation.

Mon	Tues	Wed	Thurs	Fri	Sat	Sun
1 OFF DAY	2 Practice	3 Practice	4 Game	5 Practice	6 Practice	7 Game
8 Practice	9 Practice	10 Game	11 Practice	12 Practice	13 Game	14 OFF DAY

During the nontraditional season and outside the NCAA designated athletic days, a coach is restricted to work his team a maximum of eight hours a week. This includes all countable athletic related activities; but because it is outside of the designated countable days, competition is not included. Some sports do allow limited competition in the nontraditional season.

These hourly restrictions occur during the academic semesters only. Fall sports that necessitate players' early return to campus have a maximum amount of training opportunities prior to the start of the season. For sports that play during any given institutional break (Summer Break, Fall Break, Thanksgiving, Winter Break, Spring Break, etc.) the rules change. The NCAA does not restrict the coach during institutional vacation. The amount of work and rest is each coach's decision. A coaching staff should know what is best for their student-athletes at that particular time of year.

Some student-athletes may want access to the sport facilities and equipment to do additional work or training. These voluntary workouts are not counted toward the team's maximum hours as long as there is no coaching taking place. Any optional or voluntary training where a coach is present (with the exception of swimming for safety reasons) will be counted toward the maximum hours of CARA.

Each sport has a designated number of days that are used for practice, training, conditioning and other athletic related activities. The total numbers of days are part of the 20-hour-per-week restriction placed upon the coaches and student-athletes by the NCAA.

Sport	Practice Days	Contests	Non-Traditional Contests
Archery	144 days	15 dates	
Badminton	144 days	15 dates	
Baseball	132 days	56 contests	8 contests
Basketball	*	27 contests	
Bowling	144 days	26 dates	
Cross Country	144 days	7 competitions	
Equestrian	144 days	15 dates	
Fencing	144 days	11 dates	
Field Hockey	132 days	20 contests	5 dates
Football	**	12 contests	
Golf	144 days	24 dates***	
Gymnastics	144 days	13 dates	
Ice Hockey	132 days	34 contests	
Lacrosse	132 days	17 contests	5 dates—women
Rifle	144 days	13 dates	
Rugby	132 days	11 contests	
Skiing	144 days	16 dates alpine 16 dates nordic	
Soccer	132 days	20 contests	5 dates
Softball	132 days	56 contests	8 contests
Squash	144 days	15 dates	
Swim/Diving	144 days	20 dates	
Synch. Swim	132 days	15 dates	
Handball	132 days	20 dates	
Tennis	144 days	25 dates	

Sport	Practice Days	Contests	Non-Traditional Contests
Track & Field	156 days	18 dates	
Volleyball	132 days	28 dates	4 dates
Water Polo	132 days	21 dates	
Wrestling	144 days	16 dates	

*Basketball practice begins on the Friday closest to October 15 and lasts until the end of the regular season.

** Football practice can include 40 practice opportunities prior to the first regular season game.

*** Golf contests can be broken into nine tournaments, each lasting 3 days (54 holes).

Sports other than basketball and football can divide their 132, 144 or 156 days into two different seasons. Sports that play in the fall will use the majority of these dates in the fall and use the remainder of these dates in the spring. Sports competing for their national championship in the spring will use the majority of their days in the spring, having used the other portion of their days the previous fall.

For some sports, a two-day event, such as wrestling or track & field, is counted by the NCAA as only one competition date.

GAVIN'S STORY

An excellent baseball player, Gavin was also a very good student who excelled academically in high school. His parents, teachers and coaches all helped Gavin succeed. His parents woke him up in the morning, and along with his teachers and coaches, they told him what, when and where to study and they kept him on schedule. His coaches had him on the field as soon as he had recovered from the previous game. He was the star of his high school—both academically and athletically.

As a freshman pitcher for Home Run University, Gavin felt overwhelmed by the amount of work he had to do in the classroom and on the field. Even though he had chosen Home Run University because of the academic rigor, he was lost without constant management and supervision. Gavin was not prepared for the work load and self-discipline he needed to succeed and he panicked after the first few weeks of school. Gavin's poor results started piling up.

The good news for Gavin was that he had drive and he was intelligent. Gavin wanted to change before his stumble downwards spiraled out of control. He knew there were resources available to him on campus and approached his coach for help. Gavin was concerned about his ability to discipline himself to go to bed early at night and to wake up in the morning. Most importantly, Gavin was disappointed that he was not getting the grades he desired. To top that off, Gavin's anxieties over these issues were severely affecting his performances on the pitching mound.

Coach Ruth explained to Gavin that there was a relationship between all the things that he was worried about. He pointed out that if Gavin could get one thing under control, then everything else would be easier. The first thing Coach Ruth asked Gavin to focus on was his sleep. Gavin had to get to bed early enough to get enough sleep. To ensure that he would not sleep through his alarm, Coach Ruth made arrangements for Gavin to have breakfast every morning with a senior captain who had conquered similar issues three years previously.

Coach Ruth also asked Gavin to meet with an academic counselor in the Academic Support Center. The counselor would help Gavin create a schedule and manage his time more appropriately. Gavin called and set up a meeting with Dr. Newton which he hoped would help him get his life back on track and his grades up. Prior to the meeting, Dr. Newton asked Gavin to keep a daily diary of his activities for four days. In this diary, Gavin wrote down everything he did—the time it took him to eat, walk to class, sleep, his class and study schedule and his baseball commitments. As Coach Ruth had relayed to Gavin, everything was interdependent and Dr. Newton planned to help Gavin help himself. After all, Gavin had to manage *his* own life better.

Dr. Newton examined Gavin's diary and asked him to point out where he felt the hardest change in his daily routine occurred. Gavin knew—he was tired in the afternoon, took a nap after practice, and was not tired when he should have gone to sleep at night. Confirming the problem, Dr. Newton planned a daily schedule, starting with an appropriate time for Gavin to go to bed. Working backwards toward morning, Dr. Newton fit everything else into a suitable time frame. Following this schedule, Gavin would get enough sleep at night, get up for class in the morning, and manage enough time to study and do any extra training that he felt was necessary.

Dr. Newton taught Gavin an effective way to create a schedule. This skill was an asset to Gavin because he could apply the same strategies to making a weekly and longer-term schedule for himself. Using the system, Gavin got his academic life back on track. Dr. Newton shared the following tips:

- **Use "In-Between" Hours:** Dr. Newton found time that Gavin did not know was available. Gavin normally spent the hour between classes walking back to his dorm. Once he got to his room, he watched TV for 30 minutes and then headed back to his next class. Dr. Newton changed this walking and TV time to study time. Instead of going back to the dorm, Gavin was to find a quiet classroom between his classes and study. This added approximately five hours of study time to Gavin's weekly schedule.

- **Prepare Before Class:** Studying between classes gave Gavin the opportunity to review what he had just learned in the class he had attended. It also helped Gavin prepare for his next class. Being ready for class helped him learn new material more easily.

- **Have Enough Study Time Scheduled:** Dr. Newton explained to Gavin that he should schedule a minimum of *two* hours of study and preparation for each *one*-hour class he was taking. Because Gavin was taking 15 hours that semester, he should schedule a minimum of 30 hours of study and class preparation each week. When those two numbers were added, that gave Gavin the time he needed to dedicate to academics each week—a total of 45 hours class time and study/preparation. When Gavin designated study time on his written schedule, he further broke down the assigned study periods so that he was sure to spend an adequate amount of time preparing for each individual class. Gavin realized, however, that some classes would demand more attention at certain times and he would need to remain flexible.

- **Make Use of Athletic "Off" Day:** Gavin designated the off day to schedule his studying or preparation—utilizing his time effectively.

- **Study at the Same Time:** Dr. Newton recommended that Gavin study at the same time every day whenever possible. This scheduling would create a habit, allowing Gavin to develop his study skills and learning habits.

- **Schedule Study Breaks:** A recommended study period of 50 to 90 minutes should merit a break of 10 to 15 minutes. Dr. Newton explained to Gavin that a well placed break provided physical relief from boredom and in the long run it would help him to remain focused and attentive during the study period. Simply put, Gavin's eyes and brain occasionally needed a break!

Using these tips from Dr. Newton, Gavin set up his daily study schedule around his academic and athletic commitments. He filled in all the gaps with study, eating, rest and recreation times. Gavin was amazed at how much time was available to him. He realized that he just needed to use his time more wisely and stick to a schedule. Developing his weekly and semester schedules alleviated a lot of anxiety. Gavin felt more in control of his time. He was more efficient and had more time to do the things that were important to him.

Dr. Newton also signed Gavin up for study skill classes through the Academic Support Center. Those classes taught Gavin how to create a study environment for himself, how to take better notes, and how to arrange his study material. These were strategies that continued to help him in his growth as a student throughout his college years.

Additionally, Gavin was able to relax more while at baseball practice because he could focus all his energies on his baseball performance. He did not need to worry about his class preparation during baseball time because he had everything planned out. This increase in focus and confidence helped Gavin tremendously while he was pitching.

Coach Ruth had been right—Gavin's distractions and frustrations were linked. Taking care of the small stuff like sleep and study habits while creating an efficient schedule helped Gavin become a successful student and an even more successful baseball player.

Gavin's Weekly Schedule

	Mon	Tue	Wed	Thu	Fri	Sat	Sun
7am	Wake	Wake	Wake	Wake	Wake		
7:30am	Eat	Eat	Eat	Eat	Eat		
8am	Math	Psyc	Math	Psyc	Math		
9am	SH	SH	SH	Wake	Wake		
9:30am	Bus	Bus	Eat	Eat			
10am	Eng	Eng	Eng	Rec	SH		
11am	Hist	SH	Hist	SH	Hist	Rec	SH
12pm	Lunch	Lunch	Lunch	Lunch	Lunch	Lunch	Lunch
1pm	Rec	Rec	Rec	Rec	Rec	G	G
2pm	SH	P	P	P	P	G	G
3pm	SH	P	P	P	P	G	G
4pm	SH	P	P	P	P	G	Rec
5pm	SH	C	Rec	C	Rec	G	Rec
6pm	Eat	Eat	Eat	Eat	Eat	G	Eat
7pm	Rec	SH	SH	SH	Rec	Eat	SH
8pm	Rec	SH	SH	SH	Rec	SH	SH
9pm	SH	SH	SH	SH	Rec	SH	SH
10pm	SH	SH	SH	SH	Rec	Rec	SH
11pm	Rec	Rec	Rec	Rec	Rec	Rec	Rec
12pm	Sleep	Sleep	Sleep	Sleep	Sleep	Sleep	Sleep

SH = Study Hall/Study
Rec = Recreation Time
C = Conditioning
P = Practice
G = Game
Math = Math 101
Bus = Intro to Business
Hist = World History
Eng = English Composition
Psyc = Intro to Psychology

DAILY SCHEDULES

Each sport or program has a different schedule. Coaches make the team's schedules dependent on many factors:

- **Class Schedules**—A coach will want to have as many of the student-athletes at training as possible.

- **Game Schedules**—Many coaches like to train as close to their *normal* game time as possible. For example, a team that traditionally plays at 7:00 p.m. may train from 7:00 – 9:00 p.m. during the week.

- **Facility Availability**—It is very common for different sports and/or programs to share facilities. For example, the institution may have one indoor gym facility with two basketball teams and a volleyball team needing to use the same facility.

- **Environmental Factors**—Some areas of the country experience extreme weather difficulties and the coaches may choose to work around these. For example, a soccer or football team in the south may choose to train earlier in the morning, before classes, to avoid extreme temperatures later in the afternoon or evening.

- **Support Staff Availability**—Many institutions share support staff and have to work with everyone's schedules. For example, an athletic trainer may have to cover football and swimming or a strength coach may have to work with both the men's and women's soccer programs.

- **Coaches Importance/Priority**—Some coaches may put emphasis on certain things within their programs that not all coaches do. For example, a coach may want the student-athletes to spend more time in the weight room than on the field, court or track. This may vary depending on the time of year—traditional or non-traditional season—or within smaller sections of larger training and competition segments.

During the recruiting process, it is important for the prospects to ask the coach and the currently enrolled student-athletes what a typical day, week and season is like as a student-athlete in that specific program—each coach differs. Sample schedules for several different sports follow.

Baseball: Rich Hill, University of San Diego

Fall	6:00 a.m.:	Weight Training/Conditioning, then breakfast
	Morning/Early Afternoon:	Classes
	Afternoon:	Skill Instruction/Practice (depending on NCAA limits)
	Evening:	Study Hall
Spring	Morning/Early Afternoon:	Classes
	2:00 – 6:00 p.m.:	On-Field Instruction/ Practice—includes some individual skill conditioning
	Evening:	Study Hall

During the traditional season (spring), the team has Monday as their off day and normally plays three games over the weekend—a double header on Saturday and a single game on Sunday.

Basketball: David Hixon, Amherst University

All Year	Early Morning:	Breakfast
	Morning/Early Afternoon:	Classes Individual Practice and/or Strength Training (Optional)
	4:30 - 6:30 p.m.:	Team practice Watch film—when scheduled
	Evening:	Study time

During the season, Coach Hixon limits team practice to 1.5 hours. During pre-season, training may last 2 hours and 15 minutes.

Cross Country and Track & Field: Matt Morris, Western Illinois University

All Year	Early Morning:	Morning Run (2x week) or Strength Train (2x week)
	Morning/Early Afternoon:	Classes and academic work
	Afternoon:	Afternoon workout (1.5 - 2 hours in length)
	Evening:	Study Hall (2x week) or team time (1x week)

Every member of the WIU Cross Country and Track program is required to go to study hall twice a week, no matter what his or her grades are. In addition, one night a week, the members of both the men's and women's programs get together and hang out. On the weekends, longer training sessions take place.

Golf: Mike McGraw, Oklahoma State University

All Year (within NCAA limits)	
Early Morning:	Conditioning and workout with strength coaches
Morning:	Classes
Lunch:	As a team every day when possible
Afternoon:	2–3 hours practice and play
Dinner:	As a team everyday when possible
Evening:	classes and/or study hall/tutoring

When traveling to tournaments, Coach McGraw and his golfers try to keep their routine the same as it is when they are at home. The golf team uses a short practice the day before a tournament and study in the evening when their schedule allows.

Women's Lacrosse: Mike Scerbo, Duquesne University

Fall	Early Morning (7:00–9:00 a.m.): Morning Training (includes weight training, conditioning and practice)	
	Morning and Afternoon:	Classes
	Evening:	Study Hall/Study Time
Spring	Morning/Early Afternoon:	Classes
	3:00–6:00 p.m.:	Practice and Conditioning
	Evening:	Study Hall/Study Time

Coach Scerbo likes to practice around game time during their traditional season (spring) whenever possible. He is also aware of travel schedules and how it affects his student-athletes and will adjust the practice and conditioning schedule when necessary. In addition to the daily training, the team spends two days a week reviewing video analysis of their team and opponents.

Rowing: Doug Wright, Southern Methodist University

All Year (except November and January per NCAA Limitations)	
5:30–7:30 a.m.:	Morning Training
9:00 a.m.–3:00 p.m.:	Classes
4:00–6:00 p.m.:	Afternoon Training
6:00–11:00 p.m.:	Study Hall/Recreation
11:00 p.m.:	Sleep

Coach Wright acknowledges that the schedule of a rowing athlete can cause a high attrition rate, especially for rowers who are new to the sport. Rowing is a lifestyle, and to succeed at the college level, a rowing student-athlete must enjoy the life style of competing at a high level.

Women's Soccer: John Cossaboon, Gonzaga University

Fall	Morning/Early Afternoon:	Classes
	Before Practice:	Training Room/Meetings
	Late Afternoon:	Practice including coach-led conditioning (2 hours)
	Post Practice:	Therapy (if needed)
	Evening:	Study Hall/Study Time
Spring	Similar schedule as the fall, dependent on whether the team is utilizing the 20-hour or 8-hour per week training schedule and has training games. A larger emphasis is placed on soccer-specific conditioning and physical development.	

During the season, Monday is the team's off day, followed by two hard ("meat and potato") days on Tuesday and Wednesday. Thursday is a game preparation day (and may be a travel day) for games on Friday. Saturday is a recovery day and preparation for Sunday's game.

Softball: Glenn Moore, Baylor University

All Year	8:00 a.m.–1:00 p.m.	Classes and study time
	2:15–5:00 p.m.	Practice
	5:15–6:15 p.m.	Strength training and conditioning
	Evening:	Study Hall (freshmen and S-A's below 3.0 GPA)

Coach Moore gives student-athletes two days off a week—Sunday is family day and Wednesday is for academic work. During the season, athletes have the opportunity to train in the early morning if they are early morning personalities. During the off-season, student-athletes will condition three times and strength train three times in a week (over five days). During the season, student-athletes will strength train and condition twice each week.

Swimming: Steve Collins, Southern Methodist University

All Year (within NCAA Limitations)	
6:00–8:00 a.m.:	Swimming Workout
Morning/Early Afternoon:	Classes
2:00–4:00 p.m.:	Dry Land Training
	Swimming Workout
Evening:	Study Time

Coach Collins utilizes a "dry" land workout daily to strengthen the student-athlete's core and to work on total body strength and power. The swim team is not required to complete study hall hours but must check in weekly with their advisor at the university's Learning Enhancement Center (Academic Support Center).

Swimming is a year-round commitment for student-athletes. After the NCAA championships, they have the *Nationals* (where the Olympic team is selected) and then the *Worlds*.

Tennis: Debbie Southern, Furman University

All Year	6:30–7:30 a.m.:	Strength and Conditioning
	Morning/Early Afternoon:	Classes
	2:30–4:30 p.m.	Tennis Practice
		Conditioning may follow
	Evening:	Dinner together
		Study and recreation time

In addition to the scheduled practice and training sessions, members of the program may request additional/individual hitting practice with or without the coaching staff.

Volleyball: Chris Herron, Washburn University

Fall	Morning–1:30 p.m.:	Breakfast/Classes/Lunch
	1:30–2:30 p.m.:	Training Room
	2:30–3:10 p.m.:	Strength Training (twice weekly)
	Or	
	2:30–2:45 p.m.:	Stretch/Warm-up
	2:45–4:45 p.m.:	Team Practice
	After Dinner:	Study Hall
Spring	6:00–7:20 a.m.:	Strength and Conditioning (3 days per week)
	From March 1:	Position specific training (3 days per week)

SUMMARY

SCHEDULES–TO-DO LIST

- Keep a complete schedule—include meetings, training, classes, study hall, conditioning, travel, recreation time, eating and sleeping—everything!

- Be organized.

- Remain flexible.

- Understand the time commitment that the coach places on his or her athletes—ask about this during the recruitment process.

- Understand countable activities (and what are not) in your daily and weekly schedule.

- Use travel days effectively—study!

- Utilize your off days effectively—study!

- Talk to your coach, or an administrator, if you believe you are not getting time off.

- Utilize academic support resources if/when you need them.

- Use teammates as a support/buddy system, especially upper classmen.

- Take a time management class/seminar to help create an effective schedule for yourself.

- Take a study skills class/seminar to learn how to create an effective learning environment.

- Stay away from the nap-trap.

- Use in-between hours to review/study/prepare for class.

- Designate two hours of study/preparation time for every one hour of class.

- Schedule study breaks—keep your mental focus.

- During the recruitment process, ask about schedules—academic, athletic, study, etc.

SAMPLE CARA FORM
COUNTABLE ATHLETICALLY RELATED ACTIVITIES

Team: Men's Soccer Dates of Week 10/30 To 11/5

COACH'S WEEKLY SCHEDULE (Hours)

DAY OF THE WEEK	Mon	Tue	Wed	Thu	Fri	Sat	Sun	
Practice	0.0	2.0	2.0	1.5	1.5			
Meeting	0.5	0.5	0.5					
Weight Training/								
Conditioning	1.0	1.0	0.5					
Film/Video	0.5	0.5	0.5					
Competition		3.0	3.0					
Other Countable Activities								
TOTAL HOURS								
FOR WEEK								
TOTALS	0.0	4.0	3.0	3.5	3.0	2.5	3.0	19

20 Hour Week: X STUDENT-ATHLETE SCHEDULE 8 Hours Week:
(make changes if different from above)

NAME	Mon	Tue	Wed	Thu	Fri	Sat	Sun	Comments
Jimmy Scorer	0.0	3.0	3.0	2.5	3.0	2.5	3.0	Left practice early for class Tues and Thurs
Fred Back	0.0	2.0	3.0	3.5	3.0	2.5	3.0	Had Lab on Tuesday
Frank Hurt	0.0	4.0	3.0	3.5	0.0	0.0	0.0	Was injured and did not travel to games
Roy Anger	0.0	4.0	3.0	3.5	3.0	0.0	0.0	Suspended for game, did not travel

Head Coach Signature _____

Date _____

CHAPTER TEN

THE RULES ARE THERE TO PROTECT YOU

Very few coaches will blatantly tell prospects lies to get them to commit to an institution, but it does happen. That is why it is important that as a prospect, you ask many questions. Do not just question the coaches and support staff, ask the current student-athletes questions such as these:

- Did the coach and his or her staff paint a true and accurate picture during the recruitment process?

- Were the coaches true to their words once you became a student-athlete?

During the recruitment period, every college coach is going to emphasize the best part of their team, program and institution to prospects and parents. Some are more truthful than others, while others may tell the prospects whatever they want (or need) to hear. They tell prospects they are a "perfect fit," that they are great athletes and how successful they will be within their program.

The following stories of Nick, Erica, Lynn and Jeff illustrate examples when life as a student-athlete does not go as planned and what options are available. The NCAA has rules in place to protect student-athletes.

Stories like these are the exception rather than the rule. The vast majority of collegiate coaches have the best interest at heart for all their student-athletes and recruits.

Beware of your options before you become a student-athlete. The more prepared you are, the less likely you are to be in one of these situations. And remember to use common sense. If someone tells you something that sounds too good to be true, it might just be!

NICK'S STORY

During the recruitment process, Coach Owens targeted Nick as a starting quarterback for Football University. Nick fully believed that he would have the opportunity to play as a starter all four of his years at FU. Despite all the offers from other schools that came his way, Nick chose Football University because of the promises made to him during his high school years.

During the recruiting process, Nick asked all the coaches to clarify his future position via email, on the phone and in person. The coaches told him that he would start, that they were not recruiting another quarterback, and that he was better than all the other quarterbacks. The coaches continuously told Nick that he possessed more potential and was more accomplished than any of the quarterbacks that were already on the team.

In early August, Nick arrived at FU for the start of preseason training. Excited about the prospect of starting as a freshman on national television, Nick arrived ready to play. However, during the first scheduled preseason practice, Nick discovered he was one of three freshman quarterbacks. Nick quickly realized that the coaches had told the same story to everyone—that each one of them would start for four years!

Tension mounted throughout the training session between the three freshmen quarterbacks, which led to further tension off the playing field. Each quarterback believed the coaching staff had lied to them. Each new quarterback agreed that had he known the real situation, he could have either mentally prepared himself for the additional competition, or made a choice to attend a different university. Knowing that he had been lied to, Nick had a tough time respecting his coaches. He did not appreciate being brought to Football University under false pretenses.

Nick had difficulty during the training sessions and allowed the situation to bring him down. During a water break at one training session, Nick asked Coach Owens, the Quarterback Coach, if they could meet after practice—alone—to discuss the situation. Coach Owens agreed, especially since he had noticed the tension between the three athletes and wanted it cleared up before any more damage occurred.

During his meeting with Coach Owens, Nick explained what he was told during the recruiting process—that he would be the only freshman quarterback and that he would start. Nick expressed that he felt lied to and that if he had known the truth, he might have made another choice.

Coach Owens explained to Nick that he was recruited just like everyone else. Nick was there to do a job and he had to get over his personal disappointment and think of the team. He also reminded Nick that he was receiving a very good scholarship. The coaches felt they did not need to explain themselves to Nick or any of their recruits. The coaches were just doing their job—trying to build a winning and successful program. Nick was recruited to play football, whether he started or not, and he should fight for his starting position. Even if he did not make it to the starting offensive group, the coaches expected him to do what he was told—period!

Nick wasn't happy. Coach Owens' explanation did not make him feel any better. Nick still believed the coaches misled him and lied to him during the recruitment process and their behavior was not professional. So, he complained to the Compliance Department.

The Director of Compliance listened to Nick's complaints and took them back to Coach Owens. He told Coach Owens he needed to get Nick back on board with a positive attitude. Coach Owens told Nick in no uncertain terms that unless his attitude changed, the coaches would have no option but limit his playing time, if he played at all. Nick refused to back down and was black-listed by the coaches.

As the season progressed, Nick received no playing time at all and spent practice standing alone. Frustrated at the situation, Nick arranged a meeting with the Head Coach, Coach Perry, to discuss his future. Coach Perry abruptly told Nick that he had no future at FU and that he might as well stop showing up for practice. Stunned, Nick asked Coach Perry to release him from the program so that he could transfer to another school.

Coach Perry explained to Nick that he would not be released and that he would not be allowed to transfer. However, if Nick felt he was being singled out at training, then he should quit the team and stop going to training. This was probably Coach Perry's way to get Nick to quit so he could take back his scholarship money.

Forcing a student-athlete to quit can be an approach made by some unethical coaches so the heat is off them and they get their scholarship money back.

This denial was the final straw for Nick. He believed that he had no option but to quit the team and find another way to pay for school. Fortunately, Nick called his high school coach and talked to him about his dilemma. Nick's high school coach advised Nick to document the situation and go to the Compliance Office where they could help him manage the situation.

The following day, Nick met with the Director of Compliance again. He explained the situation and told the director that Coach Perry explained there was no way he could be released to transfer to another institution. After listening to Nick, the director encouraged him to stay with the program and follow the correct procedure for a transfer. If Nick voluntarily left the program, he would sacrifice all his scholarship money for the current semester and the remaining year. The Compliance Director explained to Nick the correct procedure for requesting a transfer:

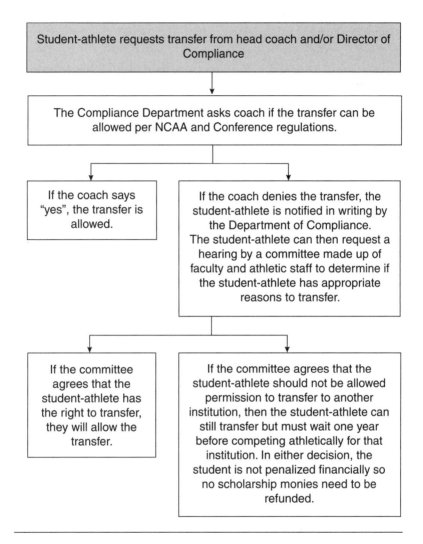

Student-athlete requests transfer from head coach and/or Director of Compliance

The Compliance Department asks coach if the transfer can be allowed per NCAA and Conference regulations.

If the coach says "yes", the transfer is allowed.

If the coach denies the transfer, the student-athlete is notified in writing by the Department of Compliance. The student-athlete can then request a hearing by a committee made up of faculty and athletic staff to determine if the student-athlete has appropriate reasons to transfer.

If the committee agrees that the student-athlete has the right to transfer, they will allow the transfer.

If the committee agrees that the student-athlete should not be allowed permission to transfer to another institution, then the student-athlete can still transfer but must wait one year before competing athletically for that institution. In either decision, the student is not penalized financially so no scholarship monies need to be refunded.

Keep a file of all correspondence that occurs during your recruiting process—especially of promises made. Transcribe phone conversations, verbal agreements and print out emails. Try to get every important issue confirmed in writing such as playing time, starting positions, scholarship monies, class times and practice schedules. Print out and bring copies with you when you go to school so you are prepared for any misunderstanding that might occur.

ERICA'S STORY

Erica decided to attend Women's Lacrosse University for several reasons. The engineering program allowed her to follow her academic dream, the lacrosse program was competitive and she would play as a freshman. Plus, she received scholarships from the lacrosse program, the engineering program and an academic scholarship from the Admissions/Financial Aid Department. It seemed WLU was the perfect fit!

Erica was very excited that everything she had set her sights on was now a reality. Her hard work had paid off and she was ready to take full advantage of a great education as well as a fantastic opportunity to play lacrosse. Erica could not imagine things not working out more perfectly. Her college coaches had promised her she would live her dream—get a degree in engineering and play college lacrosse.

During her freshman year, Erica's plan was straight forward. She would start with her core classes, receive good grades and create a solid foundation for the engineering classes that were to come later in her academic career. As athletes, Erica and her teammates enjoyed the luxury of preferred class registration so they scheduled morning classes to allow freedom for afternoon training and practice. Additionally, WLU offered most core classes during a variety of times, so they never had to worry about missing practice because of class.

As a lacrosse player, Erica had made the impact that she and her coaches had anticipated. Erica was selected All-Conference by opposition coaches and both Erica and Coach Stein refocused Erica's goals to become an All-American and Academic All-American. Erica's future continued to look very bright!

During Erica's sophomore year, she was required to take a class that had a laboratory section during the afternoon practice. In addition, she was required to take an introductory engineering class that only had one time slot available– twice a week during afternoon lacrosse practice. In all, Erica's class schedule made her miss three team practices per week.

The coaches began to get frustrated with Erica's absences and discussed having her reschedule her classes. The coaching staff explained to Erica that she was simply missing too much practice and she was in danger of losing her starting role. Additionally, the coaches told Erika that she would never make her goal of being an All-American if her class schedule remained the same. They were forceful in their argument and attempted to pressure

Erica into making the change that they wanted. However, Erica told the coaches that there were no other class options because her engineering classes were only offered at one time. Since the coaching staff understood when they recruited her that she planned to major in engineering, Erica insisted they should have known about any schedule conflicts.

Coach Stein approached Erica's academic advisors and asked them to find suitable alternatives for Erica because her class schedule did not permit her to be a member of the women's lacrosse program. Coach Stein was told that as an engineering student, Erica had few options. With this confirmation, Coach Stein advised Erica that she needed to find a different major. Missing practice was not acceptable, and since she was a scholarship athlete, she needed to find a more accommodating academic pursuit. Her sophomore year had to be the last as an engineering student.

As the semester continued, Erica missed more practice and received no flexibility from her coaches. Attempting to appease the situation, Erica increased her strength-training schedule. But the coaches still were not happy. The tension between Erica and the lacrosse staff mounted and Erica saw her playing time dwindle to almost nothing. This caused tension between Erica and her teammates. Her team wanted Erica on the field, not on the bench.

The coaching staff attempted to use peer pressure to make Erica change her mind regarding her educational path. Midway through the season, the team captains approached Erica. They asked Erica to withdraw from her classes for the good of her team. They needed her at practice and then Coach Stein would then let her play. The captains warned Erica that Coach Stein would not renew her scholarship the following year unless she changed her major and committed 100 percent to the program.

At that point Erica asked to meet with Coach Stein and her staff. She explained to Coach Stein that she had also received a scholarship from the Engineering Department and that the coaching staff had known from her recruitment that Erica wanted to be an engineer. She asked Coach Stein if they could change their practice to a later time, which would allow Erica to be at practice at least a couple of times a week. Erica's academic schedule was not flexible, but maybe the practice schedule could be. Coach Stein bluntly told Erica she had to change her major if she wanted to play lacrosse *and* keep her scholarship.

Frustrated, Erica met with the Senior Woman's Administrator (SWA) and explained the situation. Erica wanted to play lacrosse at WLU, but she also wanted to major in engineering. Erica explaining the pressure that her coach and team captains placed on her to change majors, and how she felt extremely overwhelmed and disappointed.

Erica met with Coach Stein again and brought the SWA along for support. Erica took with her a well-documented case in an attempt to help Coach Stein understand her desire to be at WLU and to be part of her program. Erica's documentation included the following:

- Copies of recruiting emails outlining her desire to major in engineering, with Coach Stein's positive responses

- A copy of an email from Coach Stein that stated when there is a class-practice conflict that classes always come first

- Coach Stein's statement that the coaches always find a time when everyone can practice together

- A copy of the student-athlete handbook from WLU that states that if there is a conflict, classes always take priority

- An email from the strength coach, showing Erica's workout routines were over and above what was required

- Documented support from the SWA that a coach could not take a scholarship away from a student-athlete because of a class conflict, the inability of the student-athlete to practice or because the student-athlete did not play as often as anticipated

- Available practice times furnished by the SWA that were conflict free for all Coach Stein's student-athletes

Finally, Coach Stein was willing to listen to Erica. Coach Stein admitted her inflexibility. She agreed to change the training schedule, welcome Erica back to the team in a fulltime capacity and she promised Erica that she would be more open to communicating at an appropriate level.

Erica was very fortunate that she had strong support from the SWA and strong guidance from people around her. Keeping her emails and letters from coaches was a habit she developed during the recruitment process to keep everything straight in her mind. This habit had helped her maintain her goal of becoming an All-American lacrosse player at WLU and of graduating with a degree in engineering.

Keep all written promises and statements and do not be afraid to ask for help from your athletic administrators. Finally, if you believe you are doing everything you can to keep things positive, ask the same from your coaches. Good coaches would be more proactive than Coach Stein was and this conflict could have been prevented. Communication is the key to a good coach-athlete relationship.

LYNN'S STORY

Voted captain by her teammates and supported by the coaching staff, Lynn was a stand-out her junior and senior years on the State Rowing University's women's team. As captain, she helped create and administer the program's rules. Every year, under strict guidelines from the coaching staff, the team captains tweaked the guidelines for consequences to teammates who broke the rules.

Believing that a sense of empowerment and control for the student-athletes created a stronger bond and commitment from her athletes, Coach Redgrave was happy to allow the athletes within her program the opportunity to develop and create the rules. She had noticed over the years that student-athletes followed their own rules better and often created rules that were more stringent than ones developed by the coaching staff. Team empowerment also proved a positive recruiting point for most prospects.

The team rules covered everything from academics and tardiness to alcohol, drugs and breaking the law. Clearly developed by the captains in collaboration with the coaching staff, the team rules produced a strong guideline for living as a rowing athlete at State Rowing University. Each student-athlete was required to agree to all the rules and sign a statement to assure that they all understood each rule. Simply by being part of the program, they agreed to live under the direction of the rules.

The captains were required to administer the rules as well as make them. If rules were broken, it was their responsibility to insure that the offender admitted her wrongdoing to the coaches, and then the coaching staff would administer any consequences. The penalty for breaking a rule varied, depending on the coach's discretion and severity of the violation.

On the Thursday night of her 21st birthday, Lynn went out to celebrate with a few friends. Even though there was training the following morning at 6:00 a.m., Lynn did not want to miss the opportunity to celebrate her birthday. Because she believed that her rowing career had been stellar to that point, Lynn felt that she could afford one mediocre day. Although she celebrated until 2:00 a.m., Lynn was sure that she would receive a break from the coaching staff—after all, she was the team captain!

The following morning, the rowing team began their usual warm-up prior to entering the boats and getting on the lake. However, there was no sign of Lynn. Coach Redgrave asked several of the upper classmen if they had seen Lynn and if she was okay. Coach Redgrave was concerned because it was very unlike Lynn not to be at practice on time, leading the team as they prepared for their morning workout. Some of Lynn's teammates said that they had seen her the previous night, heading out to celebrate her birthday.

At 6:15, Lynn showed up for practice. Disheveled, Lynn was anything but at her best. She still smelled of alcohol from her birthday bash. Coach Redgrave asked Lynn if she had been drinking the previous night. Lynn knew she could not hide the truth from her coach and admitted to celebrating her birthday. She also apologized for being late and asked if it was okay for her to start training.

Coach Redgrave explained to Lynn that she had broken the team's rules—the rules that she helped develop and administer. In addition, he explained that training in the physical state that she was in would not be advantageous to her health or for her teammates' training intensity. Coach Redgrave asked Lynn to leave with the directions to meet with her that afternoon in her office.

When Lynn showed up for her meeting, Coach Redgrave was very willing to listen. Coach Redgrave's first priority was the well-being of her student-athletes and she asked many probing questions to make sure that this was not a common occurrence. Coach Redgrave wanted to make certain that Lynn did not have a drinking problem. Lynn assured Coach Redgrave that the incident was associated with her 21st birthday and the celebration of "being of drinking age" rather than an indication of a chronic drinking problem. Lynn promised her coach that she would learn from her one-time mistake.

Still, Coach Redgrave had no option but to follow the team guidelines created by the captains. Lynn had been part of the group that wrote the team rules and Lynn had signed them. Any consumption of alcohol during a competition week was a serious violation of team rules. Additionally, the consequences were clear—Lynn could not compete in the upcoming event and she would resign as team captain for the remainder of the year.

Even though she was a potential Academic All-American, Lynn had broken the rules set forth by the program she captained. Even with parents' weekend upon her—and the visit of her parents and immediate family—Lynn could not compete for her university. Lynn asked her coach if there was any way she could row that weekend since her family was on their way to watch her compete. The answer was a firm "no."

Regarding Lynn's suspension from all team activities, Coach Redgrave explained to Lynn that she had no option other than the punishment set forth in the guidelines. Coach Redgrave explained that she would receive written notification of the decision via email by the end of that day. Lynn was also notified that a memo would be sent to the Compliance Department and the Senior Woman's Administrator regarding the incident and the memo would remain in her permanent file.

Coach Redgrave stated that she did not want to lose Lynn and reaffirmed that she was an important part of the team. However, Lynn had broken team rules and Athletic Department guidelines. Unfortunately, there was no other option for her. Even though Coach Redgrave liked Lynn, she had to look at the program before the team and the team before the individual student-athlete. Lynn had to live with the fact that her family had spent time and money to come and watch her compete, but her actions would not allow that to happen. Lynn had let herself down primarily, but she also let down her coaches, teammates, friends and family.

Make sure to celebrate during appropriate times that do not conflict with your athletic schedule. In addition to not suffering negative consequences, you will be able to have more fun knowing you aren't doing something wrong.

JEFF'S STORY

Jeff spent the majority of his junior and senior year in high school being pursued by some of the best collegiate track and field programs in the country. Jeff had created a very good relationship with Coach Coe, the head coach at UTS, throughout the recruitment process and he eventually decided on the University of Track Stars. After signing with UTS, Jeff continued to work hard in preparation for four stellar years under the direction of the coach he admired and trusted.

Coach Coe and his support staff created a specific throwing program to help Jeff prepare for his freshman year. Following the program diligently, Jeff felt an immediate benefit. He finally felt that his body was starting to catch up with his determination for success. Both Jeff and Coach Coe set high goals for his four years at UTS and both looked forward to Jeff achieving these goals.

As the first season began, however, Jeff fell into a funk and could not understand why. He had trained hard and was physically stronger. As instructed by his coaches, he had worked on his throwing technique. Because he had done all that was expected of him, Jeff was sure he would rise to the top. But when immediate success did not present itself, Jeff became frustrated. He tried harder and harder but did not improve. The more he tried, the shorter his throws were. The shorter his throws were, the more pressure he placed on himself and the more disappointment he felt from Coach Coe.

Coach Coe approached Jeff on several occasions in an effort to figure out why he was not performing up to his expectations. At every meet, an even greater slip and even greater amount of frustration from both parties ensued. First it was in competition, then practice and finally in the weight room.

Despite all the changes that both men made, Jeff could not get himself moving in a positive direction. He felt like a complete failure. It did not help when Coach Coe gave up on him and started to focus his attention on other athletes. Coach Coe believed that he had spent enough time on Jeff and that he had made a bad recruiting decision. He was disappointed that Jeff was not performing at the level he had anticipated.

As the season came to a halt, Coach Coe explained to Jeff that due to his poor performance and lack of improvement, the program would not award his scholarship the next year. Jeff was no longer part of the track and field program at UTS. Coach Coe told Jeff that he should transfer and give up his dream of being a successful collegiate thrower.

Devastated, Jeff withdrew from classes. He did not understand his options and the rules that protected him and his scholarship. He believed that he had no other option but to leave UTS. Because Jeff believed his only option to attain a college degree was through an athletic scholarship, he dropped out of school and never returned.

What Jeff should have known was that Coach Coe could not have taken away his scholarship due to poor performance. The NCAA protects athletes and states that it is the recruiting coach's responsibility to determine if the level of an athlete is good enough for their program. If the student-athlete does not perform at a predetermined level, then the coach has made the mistake and has to continue to work with the student and provide the same amount of aid.

Jeff had done everything that the coaches asked of him from an athletic and academic perspective. For him to lose his scholarship and stop being an athlete at UTS, Coach Coe would have needed to prove that Jeff…

- Did not receive the minimum GPA/number of hours determined by his year in school.

- Broke team rules/Athletic Department rules.

- Had a bad attitude and was disruptive to the team.

- Failed a drug test in regulation with NCAA/institutional policies.

- Violated NCAA rules and/or institutional policies.

Jeff followed all team rules and policies, had above the minimum GPA and semester hours and trained very hard. Unfortunately, Jeff did not know that Coach Coe could not take his scholarship away. He could have made an appeal to the Director of Athletics and/or the Compliance Department to keep his scholarship. Coach Coe could determine that he did not want Jeff in the program, which is the coach's decision, but Jeff would have kept his scholarship money—there must be a valid reason for not renewing scholarships.

These stories are not very common but they happen. The important thing for every student-athlete to know is that there are always plenty of people at the university and in the school's athletic department that can help. If a student-athlete is experiencing problems with teammates, coaches, professors or other people associated with the institution, the student-athlete should seek help.

Even during times of uncertainty and frustration, the student-athlete should never be afraid to talk with the coaches. In most situations, any perceived problems are the result of miscommunication between parties. When everyone gets the opportunity to talk, and more importantly, to listen, problems can be solved. A student-athlete should always take a proactive approach to dealing with any conflict and it is always better to ask than to guess. Coaches would rather you address any perceived issues than to let a problem fester so that they must deal with it when it has spiraled out of control.

It is always okay for a student-athlete to ask a team captain to accompany him or her when going to talk with a coach, especially when the captain has had discussions with the teammate and/or coach regarding the given situation. The captain(s) may be able to add another perspective to an issue that neither party has considered.

If a coach is not responsive to open communication, it is then appropriate for the student-athlete to talk with someone else associated with the program and ask for help. Please remember, athletic departments and educational institutions in general believe firmly in a chain of command. Directors of Athletics will make time for major conflicts if people further down the chain cannot solve them, but they are very busy people.

Below are selected situations and a suggested order of conflict resolution. If there is no positive outcome from the first person on the list, move to the next.

Issue	Chain of Command
Teammate issues	Team Captain—Assistant/Head coach
Medical problems	Trainer—Team Physician
Trainer/Physician problems	Coach—Associate AD
Captain	Assistant Coach/Head Coach—Associate AD/SWA
Assistant Coach	Team Captain/Head Coach—Associate AD/SWA—Director of Athletics
Head Coach	Team Captain—Associate AD/SWA/Compliance Department—Director of Athletics
Professor	Coach & Academic Advisor
Academic Advisor	Coach & Trusted Professor
Athletic Booster	Coach & Compliance Department
Roommate/Other Students	Coach & Residence Life/Counselor
Law	Parent & Coach

THE ROLES AND EXPECTATIONS OF ATHLETIC DEPARTMENT PERSONNEL

Student-Athlete: A student playing sports for a college or university must adhere to all NCAA, institutional and athletic department regulations regarding academics and athletics.

Captain of Team/Program: Each coach will define different roles for a team captain. Generally, a captain will act as a liaison between the members of the team and the coaches.

Assistant Coach(s): These coaches help administer the program under the direction of the head coach. Assistant coaches may have specific jobs within the program (for example, recruiting).

Head Coach: This adult has complete management of the athletic program he or she heads up, including supervision of all assistant coaches, support staff and student-athletes. A head coach's first priority is the well-being of the student-athlete.

Volunteer Coach: A non-paid member of the coaching staff, a volunteer cannot recruit in any capacity but can perform other duties that assistant coaches are able to perform.

Booster: This individual or corporation donates money to the athletic program(s). A booster is also known as a Representative of Athletic Interest.

Agent: This adult acts on behalf of a professional sport team or corporation in a bid to secure the athletic services of an athlete.

Strength and Conditioning Coach: A member of a head coach's support staff, he or she is qualified and certified as a strength and conditioning professional. A head coach may use the strength coach in many non-sport related athletic activities.

Athletic Trainer: This adult is a member of the athletic department's support staff and is qualified and certified to administer medical treatments under the direction of a physician. An athletic trainer evaluates, treats and rehabilitates injured athletes.

Student Athletic Trainer: A student member of the athletic staff, this young person is training to become a certified athletic trainer.

Sports Psychologist/Counselor: This adult is a member of an athletic department's support and medical staff. A coach may utilize the counselor/psychologist for performance enhancement or the student-athlete may utilize the counselor to help with personal problems.

Sports Nutrition Expert: As a member of an athletic department's support and medical staff, a nutritionist may work in conjunction with the athletic training staff to provide nutritional education for student-athletes. The nutrition expert may work in conjunction with the counseling staff or additional medical staff in the treatment of eating disorders or weight management issues.

Team Physician: A qualified and licensed medical doctor oversees the medical care of the student-athletes. An athletic program may have a variety of different specialists on staff (i.e. orthopedic, family practitioner, dentist, etc.).

Academic Support Coordinator: As a member of an athletic department's support staff, this person supervises student-athletes in all academic areas. The function of an Academic Support Coordinator may include class scheduling, study hall supervision, tutoring and any additional academic related functions (i.e. time management, study skills, etc.).

Senior Woman's Administrator: This member of the school's personnel assists the senior athletic department staff to insure the representation of women's interests, including equity and gender-based issues.

Director of Compliance: The role of the Compliance Department is to monitor, assist and administer all conference and NCAA rules and regulations. All department staff and student-athletes are required to follow all rules including eligibility, financial aid, recruitment, etc. The Director of Compliance may also function as a liaison between the Department of Athletics and the Offices of Admissions, Registrar, Financial Aid and any additional administrative offices.

Sports Information Director: The SID is responsible for all media publications and press releases regarding athletics and student-athletes.

Director of Facilities: This member of the school's staff is responsible for the up-keep, scheduling and usage of an athletic department's facilities.

Faculty Athletic Representative: The FAR is a full-time member of the institution's faculty who works with the senior members of the athletic department to uphold the academic integrity of the institution. The FAR also insures the welfare of the student-athlete and makes certain that academic services are available to all student-athletes at the institution. In addition, the FAR sits on any committee formed to address any student-athlete appeals (for example, transfer requests).

Associate/Assistant Athletic Director: This member of the school's personnel assists the Director of Athletics in overseeing designated areas or sports of the Athletic Department. The Assistant AD may act as a liaison between the Director of Athletics and the coaching staff. Additionally, the Assistant AD is the first administrator above the coach that will be available to help student-athletes.

Athletic Director/Director of Athletics: The AD is responsible for the overall management of the department, including the supervision of the Compliance Office, all coaches and support staff. The AD reports directly to the President/Chancellor of the institution.

President/Chancellor: The President of the college or university administers the total program of the academic institution, including athletics.

SUMMARY

- Clarify your status with regard to the team early on in the recruitment process. The coaches should tell you where you will fit in.

- Be prepared for changes in your coach's opinions—good and bad.

- Do not expect special treatment when you arrive on campus.

- If you are having trouble establishing yourself as a student-athlete, ask the coaches for help and clarification.

- If you decide you want/need to transfer to another institution, seek help from the school's athletic department administrators (Faculty-Athletic Representative or a member of the Compliance Department).

- Do not allow a coach to make you quit.

- Keep documentation of recruiting correspondence—letters, emails, phone calls and any additional material.

- If you know your academic intentions during the recruiting process, state them to the coaching staff at that time.

- Ask the coaches if your academic choice or field of study will effect your standing as a student-athlete.

- Do not take classes during practice time unless you have no other options. Try hard to establish a schedule with no conflicts. Student-Athletes have priority registration at most institutions.

- Do make up missed practice times with individual skills sessions and/or strength and conditioning sessions.

- Do not allow a coach to dictate your choice of academic study.

- Be proactive with any conflicts you may have. The sooner a coach knows, the easier it is for him or her to make adjustments.

- If you do not want to meet with a coach by yourself, it is okay to bring support in the form of a teammate, captain and/or administrator.

- Understand what the team rules expect from you as a student-athlete. Ask for a copy of guidelines early in the recruitment process.

- Do not expect preferential treatment from the coaching staff because you are a senior, a captain or their star player.

- Understand what options are available to you if coaches want to take away your scholarship monies. They must have valid and documented reasons.

UNIVERSITY ONE: TEAM RULES

Academics

1. Academics are your first priority. You are responsible for attending every class, unless we are traveling to a competition.

2. It is your responsibility to inform your professors of any potential class misses and ask for potential missed work prior to leaving on an athletic trip.

3. Study hall, Academic Support Center meetings and any tutorial work must be followed through with appropriate and consistent focus under the direction of all Academic Support Center staff members.

Tardiness

1. It is your responsibility to be on time to every training session, every team meeting, game and travel leave time.

2. If you are going to be late or miss any team function, you must notify a member of the coaching staff in an appropriate and timely manner.

Travel

1. No one other than team members (players, trainers, coaches) are allowed in your room.

2. Do not leave the hotel unless directed to do so by coaching staff.

3. Dress appropriately for each situation.

4. University One will pay for your hotel accommodations (plus taxes). You are responsible for any incidentals attached to the cost of the room (i.e. phone, movies, room service, etc.).

5. From the time we leave until the time we return, all travel is done with the team.

Equipment

1. Team issued attire will be worn at all team functions: travel, training, meals and games.

2. Your equipment is your responsibility and you must follow instructions for proper care and management of individual equipment.

3. Team equipment (balls, goals, cones, sticks, etc.) are for the team and must be cared for by the team.

Medical

1. You must comply fully with all medical directions when deemed necessary by medical staff.

2. Missing appointments is unacceptable. If you cannot make an appointment, proper notification must be given to medical staff and you must reschedule as soon as possible.

3. Any injury and/or illness must be reported to the medical staff in a timely manner to insure proper care.

Recruiting

1. It is the team's responsibility to make Potential Student-Athletes (PSAs) welcome during any visit.

2. Spend time with each PSA and answer every question honestly and positively.

3. When hosting a PSA, you are responsible for the welfare of the PSA. You must comply fully with rules/guidelines set forth by the NCAA, University One and the University One Department of Athletics.

Alcohol and Drug

1. The team will follow all drug and alcohol polices set forth by the NCAA and University One Athletics.

2. A team-determined "1 Week" policy is in place for all competition. (Note: If you are under the age of 21, it is illegal for you to buy and/or consume alcohol at any time.)

Additional: You represent University One at all times. Go out of your way to be courteous to the people you meet and those who are helping our effort to be a national powerhouse. These include University One faculty/staff, bus drivers, airline crew, hotel staff and wait staff, alumni and supporters of University One and University One Athletics.

By signing the "Team Rules" I understand and I am willing to comply with each and every team rule for the benefit of myself, team and program:

Name: _____

Signed: _____

Date: _____

UNIVERSITY TWO: TEAM RULES AND EXPECTATIONS

Expectations

1. Freshman are responsible for setting up and taking down goals, looking for and counting all the balls, cleaning the bus after away games and carrying the video camera.

2. Please arrive 15 minutes early to practice (if you have class, we understand).

   ✔ Ex. If practice starts at 6:00, be there at 5:45.

3. Always wear University Two Colors at practice, during lifting and conditioning.

   ✔ Ex. Red, Navy, Blue, White

4. Do not wear any University Two apparel out on the weekends.

5. Come prepared for practice. This means having all equipment (stick, mouth guard, pinnie, goggles, water bottle and appropriate footwear). This also means removing all jewelry before practice begins.

6. Come to practice with a positive attitude.

7. Do not skip training room time. If you are hurt and need rehab, go see our trainer.

8. Dress appropriately for traveling.

9. Go to practice if you get out of class early.

   ✔ Ex. If your class is scheduled to end at 6:00 but you get out at 5:30 and we are still practicing, you need to be there.

10. Prior to games, make sure you take care of yourself (sleep, water, food, etc.).

   ✔ Ex. Do not stay up to 4:00 a.m. with friends.

Rules

1. There will be a 48-hour rule in effect for both the fall and the spring. This means you are not allowed to consume alcohol 48 hours before a game or a scrimmage.

   ✔ Punishment: 1st offense—A game suspension

   ✔ 2nd offense—Game suspension and 6:00 a.m. Extra Instruction (EI)

   ✔ 3rd offense—Coach's discretion

2.　You must attend study hall the number of hours you are scheduled.

   ✔ Punishment: For time you missed at study hall, you will complete EI for half that time.

      ○ Ex. If you missed one hour of study hall, you will have 30 minutes of EI.

3.　Do not come late to practice unexcused. (Coach will decide if it is excused or not.) You must be there when it is time to step on the field.

   ✔ Call if you are going to be late before you are officially late.

      ○ Ex. If you come at 7:01, by Coach's watch, you are late.

   ✔ Consequence: If you are between 1-15 minutes late for practice, you will have to complete 15 minutes of EI. After 15 minutes, you will have to complete that time in EI.

      ○ Ex. If you are 20 minutes late, you will have 20 minutes of EI

4.　Do not miss practice unless excused. (Coach decides if excused or not.)

   ✔ Consequence: If you miss practice, you are suspended for the next game.

   ✔ If you miss more than once, the consequence is Coach's discretion.

5.　All legal issues will be handled by Coach.

   ✔ If you are having issues or a problem, please go to someone (coaches, captains, mentors) and talk to him or her. Go to the person(s) it concerns so that they have the opportunity to help you out.

BE RESPONSIBLE!!
By signing this, you agree to all the rules and expectations listed above.

Please read this over and sign below-

Print Name _____

Signature_____Date_____

UNIVERSITY THREE: CONTRACT FOR CODE OF CONDUCT

All athletes selected for participation in soccer at University Three agree to abide by this CODE OF CONDUCT. By signing this document, you acknowledge that you have read it, understand it and are willing to abide by this CODE OF CONDUCT. If you do not wish to sign this document, you will not be allowed to participate on this team.

I agree to the following:

- Observe and obey the general rules of good conduct and citizenship.

- Observe and obey all University Three rules and regulations.

- Comply with the UT soccer policy that *no form* of alcohol will be allowed.

- Comply with the UT soccer policy that *no form* of tobacco will be allowed.

- Unacceptable behavior will not be tolerated, including but not limited to the following:

  - ✔ Any act considered to be an offense under Federal, State, Local and/or UT laws or rules.

  - ✔ Misconduct and unsportsmanlike behavior inappropriate to a representative of UT or the sport both on and off the field, including but not limited to foul language, lying and gossip about other players.

- Attend all training sessions, training and academic appointments and meetings requested by the coaches and/or staff.

- Never use or possess any banned substances at any time.

- Observe and obey any curfew established by the coaches and/or staff.

- Attend every class. If you are unable to attend class, notify the coaching staff that day. An answering machine is available at 555-5555.

NOTE: PERSONS PRESENT WHILE ANY VIOLATION OF THE CODE OF CONDUCT OCCURS MUST IMMEDIATELY REPORT THE VIOLATION AND LEAVE THE AREA OR BE CONSIDERED A PARTICIPANT BY CHOICE.

ACTIONS: I understand and agree that any violation of the CODE OF CONDUCT may result in disciplinary action, up to and including immediate dismissal for this team and/or reduction or withdrawal of my scholarship.

Participant's Name: _____

Participant's Signature: _____

Date _____

Parent/guardian Signature: _____

_____

RESOURCES

ATHLETIC WEB SITES

National Letter of Intent	www.national-letter.org
NCAA	www.ncaa.org
NCAA Eligibility Center	www.ncaaclearinghouse.com
NCAA Initial Eligibility Review worksheets	https://web1.ncaa.org/eligibilitycenter/hs/wksheet.pdf
NCAA Sports	www.ncaasports.com
NAIA	www.naia.cstv.com
Junior College	www.njcaa.org
Velocity Sports	www.velocitysp.com

FINANCIAL AND EDUCATIONAL RESOURCES WEB SITES

www.fafsa.ed.gov

www.fafsa4caster.ed.gov

www.supercollege.com

www.studentathletesguide.com

COLLEGE COACHES' WEB SITES

Athletic Training Bill Currie, Southern Methodist University
www.smu.edu

Baseball Rich Hill, University of San Diego
www.sandiego.edu

Basketball Dave Hixon, Amherst University
www.amherst.edu

CC/Track Matt Morris, Western Illinois University
www.wiu.edu

Football Phil Bennett, Southern Methodist University
www.smu.edu

Golf Mike McGraw, Oklahoma State
www.okstate.com

Women's Lacrosse Michael Scerbo, Duquesne University
www.duq.edu

Rowing Doug Wright, Southern Methodist University
www.smu.edu

Soccer John Cossaboon, Gonzaga University
www.gozags.com

Softball Glenn Moore, Baylor University
www.baylor.edu

Swimming Steve Collins, Southern Methodist University
www.smu.edu

Tennis Debbie Southern, Furman University
www.furman.edu

Volleyball Chris Herron, Washburn University
www.washburn.edu

COLLEGE COACHES' BIOGRAPHIES– SNAPSHOT

Baseball: Rich Hill, University of San Diego

- Twenty-one years of collegiate baseball coaching

- More than 600 Career Wins

- West Coach Conference Coach of the Year (2002)

- WCC Championship (2002, 2003)

- National Ranking as high as number 8

- Two NCAA III World Series appearances (Cal Lutheran)

- Thirteen former players drafted to professional ranks

- ABCA West Region Coach of the Year

- Two-time Southern California Intercollegiate Athletic Conference Coach of the Year

- Other places coached: Cal Lutheran, University of San Francisco

Basketball: Dave Hixon, Amherst College

- NCAA Championship
- NABC National Coach of the Year
- Three-time NABC Northeast Region Coach of the Year
- Ten NCAA Tournament Appearances
- Thirteen ECAC Conference Championships
- Fifteen Little Three Titles
- Four NESCAC Championships
- More than 550 Career Wins

CC/Track: Matt Morris, Western Illinois University

- Mid-Continent Conference Champion (2007)
- NCAA Regional Qualifying
- Ten-time Montana Coaches Association Cross-Country Coach of the Year
- Coached at the 2001 World Track and Field Championships

Golf: Mike McGraw, Oklahoma State University

- Two NCAA Championships (one as head coach, one as an assistant)
- NCAA National Coach of the Year (Dave Williams Award)
- National Assistant Coach of the Year (Jan Strickland Award)
- Big 12 Championship (2005, 2007)
- Coached two National Players of the Year
- Coached 19 All-Americans

Women's Lacrosse: Michael Scerbo, Duquesne University

- IWLCA Women's Coach of the Year nomination (2001)
- Coached several All-Americans
- National Ranking as high as Number 2 In 2001 (Limestone College)
- American Lacrosse Conference Championship (Ohio State)
- Other places coached: SUNY Oswego, Limestone College, Ohio State University

Rowing: Doug Wright, Southern Methodist University

- Numerous medal and event winners
- Coached five CRCA National Scholar Athletes
- Coached All-American rowers
- Other places coached: Hobart College, William Smith College, North Carolina State University

Soccer: John Cossaboon, Gonzaga University

- Two C-USA Coach of the Year Awards (Southern Methodist)
- Two C-USA Regular Season Championships (SMU)
- Two WAC Regular and Post-Season Championships (SMU)
- Eight consecutive NCAA Tournament appearances
- Coached in Japanese professional league
- Coached NCAA All-Americans, National Team Players, and Olympic and World Cup Winning players
- Other places coached: University of North Carolina, Duke University, Cal State Hayward, University of San Diego, Southern Methodist University

Softball: Glenn Moore, Baylor University

- NCAA World Series participant
- Big 12 Championship
- NCAA Regional Championship
- National Ranking as high as 7
- Two SEC Championships (LSU)
- Other Places Coached: Louisiana State University, William Carey College

Swimming: Steve Collins, Southern Methodist University

- Two-time NCAA Coach of the Year (1991, 1996)
- Ten consecutive Conference Championships
- Six Conference Coach of the Year Awards
- Nine Top 5 finishes at the NCAA Championships
- Coached eight Conference Swimmers of the Year
- Head Coach—Slovakian Swim Team (2004 Olympics)
- Coached 27 Olympic swimmers (including medal winners)
- Coached one National Swimmer of the Year
- Other places coached: University of South Carolina

Tennis: Debbie Southern, Furman University

- Ten Southern Conference Coach of the Year Awards
- Fifteen Southern Conference Championships
- Seven NCAA Tournament appearances
- Coached National Sportsmanship Award winner
- Member of the South Carolina Tennis Hall of Fame
- Other places coached: Austin Peay University

Volleyball: Chris Herron, Washburn University

- NCAA Final Four (2007)
- Four NCAA Tournament Appearances
- Two MIAA Coach of the Year Awards
- Two HACC Coach of the Year Awards
- Coached ten All-Americans and 23 All-Region Players
- Other places coached: Benedictine College

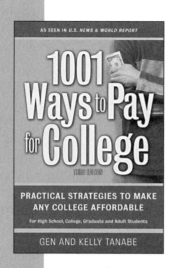

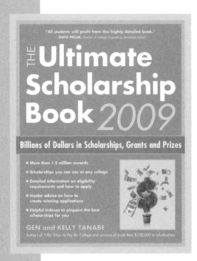

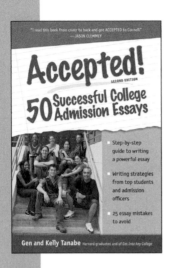

WWW.STUDENTATHLETESGUIDE.COM

The recruiting process can be a daunting time, especially when rules, trends and calendars change often—and sometimes change back. The NCAA decision makers, with input from college coaches and administrators, are always looking to make rule changes that keep the playing field level for all recruiting institutions and, more importantly, for the welfare of the prospective student-athlete and current student-athlete. It is important that everyone understands what is expected and when—and **www.StudentAthletesGuide.com** can be a helpful resource.

Gain additional knowledge and skills to initiate and develop recruiting strategies, find up-to-date information on rules and trends, plus much more at **www.StudentAthletesGuide.com**.

* Updated recruiting rules and calendars

* Current communication allowances (per calendars) for prospects and coaches

* Recruiting—What you should be doing at that time of year (per HS grade and sport)

* Conditioning—What you should be doing at that time of year (per season and sport)

* Ask-an-expert area

* Featured experts

* Sports Features

* FAQs and answers

* Plus much more

Together, *The Student Athlete's Guide to Getting Recruited* and **www.StudentAthletesGuide.com** will help prepare you for the exciting transition from high school athletics to becoming a collegiate student-athlete.

GET MORE TOOLS AND RESOURCES FROM SUPERCOLLEGE.COM

Visit www.supercollege.com for more free resources on admission, scholarships and financial aid. And, apply for the SuperCollege Scholarship.

STEWART BROWN

After spending thirteen years coaching collegiate and youth soccer, Stewart Brown wrote this book in a bid to relieve the Prospective Student-Athlete and collegiate Student-Athletes of common frustrations he has seen them encounter. This writing combines his knowledge as a recruiting college coach, a youth coach helping his players reach their goal of playing college soccer, his own playing career and finally, his educational background.

Brown currently resides in Dallas, Texas where he teaches and coaches at the Blue Ribbon award-winning school, Highland Park High School. Additionally, Brown coaches youth soccer in north Texas.

Prior to teaching, Brown was an assistant coach for the Southern Methodist University women's soccer program. Brown played a major role in the evaluation and recruitment of high school athletes that were soon to enroll at SMU. During these four successful years, Brown helped lead the program to four consecutive conference titles and four trips to the end of season NCAA Tournament. In addition to the team success, many student-athletes won individual awards, including an NSCAA All-American (2006), and the team consistently carried a combined GPA over 3.0.

It was at Limestone College in Gaffney, South Carolina where Brown was introduced to coaching and teaching. Arriving at Limestone in the fall of 1996 as the Assistant Athletic Trainer, it was not long until Brown was asked to assist the newly formed women's soccer program. Within a year Brown added head women's soccer coach to his assistant athletic trainer title. In 2000, Brown added adjunct faculty to his resume by teaching various athletic training and physical education classes. Additionally, Brown became the head coach of the men's soccer program in the same year. In 2001, Brown was selected as the Coach of the Year by the Carolinas' Virginia Athletic Conference for both his men's and women's programs.

Educationally, Brown attained a Bachelor of Science degree in Sports Medicine from Alderson-Broaddus College (Phillipi, West Virginia) in 1996 and a Masters of Arts degree in Health and Exercise Science from Furman University (Greenville, South Carolina) in 2000. In addition, Brown attained national certification as an athletic trainer in 1996 and a certified strength and conditioning specialist in 1997. Brown also holds the NSCAA Premier Diploma for coaching.